PRAISE FOR *CAN WE BELIEVE IN PEOPLE?*

"In this culmination of a lifetime's philosophical investigations, Stephen Clark insists that far from dangling above a limitless existentialist abyss, we are invited to join the dance of a participatory creation. In his gentle, sometimes ironic, interrogation of received shibboleths, Clark delineates a world that may lie at the very edges of our imaginations, one that depends on a holy interdependence grounded on the bedrock of immutable moral realities. In our current anomie, such a book has never been more urgently needed to reinvigorate our intuition that reality, our long-desired home, is one of coruscating beauty."
—SIMON CONWAY MORRIS, Emeritus Professor of Evolutionary Palaeobiology, University of Cambridge

"I hope this is not really Stephen R. L. Clark's last book, as he suggests it may be. If it is, it constitutes a particularly elegant, rigorous, and beautiful *envoi*. At once classical and original, reflective and constructive, it is philosophy of the most morally illuminating kind: a vision of the spiritual community of all living things and of the participation of all life in the dignity and glory of spirit."
—DAVID BENTLEY HART, author of *That All Shall Be Saved* and *The Experience of God*

"Those who have come to admire and appreciate a lifetime of Stephen Clark's literary as well as philosophical skills will not be disappointed with this marvelous and timely book, which differs from his prior works in more directly interrogating theological and religious ideas on what it means to be human — focusing particularly on the likeness and image of God, but also on how we human beings have come to believe in anything at all, and more especially in what our future might be like. It is not easy to preserve a strong sense of human distinctiveness alongside a clear affirmation of the worth of other creatures, in tandem also with a fluency in evolutionary and other biological accounts; yet Clark achieves this through prose that is a joy to read, making this book not just deeply thoughtful philosophically, but inspirational as well."
—CELIA DEANE-DRUMMOND, Director of the Center for Theology, Science and Human Flourishing, Professor of Theology, University of Notre Dame

"This book offers a nuanced treatment of human dignity, but without anthropocentric excess. Stephen Clark deftly denies the reality of species boundaries as well as the idea that human beings are indefinitely malleable. His treatment of *theosis* renders his religious view of human existence quite other than most accounts in contemporary philosophy. And Clark saves the best chapter for the end, where he deals with eschatology in a fascinating way."
—DANIEL A. DOMBROWSKI, Professor of Philosophy, Seattle University; author of *Not Even a Sparrow Falls: The Philosophy of Stephen R. L. Clark*

"In this visionary, provocative work, Platonism and the three Abrahamic religions come into conversation with mathematics, evolutionary biology, and even thought experiments of science fiction. With great wit—which serves well to underscore his seriousness of purpose—the author challenges the boundaries of what is commonly construed as 'rationality,' as well as what it traditionally means to be human and made in the image and likeness of God. Stephen Clark invites his readers to rethink the dignity of the human being in a much closer, yet also transcendent, relationship of love with all things existing."
—GRETCHEN REYDAMS-SCHILS, Professor in the Program of Liberal Studies, University of Notre Dame

"Stephen Clark writes with clarity and erudition on the philosophy of human nature, the nature of mind, values, our relationship to non-human animals and the divine. He enables us to see the wisdom of Plato, Aristotle, Plotinus, and others as deep resources for our thinking about the meaning of life today. Recommended to all who are looking for a rich, stimulating, mature work in philosophy, understood as the love of wisdom."
—CHARLES TALIAFERRO, Professor of Philosophy, St. Olaf College

"There is no more basic issue than that of the nature of human beings and their place in the scheme of things. This scholarly book grips our attention with incisive arguments about matters that concern us all."
—ROGER TRIGG, Senior Research Fellow, Ian Ramsey Centre, University of Oxford

Can We Believe in People?

STEPHEN R. L. CLARK

Can We Believe in People?

Human Significance in an Interconnected Cosmos

Foreword by Catherine Pickstock

Angelico Press

First published in the USA
by Angelico Press 2020
Copyright © Stephen R. L. Clark 2020
Foreword © Catherine Pickstock 2020

All rights reserved:
No part of this book may be reproduced or transmitted,
in any form or by any means, without permission

For information, address:
Angelico Press, Ltd.
169 Monitor St.
Brooklyn, NY 11222
www.angelicopress.com

978-1-62138-509-7 pb
978-1-62138-510-3 cloth
978-1-62138-511-0 ebook

Book and cover design
by Michael Schrauzer
Cover:
Henri Rousseau, "The Snake Charmer" (detail), 1907

Then God [Elohim] said, "Let Us make man in Our image, according to Our likeness; and let them rule over the fish of the sea and over the birds of the sky and over the cattle and over all the earth, and over every creeping thing that creeps on the earth." God created man in His own image, in the image of God He created him; male and female He created them. God blessed them; and God said to them, "Be fruitful and multiply, and fill the earth, and subdue it; and rule over the fish of the sea and over the birds of the sky and over every living thing that moves on the earth." Then God said, "Behold, I have given you every plant yielding seed that is on the surface of all the earth, and every tree which has fruit yielding seed; it shall be food for you; and to every beast of the earth and to every bird of the sky and to every thing that moves on the earth which has life, I have given every green plant for food"; and it was so.

Genesis 1:26–30

CONTENTS

Foreword by Catherine Pickstock   ix
Preface   xiii

1   The Image and Likeness of God   1
     Sacred Images [1]—Losing and Recovering the Likeness [5]—
     Why the Non-human is Neglected [10]—Soul, Spirit, Christ [14]

2   Hume's "Peculiar Privilege"   21
     The Merits of Evolved Intelligence [21]—The Unreasonable
     Effectiveness of Mathematics [27]—Reason, Reality and the
     Mind of God [34]

3   Moral Realism   41
     Life's Work and Symbioses [41]—The Atheistical Paradox
     [46]—A Quasi-Realist Alternative [54]—The Eternal [65]

4   Is Humankind a Natural Kind?   71
     The Problem of Darwinian Species [71]—Species-specific
     Perfections [73]—Clades and Classes [78]—Theme and
     Variation [85]

5   Human Dignity   91
     Family Disputes [91]—Preserving Human Dignity in an
     Evolutionary Cosmos [97]—The Image Reimagined [110]

6   The Roots of Religion   117
     The Reason Why [117]—The Gods of Common Stuff [125]
     —Omens and the Hidden Order [133]

7   Alien Life on Earth and Elsewhere   141
     Imagining Other Lives [141]—The Bacterial Cloud [149]
     —The Eusocial Option [152]—Climbing up to Heaven [158]

8   Do We Have a Future?   165
     Omega Points [165]—The Doomsday Argument [173]
     —In the Beginning, God [180]

Conclusion   191
Epilogue   195
Works Cited   197
Index   211

FOREWORD

by Catherine Pickstock

Maybe there are times when we should envy not merely the beasts' equanimity, but their—partial—silence. Maybe we do not become "godlike" by mastering the world, but by acknowledging that we are not masters.

What is it to be human, and how should one live? Stretched between animals and gods, human beings are easily waylaid by mirages of power and certainty. How should one occupy this distended and contradictory space, between vulnerability and majesty? How can one live as such a "mixed" creature, as Pascal called human beings? At a time when humanity is variously displaying its dissembling and ossifying tendencies in all its regions, it is timely to ask how one should believe in people.

In this moving book, which he declares is "likely enough to be [his] last," the esteemed British philosopher Stephen R. L. Clark sums up and elaborates an academic lifetime's work of reflection upon metaphysics, ancient philosophy, religion, anthropology, animal nature, ethics, science and science fiction. He does so in direct and simple terms, and yet with reference to a wide range of vivid references to ancient sources, modern science and literature. Despite its prismatic reflectiveness, a seamless thread of argument and tone yields a single enthralled and enthralling voice, which leads us as if through a library with an idiosyncratic yet wise interpreter by one's side, enabling one to see everything anew. This library is the whole body of Western wisdom, but with many reachings-out beyond the West, and many surprises.

The connecting theme is the image of God in human beings. Clark negotiates this in terms of a tension, which, if ever it is to be resolved, will be—in accord with the philosophy of his hero, Plotinus—by *living the resolution* and not only by thinking it. The tension arises between an endorsement of a humanism deriving both from classical antiquity and from the Bible, on the one hand, and a suspicion of anthropocentrism, on the other. This is a vision which, like that of Aquinas, sees the trace of God in all of reality, and is prepared to exalt as equally the humble trace or vestige of God in all creatures as the discursively-manifest image of God in rational creatures, and even to see its non-discursivity — again in keeping with Plotinus's elevation of "life" (*zoe*) as the supreme mediator of the One — as more closely approximating to the simplicity of God.

It is because he has thought through the implications for the moral life of this theology of creation that a concern with the ethical treatment of animals has been an abiding feature of Clark's remarkable *opus*. He notes that it was not just the authors of the Hebrew scriptures, but also Greek and Roman writers, who were suspicious of the Egyptian worship of animals, and tended at times to associate animals with dubious captivity to passions which human beings must seek to avoid. In consequence, the Christian religion has often enough tended to disenchant the world, removing dryads from the streams and wresting nymphs from the groves. At the same time, he explores how these concerns to distinguish the human from the animal and the natural could release the latter just to be themselves. As for Coleridge, the Bible opens up nature simply as nature, beyond its limitation as a shrine for things which may more immediately fascinate us. Equally, and crucially, Clark notes how pagan classical philosophers of several Schools could allow that animals fixed in routine habits and instincts were not for that reason in every way inferior to human beings. Rather, they might possess stronger singular capacities, such as that of smell, and their "fixity" presented an example of stability, regularity and patience which human beings could be exhorted to emulate in their own distracted lives.

This leads us to the heart of Clark's argument. One can admit that human beings have a far greater capacity for relating things together in their minds, and their open-ended choices range more widely than anyone can immediately picture in their mind, like Descartes' chiliagon. However, considered in merely secular terms, such humanism tends to what a religious attitude might see as demonic: an enthroning of discursive reason above wisdom, that condemns one to discontented uncertainty, which one then tries to resolve by seeking a grim and gritted satisfaction in dominating other creatures. It is clear that for Clark this characterizes the contemporary crisis, which has roots in ancient and excessively anthropocentric religion: with understanding human stewardship as domination, and other creatures as existing solely for one's instrumental use. Perhaps one should have had more time for the Egyptians.

All the same, Clark holds open a specifically *religious* mode of humanism which can be rescued from this anthropocentric excess. For here—as throughout his works—we see the human glory as consisting in one's capacity for *theoria*, understood by Aristotle as contemplation of cosmic beauty which unites one with intuitive *nous* in Plotinus's sense. As Henri Bergson suggested, in keeping with the latter, as pointed out by Pierre Hadot, it seems that one does not require conscious mind in order to construct an eye, or to know how to move a hand. If everything happens perfectly well and in perfectly rational terms in the unconscious sphere of life, then what, exactly, is fully-aware thinking *for*? It can only be, as Plotinus suggested, for the sake of contemplation, for the full expression of truth as a poetic turning-round upon things to appreciate their radiant gratuity. This "reversal" is a returning of things to their source in the One, or in the divine. As such, for Plotinus, it exceeds reflexive consciousness and returns to life, but at the higher level of ecstasy.

Clark points out that this contemplative ascent or rising above mere broad discursivity *connects* human beings in certain ways with the settled intuition of animals, and even the simple unity of inanimate things, as ancient thought both West and East at times indicated. This means that the distinctness of human beings (stretched between awkwardly aggrandized and genuine kinship) resides not in one's being "above" everything else, so much as being "with" everything else, and consciously within a shared reality.

When it comes to ethics, Clark sees acutely the human moral awareness, which he construes in virtue-ethical terms, as an *accentuation* of animal instinct whereby one naturally respects superiors and cares for the young. Although this process of "transition" is subject amongst human beings to uncertainty and preference, this cultural addition still builds upon a natural given.

These themes are elaborated in terms of debates with evolutionary theory and considerations and examples drawn from different religious traditions. The embedding of human distinctness in the cosmos is matched by a suggestion that the latter should be most plausibly understood (in ways that echo Stoicism and Neoplatonism, besides Bergson and Whitehead) as suffused with a causal power of "life," and structured according to intelligence which allows one to understand it in mathematical and other rational terms.

This consummating book concludes by suggesting that the "Trinitarian" divine *logos*, and the outgoing and returning "life" of *pneuma* that conveys it, are intuited in all the monotheistic faiths, and in Neoplatonism. What is unique to Christianity is the doctrine that the *Logos*—outgoing and moving life expressively "arrested" in contemplative form—became incarnate. Clark sees the Incarnation as underscoring the non-degrading of the animal, since God assumed animal human flesh.

In this deeply affecting book, Stephen Clark provides an acute meditation on our current tensions between the human and the natural, the scientific and the religious. It suggests a disclosive and abundantly helpful human as well as cosmic way forwards, beyond our current cultural and natural catastrophe.

PREFACE

In my doctoral thesis and first book I sought to outline Aristotle's conception of humanity. Human beings, he supposed, were the template for all terrestrial life, and every other creature a more or less "deformed" version of their original. Those of us who wonder how to live are best answered by identifying what it is that we, as human beings, have to do: namely to choose our particular actions and choose — or at least identify — our preferred goals in life. We are creatures (at any rate all those of us who ask the question) who must *choose* what to do, unlike either beasts or even gods, whose lives are laid out for them. What counts as thus "human" was not merely a matter of our biological kind: hydrocarbon arachnoids from Jupiter, I said, were human as much as we — if we could talk with them, and they with us.[1] Being "human" in this sense is simply being a "rational," choosing, responsive and promise-making being. That we were also upright and had hands were not insignificant factors, but there might be cognate properties allowing much the same endeavors: that is, to watch the heavens, and make many new marvelous things.

So, granted the necessity of choice, we had better also discover what information, talents and virtues we most need to help us to make sensible choices, most likely to leave us with a life "well-lived": lived, that is, in accordance with virtue — or if there is more than one virtue, in accordance with the best and most complete (*Nicomachean Ethics* 1.1098a16–18). This latter qualification led Aristotle to insist that the best life would be the life of *theoria*, which God or the gods live always, and we only for short times. When I first wrote my book the consensus seemed to be that he didn't really mean that: the best life for human beings must "surely" be the one that contained all the many different goods that we may normally desire (a notion that always struck me as absurd). Anything else could only be an occasional respite from the trials of normal, ethical and political life: maybe "*theoria*" was abstract reasoning about eternal truths. My own account, only gradually

---

[1] Stephen R. L. Clark, *Aristotle's Man: Speculations upon Aristotelian Anthropology* (Oxford: Clarendon Press, 1975), 25.

formulated, was that it was instead the enjoyment of eternal beauty—the beauty of the heavens, of numbers, and even that displayed in the smallest and least considerable of living things. The goal of all who could manage it must be "to love and serve the Lord" (*ton theon theorein kai therapeuein*): to *love*, not simply to contemplate in some neutral or unmoved manner![2]

In that first book I also pointed out that Aristotle did not suppose that the human species was wholly distinct from other animal kinds. We have the inherited qualities we do because, precisely, we have inherited them from our forebears, not because there is a clear and distinct Idea or Archetype that molds our growing lives. There are no firm boundaries in nature, and all terrestrial life is variously like our own, and possibly related to us. In later years it gradually grew clear to me that we could not reasonably insist that *human beings* were morally considerable and non-human beings not. Like other Greek philosophers, from Theophrastus to Porphyry, I concluded that our choices *ought* to take account of the lives and interests of the creatures with whom we share the world, and on whose lives and vigor we depend.

Even in writing that first book, I took more account of later Greek philosophy (especially Plotinus) and of non-European philosophy (especially Chinese) than was then usual or commended. My thought was usually that particular unfamiliar readings of the Aristotelian text could be made more plausible if *other* writers, far away in time or space, had reached some similar conclusions, for example about the possible union of subject and object in a supreme intelligence. I made less effort to draw on early Christian, Muslim or Jewish writings—an omission I have tried to remedy since then, in obedience to my conviction that honest thought about these matters of highest moment always deserves respect, and a careful avoidance of mistaken readings. In what follows here, in what is likely enough to be my *last* book, I am addressing far more directly how we should understand the notion that humankind was made "in the image and likeness of God," especially in the light of our present knowledge of terrestrial biology and the vast sweep of the heavens. In what way might we still suppose that humankind is special, and what exactly would be its role? How shall we believe in people?

---

2 See further my "Therapy and Theory Reconstructed," *Philosophy as Therapy*, Royal Institute of Philosophy Supplementary Volume 66, ed. Clare Carlisle and Jonardon Ganeri (Cambridge: Cambridge University Press, 2010), 83–102.

Preface

I have for the last several years been speaking and writing around these matters, and may often repeat myself, or at least repeat quotations from my betters. I hope that in this book I have managed to develop and explain my more baffling opinions or suggestions — but there is plainly always more to be said on everything, even if not by me. My relevant past writings include "Is Humanity a Natural Kind?," T. Ingold, ed., *What Is an Animal?* (Unwin Hyman, 1988), 17–34, reprinted in *The Political Animal* (Routledge, 1999); "Enlarging the Community," Brenda Almond, ed., *Introducing Applied Ethics* (Blackwell, 1995), 318–30, also reprinted in *The Political Animal*; "Understanding Animals," Michael Tobias and Kate Solisti Mattelon, eds., *Kinship with the Animals* (Hillsborough, OR: Beyond Words Publishing, 1998), 99–111; "Conducta decente hacia los animales: un enfoque tradicional," *Teorema* 18/3 (1999): 61–83; "The Covenant with All Living Creatures," Mark J. Cartledge and David Mills, eds., *Covenant Theology: Contemporary Approaches* (Carlisle: Paternoster Press, 2002), 1–20; "Elves, Hobbits, Trolls and Talking Beasts," *Creaturely Theology*, Celia Deane-Drummond and David Clough, eds. (London: SCM Press, 2009), 151–67, reprinted in *Philosophical Futures* (Peter Lang, 2011); "Animals in Classical and Late Antique Philosophy," in *Oxford Handbook of Animal Ethics*, Raymond Frey and Tom Beauchamp, eds. (Oxford University Press, 2011), 35–60; "God and Animals," Charles Taliaferro, Victoria S. Harrison and Steward Goetz, eds., *Routledge Companion to Theism* (Routledge, 2012), 528–40; "Does 'Made in the Image of God' Mean Humans are More Special than Animals?," Tripp York and Andy Alexis-Baker, eds., *A Faith Embracing All Creatures* (Eugene, OR: Cascade Books, 2012), 138–49; "The Ethics of Taxonomy," Evangelos Protopapadakis, ed., *Animal Rights — Animal Liberation* (Berlin: Logos Verlag, 2012), 38–58; "Folly to the Greeks," *European Journal for Philosophy of Religion* 4 (2012): 93–113; "Ask now the beasts and they shall teach thee," Celia Deane-Drummond, David L. Clough and Rebecca Artinian-Kaiser, eds., *Animals as Religious Subjects* (London: Bloomsbury, 2013), 15–34; "God, Reason and Extraterrestrials," in Andrew Moore, ed., *God, Mind and Knowledge* (London: Ashgate, 2014), 171–86; "Changing Kinds — Aristotle and the Aristotelians," *Diametros* 45 (September 2015): 19–34; "Going Beyond Our Worlds to Find the World — What Reason is Really For," *Animals: New Essays*, Andreas Blank, ed. (Philosophia Verlag,

2016), 397–418; "Animals Real and Virtual," *Science and the Self: Animals, Evolution and Ethics: Essays in Honour of Mary Midgley,* Ian James Kidd and Liz McKinnell, eds. (Routledge, 2016), 31–40; "Animals in Religion," Linda Kalof, ed., *Oxford Handbook of Animal Studies* (Oxford University Press, 2017), 571–89.

My earlier books on related topics include *Aristotle's Man: Speculations upon Aristotelian Anthropology* (Clarendon Press, 1975); *The Moral Status of Animals* (Clarendon Press, 1977); *The Nature of the Beast* (Oxford University Press, 1982); *Animals and Their Moral Standing* (Routledge, 1997); *God, Religion and Reality* (SPCK, 1998; reissued by Angelico Press, 2017); *The Political Animal* (Routledge, 1999); *Biology and Christian Ethics* (Cambridge University Press, 2000); *G. K. Chesterton: Thinking Backwards, Looking Forwards* (Templeton Foundation Press, 2006); *Understanding Faith: Religious Belief and Its Place in Society* (Imprint Academic, 2009); *Ancient Mediterranean Philosophy* (Continuum Press, 2013); and *Plotinus: Myth, Metaphor and Philosophical Practice* (University of Chicago Press, 2016). What my relevant future writings, if any, may be, I cannot be entirely sure.

To my friends and family, colleagues and critics, as always, my respect and gratitude, especially to Gary Chartier, Gillian Clark, Celia Deane-Drummond, Daniel Dombrowski, Douglas Hedley, Gretchen Reydams-Schils, Charles Taliaferro and Roger Trigg.

Stephen R. L. Clark
Bristol
June 2019

1

The Image and Likeness of God[1]

SACRED IMAGES

European civilization takes its beginnings from the Mediterranean world of two and three millennia ago, and principally from its Hebrew and Hellenic elements. Both Hebrews and Hellenes privileged the human form above all others, and found it odd, or even scandalous, that, for example, the ancient Egyptians worshipped "animals." Even such sympathetic commentators as the first-century Platonist, Plutarch of Chaeronea, thought that portraying the gods as animals must lead "the weak and innocent into 'superstition' (*deisidaimonia*), and the cynical and bold into 'atheistic and bestial reasoning' (*atheos kai theriodes logismos*)."[2] Even the author of the Wisdom of Solomon, who insisted—as I shall emphasize myself—that God hates nothing that He has made (11:24), mocked the Egyptians for their worship of "vermin" (11:15–20). Only in the human, we are to suppose, can God's likeness be found.

This opinion was not undisputed, in either Hebrew or Hellenic circles. The philosopher Xenophanes observed that "if cows and horses or lions had hands, or could draw with their hands and make things as men can, horses would have drawn horse-like gods, cows cow-like gods."[3] And the Hebrew prophets were clear that God was utterly unlike any created thing: "my thoughts are not your thoughts, neither are your ways my ways, saith the Lord" (Is 55:8). Conversely, moralists in both traditions drew lessons from the habits of "animals," even if they also denied that the animals they

---

1 An earlier version of this chapter was presented, in brief, to the Biodiversity Conference at SOAS on March 22, 2012.

2 See Ingvild Saelid Gilhus, *Animals, Gods and Humans: Changing Attitudes to Animals in Greek, Roman and Early Christian Ideas* (London: Routledge, 2006), 98, after Plutarch, *Moralia*, vol. 5, trans. Frank Cole Babbitt, Loeb Classical Library (Cambridge, MA: Harvard University Press, 1936), 167, *On Isis and Osiris* 71:379e6–10.

3 Xenophanes 21B15DK, in Robin Waterfield, ed., *The First Philosophers: The Presocratics and Sophists* (New York: Oxford University Press, 2000), 27.

admired themselves knew what they were doing. Even the Hellenes thought some animals at least were sacred, to one divinity or another. Even the Hebrews acknowledged that we had duties to the creatures in our service: "Thou shalt not muzzle the ox when he treadeth out the corn" (Deut 25:4).

Nonetheless, in both traditions—and others around the world—the ruling assumption was that human beings were special, and that they had divine permission and authority to make use of creation for their own (worthy) ends. One core text for European history, and one that is now often vilified by good environmentalists, is the concluding statement of the "Priestly" story of creation:[4]

> And God (Elohim) said, Let us make man in our image (*tzelem*), after our likeness (*demut*): and let them have dominion over the fish of the sea, and over the fowl of the air, and over the cattle, and over all the earth, and over every creeping thing that creepeth upon the earth. So God created man in his own image, in the image of God created he him; male and female created he them. (Gen 1:26–27)[5]

As many other Christian writers have pointed out, the "dominion" being conveyed is not permission to use things as we please. "Although it is true that we Christians have at times incorrectly interpreted the Scriptures, nowadays we must forcefully reject the notion that our being created in God's image and given dominion over the earth justifies absolute domination over other creatures."[6] Even permission to eat our fellow creatures

---

[4] Commentators generally distinguish the "Priestly" account of creation (Genesis 1:1–2:4) from the "Yahwist" (Genesis 2–3). See, for example, Gerhard von Rad, *Genesis: A Commentary*, rev. ed., trans. John H. Marx (London: SCM Press, 1972), 46–67, 73–96.

[5] The notion occurs much earlier, in Egyptian literature: "Well directed are men, the cattle of the god. He made heaven and earth according to their desire, and he repelled the water-monster. He made the breath of life [for] their nostrils. They who have issued from his body are his images. He arises in heaven according to their desire. He made for them plants, animals, fowl, and fish to feed them": *Instruction for King Meri-Ka-Re* [22nd century BC], quoted by Jon D. Levenson, *Creation and the Persistence of Evil: The Jewish Drama of Divine Omnipotence* (Princeton, NJ: Princeton University Press, 1994 [1985]), 115, from James Pritchard, ed., *Ancient Near Eastern Texts Relating to the Old Testament* (Princeton, NJ: Princeton University Press, 1969 [1950]), 417.

[6] Pope Francis, *Laudato Si': On Care for Our Common Home* (London: Catholic Truth Society, 2015), § 67.

is not given, in the story, till after the Flood (Gen 9:1–4) — and even that permission is strangely qualified: "this bond doth give thee here no jot of blood!" (Shakespeare, *Merchant of Venice* 4.1; Portia speaks). But something is being conveyed: human life is to be considered special "for in the image of God has God made man" (Gen 9:6). Chesterton stated this traditional opinion neatly: "cruelty to animals is cruelty and a vile thing; but cruelty to a man is not cruelty, it is treason. Tyranny over a man is not tyranny, it is rebellion, for man is royal."[7]

What is the logic of the Priestly judgment? It may be that the conjoined phrases, "in our image" and "after our likeness," are equivalent — and that is a reading to which I shall return — but both Rabbinic and Patristic scholarship made a distinction. Even Aquinas — though he insisted that human beings were essentially "like" God, and unlike "animals," at any rate in being "intelligent" — made a distinction:

> The image of one thing is present in another in one of two ways. The first, as in a being of the same specific nature, e.g., the king's image in his son; the second, as in a being of a different nature, e.g., the king's image on a coin. The Son is the Image of the Father in the first manner; man is the image of God in the second.[8]

God made us "images" of Himself rather as earthly rulers may set up statues of themselves to make their presence known, and insist that everyone pay something like the same respect to the statues as they would to the king's own person.[9] Human beings, that is, are to be reckoned sacred, and any disrespect or injury to them is taken as disrespect or injury to God. Jesus of Nazareth drew the further inference that even *neglecting* people is an

---

7 G. K. Chesterton, *Charles Dickens* (London: Methuen, 1906), 197; see my *G. K. Chesterton: Thinking Backwards, Looking Forwards* (West Conshohocken, PA: Templeton Foundation Press, 2006).

8 Aquinas, *Summa theologiae* I.35.2, cited by Celia Deane-Drummond, "God's Image and Likeness in Humans and Other Animals: Performative Soul-Making and Graced Nature," *Zygon* 47.4 (2012): 934–48, 944.

9 Tikya Frymer-Kensky, "The Image, the Glory and the Holy: Aspects of Being Human in Biblical Thought," *Humanity Before God: Contemporary Faces of Jewish, Christian and Islamic Ethics*, ed. William Schweiker, Michael A. Johnson and Kevin Jung (Minneapolis: Fortress Press, 2006), 118–38.

offence against God, not merely actively oppressing them (Mt 25:31–46).

So human beings are each, individually, representatives and — as it were — heirs of God: each is sufficient reason for the whole world to exist, according to the Rabbinic gloss.

> A man stamps many coins with one seal, and they are all identical, but the King of the kings of kings stamped every man with the seal of the first man, and none is identical with his fellow. Therefore it is the duty of every one to say: For my sake the world was created.[10]

A similar thought is given more emotional expression in the writings of Thomas Traherne, the seventeenth-century Anglican cleric:

> You never enjoy the world aright, till the Sea itself floweth in your veins, till you are clothed with the heavens, and crowned with the stars: and perceive yourself to be the sole heir of the whole world, and more than so, because men are in it who are every one sole heirs as well as you. Till you can sing and rejoice and delight in God, as misers do in gold, and Kings in scepters, you never enjoy the world.[11]

So each human life is to be reckoned sacred, and each human being is to rejoice in the beauties of the world she has been freely given. We are Kings and Queens — but not of the sort that the prophet Samuel warned against, who would enslave Israel (1 Sam 8:10–22). We human beings must consider each other sacred, but non-human animals have no such duty to revere us: any duty there is lies on our side, to be as careful of their lives as good kings are of their subjects.

---

10 *Mishnah: Sanhedrin* 4.5, in Ephraim E. Urbach, *The Sages: Their Concepts and Beliefs*, trans. Israel Abrahams (Cambridge, MA: Harvard University Press, 1979), 217; see also Mt 22:21.

11 Thomas Traherne, *Centuries of Meditations* (London: Bertram Dobell, 1908), 20. See also the classic text of Russian Orthodox spirituality, *The Way of the Pilgrim*: "When I began to pray with the heart, everything around me became transformed and I saw it in a new and delightful way. The trees, the grass, the air, the light and everything seemed to be saying to me that it exists to witness to God's love for man and that it prays and sings of God's glory." *The Way of a Pilgrim*, trans. Helen Bacovcin (New York: Doubleday, 2003), 25.

The Image and Likeness of God

LOSING AND RECOVERING THE LIKENESS

The story told in Genesis — at least for my present purposes — identifies an ethical and spiritual program: it need not be read as historical anecdote, nor explanatory hypothesis. Whatever happened or did not happen long ago, our present world is painful, and our personal characters are clearly not divine. We are still in God's image, but not in His likeness. As Chesterton — ghoulishly — observed:

> If it be true (as it certainly is) that a man can feel exquisite happiness in skinning a cat, then the religious philosopher can only draw one of two deductions. He must either deny the existence of God, as all atheists do; or he must deny the present union between God and man, as all Christians do.[12]

In our beginnings, so the story goes, we were "like" God, but are so no longer. Instead we have to be urged and harried into making an effort to grow more like Him: the Israelites are to be "holy" (Lev 20:26; see also 1 Pet 1:16), and Jesus required his followers to be "perfect" (Mt 5:48). We are, so the Church Fathers told us, to become "gods" (Ps 82:6; Jn 10:34): this is why God's Word became human, so that human beings could become divine (see, for example, Athanasius, *On the Incarnation* 54.3, written c. 318 AD). This prophecy and instruction, as it evolved in Christendom, drew on both Hebraic and Hellenic sources: Plato and Aristotle both suggested the same duty, to become godlike (Plato, *Theaetetus* 176a), to "immortalize ourselves" (Aristotle, *Nicomachean Ethics* 10.1177b31–4). But whereas they seem to have had the hope that our present, natural resources could — possibly — assist us to this goal, Christian and other Abrahamic theologians have rested their hopes entirely on God's initiative: we can only hope to be remade divine.

And what does this "divinity" amount to? One easy answer — especially for those who have neglected or ignored the distinction between "image" and "likeness" — was to say, like other pagan philosophers, that human beings were "rational beings," and so members of the same order as the gods or angels.

---

12 G. K. Chesterton, *Orthodoxy* (Thirsk: Stratus, 2001 [1908]), 6.

Can We Believe in People?

> In B'rei'shit Rabbah 8:11, four angelic qualities are seen as inherent to humans: speech, understanding (i.e., intelligence, reason), sight (perhaps also meaning "foresight"), and physically upright posture.[13]

These are also the distinctive properties identified by Aristotle—including our upright posture (*De Partibus Animalius* 2.656a11–14[14]), and the reason why that matters: "the reason why the other animals do not speak is because they cannot stand upright and so cannot behold the stars and the heavens!"[15] The world, so the Stoics said, was created solely for the benefit of gods and men, as the only "rational" creatures (Cicero, *On the Nature of the Gods* 2.133): only they can actually enjoy the world as a whole, rather than their own particular niche, as only they can even imagine such a thing as the World apart. Amongst earthly creatures only human beings have been endowed with the power to intuit eternal truths, or reason their way to theories about the world or our lives together; only they are "free" to disregard or transcend the "natural" impulses that govern other earthly life. According to the *Catechism of the Catholic Church*:

> Of all visible creatures only man is "able to know and love his creator." He is "the only creature on earth that God has willed for its own sake," and he alone is called to share, by knowledge and love, in God's own life. It was for this end that he was created, and this is the fundamental reason for his dignity. Being in the image of God the human individual possesses the dignity of a person, who is not just something, but someone. He is capable of self-knowledge,

---

13 David M. Seidenberg, *Kabbalah and Ecology: God's Image in the More-Than-Human World* (New York: Cambridge University Press, 2015), 47. One very odd development is mentioned in Seidenberg, *Kabbalah*, 90: "The Maharal [that is, Yehudah Loew of Prague, 1525–1609] states (in *Derekh Chayyim*, ch. 5, 274) that 'you will find that the human alone walks with *qomah z'qufah*, more so than all the rest of the animals. . . . [F]or the human, since he is a king/*melekh* among the lower ones, walks upright, [in] the image/*dimyon* of the king, and the rest of the creatures walk bent over before him.' Maharal also makes the astonishing claim here that 'when a person is ninety [years old] he is a partial human . . . because) he begins to walk hobbling, and this thing is as if he were no longer a complete human, since the superiority of the human is uprightness, and [so] he no longer has Elohim's image.'"

14 See also Clark, *Aristotle's Man*, 46.

15 Seidenberg, *Kabbalah and Ecology*, 319, after Zohar Chadash.

of self-possession and of freely giving himself and entering into communion with other persons. And he is called by grace to a covenant with his Creator, to offer him a response of faith and love that no other creature can give in his stead.[16]

Where we get such exact information about the abilities of other creatures, and the purposes of their Creator, is unclear: the Biblical record is far more ambiguous, and saints even of the Catholic tradition are often far more appreciative of our non-human kin. The *Catechism* goes on to insist, on the word of John Chrysostom, that man is "more precious in the eyes of God than all other creatures! For him the heavens and the earth, the sea and all the rest of creation exist"[17] (notwithstanding the fact, as the *Catechism* also notes, that the Bible records or imagines their creation, and that they were good, before ever God made humankind). Some commentators have gone further, insisting that all other created things are useful only during this earthly life, and will have no share in the coming or eternal kingdom (and this claim, like the others, seems not to be supported by any relevant revelation).

I shall return to these and other claims about the supposedly unique capacities of human beings, as constituting their "likeness" to God. But what is the likeness that we lost? And what is it that we are required to seek again? The answer to both questions lies in the declaration that God is "holy," and that we are to seek that "holiness," *qadosh* (1 Pet 1:15). It is not wrong to see that the term has associations also with "purity": God's people are to separate themselves from iniquity, from all forms of self-indulgent greed and cruelty, and adopt strict dietary and other rules to help them (see Lev 11:44). But the principal association of the term *qadosh* in the Hebrew texts is with compassion[18]: we are to seek to imitate and express God's generosity, to orphans, widows, strangers and the wild things in our country (that is, the country we are given to help guard and garden). We are not to seize all things for ourselves alone, but leave resources — or more actively provide resources — for all those in need (see Lev 19:9–10; 23:22; 25:6–7). Conversely, our failure to do

---

16 CCC 356–57 [www.vatican.va/archive/ENG0015/_INDEX.HTM].
17 John Chrysostom, *In Gen. sermo* 2, 1: *Patrologia Graeca* 54, 587D–588A.
18 See Eliezer Berkovits, *Man and God: Studies in Biblical Theology* (Detroit: Wayne State University Press, 1969).

this deserves deep condemnation. We are not to steal or cheat or keep back an employee's wages, nor deprive the poor and the stranger of the chance to glean the harvest, nor "treat the deaf with contempt nor put an obstruction in the way of the blind" (Lev 19:13–14). "This was the iniquity of your sister Sodom: she and her daughters had pride of wealth and food in plenty, comfort and ease, and yet she never helped the poor and wretched" (Ezek 16:49).

God made Man (that is, both male and female) to be generous: to live as much for others as for themselves. In our fallen state this is experienced as an instruction very hard to fulfil: the best we can usually manage is bare justice, and not love.

> You shall not pervert justice, either by favoring the poor or by subservience to the great.... You shall not nurse hatred against your brother.... You shall not seek revenge, or cherish anger toward your kinsfolk; you shall love your neighbor as a man like yourself. I am the Lord. (Lev 19:15–18)

How did we lose that likeness, according to the story incorporated into the second and third chapters of Genesis, the work now usually identified as from the Yahwist rather than the Priestly source? In the beginning (Gen 2:9) God [Yahweh Elohim] planted two trees in Paradise: the tree of life and its opposite, the tree of the knowledge of good and evil (which brings death). We were presented, that is, with an implicit choice between Life and Death (see also Deut 30:15–20), and warned off the latter. The serpent, it is said, suggested that by eating from the tree of knowledge we would be "like gods" (Gen 3:5) — but not, it turned out, like the gods we were once meant to be. What did the choice amount to? Adam had already named each living creature (Gen 2:19–20) before he was divided into male and female: that is, he already knew their names and natures. Later commentary in the Abrahamic tradition suggested that it was this knowledge that persuaded almost all the angels of God — who must, almost by definition, be both cleverer and more powerful — to acknowledge that Adam nonetheless had the higher status (*Koran* 2.31–4[19]). Only Satan and his followers resented this authority, and

---

19 See Abdulaziz Sachedina, "Human Vicegerency: A Blessing or a Curse?," in Schweiker, *Humanity Before God*, 31–54.

rebelled. Sin entered the transhuman world, that is, from intellectual pride, not bodily passion — but that is another story.

If Adam already knew the names and natures of all living creatures, what did "the knowledge of good and evil" add? We began to experience some things, some creatures, as "good" and some as "evil." We learnt discrimination, and so condemnation. And the antidote conceived, for example, in the words of Jesus is that we should not "judge," nor seek to disentangle "good" and "evil" influences, but behave "like God," so "that you may be the children of your Father who is in heaven: for he makes his sun to rise on the evil and on the good, and sends rain on the just and on the unjust" (Mt 5:45).

The effect of this in our relations with the non-human is that we think creatures "good" if they serve our purposes, and enemies or vermin if they don't. Before we began to discriminate we could acknowledge that all things created were, in their way, beautiful — and this thought does still surface in both pagan and Abrahamic literature. As Aristotle said, there is something wonderful and beautiful in even the smallest, commonest and apparently "base" of living creatures (*De Partibus Animalium* 1.645a15f.). If we are ever to be "holy" we must love even our enemies, even "vermin," and so realize that they are not essentially verminous.

Is this mere sentimentality? Consider the sardonic rhyme devised by Chesterton's friend J. S. Phillimore in response to the conclusion of Coleridge's Ancient Mariner:

> He prayeth best who loveth best
> All things both great and small.
> And Streptococcus is the test —
> I love him best of all.[20]

We are unlikely to like Streptococcus or any similar bacterial agent. But we can now see clearly what many commentators have been warning us about for decades: a battle with bacteria is one that we will lose. The misuse, the overuse, of antibiotics has imposed a fierce selective pressure on a

---

20 Quoted by Christopher Hollis, *The Mind of Chesterton* (London: Cassell, 1970), 69. Some versions give "I hate him worst of all" as the last line, but this seems to me to be an inferior reading. The verse is also widely, but wrongly, attributed to Hilaire Belloc.

population—the bacterial cloud—that is not confined, like such eukaryotic, multicellular organisms as ourselves, within a single, simple, species-specific gene pool. Bacteria are exchanging biochemical information constantly, and we are teaching them all to be resistant to our weaponry. The better solution, though it is not one that—in this age of the world—we can expect to be universally effective or even possible, must be to make friends of our enemies and come to terms with them promptly (see Mt 5:25-26). Even our occasional "victories," as we see them—for example, to eliminate the smallpox virus—may owe more to normal evolutionary change than any effort of ours.

The serpent's suggestion was that we would be "as gods" if we could discriminate between "the good" and "the evil." The alternative answer is that we should prefer to see all things as good, or at least to refrain from judgment. According to Muslim tradition, "One day Jesus was walking with his followers, and they passed by the carcass of a dog. The followers said, 'How this dog stinks!' But Jesus said, 'How white are its teeth.'"[21] "To the pure all things are pure" (Tit 1.15)—which does not, of course, deny the possibility of corruption: on the contrary, for those who are "defiled and unbelieving," everything is "impure."

WHY THE NON-HUMAN IS NEGLECTED

It has been possible for us to lose our original God-likeness, and at least to hope that we might recover it, because we are free to choose (or think we are). In this respect, "image" and "likeness"—so some have argued—are the same: whereas all other earthly creatures are moved entirely by their given natures, and whatever angelic intelligences exist are purely intellectual and "single-minded" in their decisions, human beings are intelligences housed in natural bodies, whose intellectual decisions are often at odds with their passions. "Man's freedom is at the very heart of his being; it is that which essentially distinguishes a 'rational' being from the animals."[22] This, at any

---

21 Marvin Meyer, *The Unknown Sayings of Jesus* (Boston: Shambhala, 1998), 140, after al-Ghazali, *Revival of the Religious Sciences* 3.108.

22 John Meyendoff, *A Study of Gregory Palamas*, trans. George Lawrence (Leighton Buzzard: Faith Press, 1974), 124.

rate, has been a common theme in Abrahamic and pagan thought.[23] Although tradition also contains, as I remarked before, a warning that spiritual pride has at least as dire an effect as passion, it is easy to suppose that our moral struggle is with "animal instincts" and our duty is to do what "reason" bids. When we "give in" to passion, we behave "like animals."

> When do we act like sheep? When we act for the sake of the belly, or of our sex-organs, or at random, or in a filthy fashion, or without due consideration. When we act pugnaciously and injuriously and angrily and rudely, to what level have we degenerated? To the level of wild beasts. (Epictetus, *Discourses* 2.9.2)

So although pagan and Abrahamic moralists will also often advise us to learn the virtues of fidelity or hard work from animal behavior, the more usual general precept is to remember that we are human:

> Consider who you are. In the first place, you are a man; and this is one who has nothing superior to the faculty of the will, but all other things subjected to it; and the faculty itself he possesses unenslaved and free from subjection. Consider then from what things you have been separated by reason. You have been separated from wild beasts: you have been separated from domestic animals.[24]

That is, we must stand aside both from the aggressive, greedy passions attributed to "wild beasts" and also from the stupid servility of the domestic kind. No merely "natural" passion or instinctual behavior pattern is to

---

[23] John Scotus Eriugena used the two accounts of the creation of humanity to signify a distinction between the *spiritual* and the *animal* aspects of humanity (*On the Division of Nature* 750–53): see Henry Bett, *Johannes Scotus Erigena: A Study in Medieval Philosophy* (Cambridge: Cambridge University Press, 2014 [1925]), 59. We are to suppose ourselves joined with angels on the one hand, and animals on the other, so acting as the representative of all creation. Gregory of Nyssa even proposed, without clear textual excuse, that sexual differentiation was subsequent to the Fall, that the distinction of male and female "was not in the prototype" (*On the Making of Man*, trans. W. Moore and H. A. Wilson [London: Aeterna Press, 2016], §16, p. 32), signifying, one may suspect, the alienation of "emotion" from "reason."

[24] Epictetus, *Discourses*, vol. 1, trans. W. A. Oldfather, Loeb Classical Library (Cambridge, MA: Harvard University Press, 1956 [1925]), 269 [2.10].

be taken as our rule. This advice may still apply even when more careful investigation reveals that "animals," even wild animals, are not intrinsically greedy and aggressive. It may well be true, as recent ethological study has suggested, that many or most of the "higher vertebrates" have some sense of "fair play," that they cooperate as often as they compete, and are affectionate or kindly creatures. Hesiod, the eighth-century Greek poet, was wrong to say that "the son of Kronos [that is, Zeus] has ordained this law for men, that fishes and beasts and winged fowls should devour one another, for right [*dike*] is not in them; but to mankind he gave right which proves far the best" (*Works and Days*, 1.275ff.). Right, or a sense of what is right, is not exclusively human. It does not follow that these emotions and behavior patterns — even indignation — are unequivocally "good," or that human behavior could be magically improved by appropriate medication. The violent and greedy are not the only sinners: more of us are led astray, perhaps, by a wish not to offend. Even "a sense of justice" and such cognate emotions as indignation and anger are no guarantee of good behavior, or right motivation.

Human beings, so Aristotle taught us, are creatures who must choose how to live their lives, and need, if they are to choose well and wisely, to put limits even on their quieter impulses (see *Nicomachean Ethics* 1.1098a3–18). We need to have some conception of the wider world in which our actions have their effects, and need to be prepared to control our impulses in the light of our best grasp of what would be right for anyone to do here-now. Is this a condition that marks us out as godlike? Aristotle himself denied it: we can't really suppose that God or the gods have any need to control their impulses, nor that they need fear the consequences of their actions (*Nicomachean Ethics* 10.1178b10–16). God has no need of moral virtue. Nor is it obvious that the truly saintly need to think carefully before they do whatever it is that, for them at least, comes easily. To be "holy" is something different from being merely "moral" and "self-restrained." In short, it seems unreasonable to suppose that we are "like God" even in our potential for free and rational action. We have to reason our way to our conclusions, whether in matters of fact or of morals: God does not. We must pause to consider what would happen next, and must struggle — at any rate since the Fall — with treacherous impulses and diabolical temptations. God does not. The very features of existence that supposedly distinguish our condition from that of "brute beasts" are ones that render us also very unlike God.

There are at least two other problems with the notion that our duty is to distance ourselves from merely "animal" behavior. Because we identify our passions with the emotions and behavior of the beasts, those creatures come to stand for everything that we should consider "evil." Other Mediterranean peoples found the Egyptians' practice strange, or even wicked. Because they seemed to worship "animals," they were presumed to be worshipping "animal behavior" (though in fact it does not seem that the Egyptians imitated animals), and so to be failing in "humanity." The Roman poet Virgil cast the Battle of Actium as something more than a squabble between rival Roman factions: it was the defense of Roman virtue against "every kind of monstrous god and barking Anubis too" (*Aeneid* 8.946). Later Christian moralists have supposed that non-Egyptians also

> deified their passions. They worshipped the animals within themselves. They bowed down before the passions of their own natures, which they could not control or understand. Bacchus was the deification of appetite. Aphrodite was the deification of the passion of lust. Jupiter the deification of war.[25]

This is unfair to the ancients who actually shared, exactly, the moralist's disapproval of "animal" behavior, and sought ways of accommodating and controlling the passions quite as vehemently as Christians. Unsurprisingly, they often failed.

Correspondingly, anyone who finds it important to consider the feelings and needs of "animals" is presumed to think those needs and feelings worth considering—in humanity as well as in the animal creation. If we are not ourselves to think that food, sex and safety are morally compelling reasons for our action, how can it be important that "mere animals" should enjoy them? If pain and pleasure were all that mattered to us, we might be compelled to agree that the pains and pleasures felt by "animals" are also worth considering. If we should disregard such pains and pleasures in ourselves,

---

25 Anthony M. Coniaris, *Philokalia: The Bible of Orthodox Spirituality* (Minneapolis: Light & Life, 1998), 150.

but rather pursue our duty, why should we suppose that animal pains and pleasures matter? Plainly, it can be argued, the Creator doesn't much care. And if we are to think and feel as that Creator does we will ourselves be as careless of the animal creation, save only that — being animals ourselves — we shall be tempted by the example of their lives, and should distance ourselves more firmly from them.

Or rather we shall attempt to do so. For the second great problem with the Stoic or Rationalist advice is that it is strictly impossible. Advising us to discount all our own "animal" feelings and desires, and bind ourselves to act only and entirely as "reason" demands, is very much like advising someone clinically depressed to "snap out of it," or an addict "simply to say No." We cannot, on the available evidence, expect to stand aside from our own natures and act as "reason" dictates, even if we always knew what "reason" was. We usually do not even know what it is that we accomplish in the world by our own actions: we do not know, for a simple example, how an audience will hear or read our words, and therefore do not know what it is that we succeed in saying. Stoics like Epictetus, indeed, knew very well that we cannot dictate what happens: the most that even he supposed (see *Discourses* 1.1.7–12) that we could ever manage was merely to "accept" whatever happened, without complaint or quarrelling (and without exclaiming "It's not fair!"). Even this is more than most of us can manage.

SOUL, SPIRIT, CHRIST

Rationalists have assumed too easily that human beings — or at least some human beings — are godlike in their intellects, and so in their capacity to disregard mere "animal" emotions and merely bodily affairs. They have assumed, in effect, that the serpent was correct: being able and also eager to discriminate between good and evil allows us to live "as gods." The effect is twofold. On the one hand, this is to encourage us to despise — or at least to patronize — all those, human or non-human, whom we suppose to be driven by desire and fear, in ignorance of true, rational values. Plato did not agree, warning that other "rational creatures" might do the same to us:

> This kind of classification might be undertaken by any other creature capable of rational thought — for instance cranes are reputed to be

rational in this way and there may be others. They might invest themselves with a unique and proper dignity and classify the race of cranes as being distinct from all other creatures; the rest they might well lump together, men included, giving them the common appellation of "the beasts." So let us try to be on the watch against mistakes of that kind. (Plato, *Statesman* 263d)

On the other hand, by promoting an impractical division within the human heart, we either sadly fail entirely to live up to the standards set or — worse still — convince ourselves that we have succeeded. In both aspects — the external and internal — we are deceived by a mistaken account of "intellect." "If we say that we have no sin, we deceive ourselves, and the truth is not in us" (1 Jn 1:8).

The great third-century Platonist, Plotinus, also said that "Intellect (*nous*) is our king. But we too are kings when we are in accord with it; we can be in accord with it in two ways, either by having something like its writing written in us like laws, or by being as if filled with it and able to see it and be aware of it as present" (*Ennead* V.3 [49].3, 46ff.).[26] But in translating "*Nous*" as intellect we run the risk of confusion, precisely because we have associated "intellect" — against Plotinus's own intention — with abstract reasoning. A less misleading — because also more ambiguous — translation would be "Spirit." What mattered to Plotinus was a sudden wakening, a reversal of our ordinary attention.

> If someone is able to turn around, either by himself or having the good luck to have his hair pulled by Athena herself, he will see God and himself and the all.... He will stop marking himself off from all being and will come to all the All without going out anywhere. (*Ennead* VI.5 [23].7, 9f.)

The reference is to an episode in Homer's *Iliad* (I.197f.), in which Athena (the goddess of good sense) recalls Achilles from a murderous rage. We are to hope for that awakening, and hope to be able afterwards to live in

---

26. All translations of Plotinus are from *Plotinus: The Enneads*, trans. A. H. Armstrong, Loeb Classical Library (Cambridge, MA: Harvard University Press, 1966-1988).

accordance with the vision. But of course those of us without experience of Plotinus's own revelation will still have questions. What exactly is it that we might hope to see, and what effect should that seeing have on us? Plotinus himself acknowledged that even those who have seen easily forget. "It is as if people who slept through their life thought the things in their dreams were reliable and obvious, but, if someone woke them up, disbelieved in what they saw with their eyes open and went to sleep again" (*Ennead* V.5 [32].11).

One route to a partial awakening that he proposed was to realize, not merely as an abstract theory but as an imaginative exercise (*theoria*, in the original sense of awestruck contemplation) how "soul" has made and still makes the worlds.

> Let every soul first consider this, that it made all living things itself, breathing life into them, those that the earth feeds and those that are nourished by the sea, and the divine stars in the sky. (*Ennead* V.1 [10].2)

This is true on two levels. First, the living earth, at least, has been built up over many millions of years by the action of living creatures: the very soil beneath us is an artifact as well as a place to stand. In Plotinus's day it was not unreasonable to suppose that the same rule must apply elsewhere: the fixed and planetary stars were also reckoned living. We prefer to suppose that "life" has much less influence, and that the vast extent of the cosmos is "mere matter."[27] But our conviction in this has little rational basis: it is far more likely that the cosmos is indeed a complex of changeful, self-moving, self-reproducing creatures, or even that it is a single interconnected whole. "Why should the world not be judged animate and wise, when it engenders the animate and the wise from itself?" (Cicero, *On the Nature of the Gods* 2.22). It is true that Hebrew and Christian teaching has usually been opposed to any suggestion that we should attend to the spirits of wood and stream:

---

27 Though some recent cosmological speculation suggests that even large-scale features of the cosmos — including its fundamental laws and particles — have been established by living beings. See James N. Gardner, *The Intelligent Universe: AI, ET and the Emerging Mind of the Cosmos* (Franklin, NJ: Career Press, 2007).

The Image and Likeness of God

> In former times every place was full of the fraud of oracles, and the utterances of those at Delphi and Dodona and in Boeotia and Lycia and Libya and Egypt and those of the Kabiri and the Pythoness were considered marvelous by the minds of men. But now since Christ has been proclaimed everywhere, their madness too has ceased, and there is no one left among them to give oracles at all. Then, too, demons used to deceive men's minds by taking up their abode in springs or rivers or trees or stones and imposing upon simple people by their frauds. But now, since the divine appearing of the Word, all this fantasy has ceased, for by the sign of the cross, if a man will but use it, he drives out their deceits. (Athanasius, *On the Incarnation*, ch. 8, par. 47)

In driving away those spirits we gave ourselves permission to cut down forests, divert streams and gouge metals from the living earth without feeling any of the guilt—or simple fear—that other more pagan engineers once felt. For good or ill too many thought that *only* human purposes were sacred. On the other hand, by emptying the phenomenal world of such fancies we have also permitted the things themselves a voice: we can see places as more than historical sites and living creatures as something more than symbols.

The second way of understanding Plotinus's account is to acknowledge that it is through conscious experience that the phenomenal world is made. The world as we experience it, as every sentient creature experiences it, is the product of selective attention.

> We may, if we like, by our reasonings, unwind things back to that black and jointless continuity of space and moving clouds of swarming atoms which science calls the only real world. But all the while the world we feel and live in will be that which our ancestors and we, by slowly cumulating strokes of choice, have extricated out of this, like sculptors, by simply rejecting certain portions of the given stuff. Other sculptors, other statues from the same stone! Other minds, other worlds from the same monotonous and inexpressive chaos! My world is but one in a million alike embedded, alike real

to those who may abstract them. How different must be the worlds in the consciousness of ant, cuttlefish or crab![28]

All these worlds of experience are real, and all stem from the choices — even if not always the principled choices — of living things. The single physical world that we construct together is also a complex of interwoven mental worlds. By envisaging this complexity, by realizing the world as it were as a statue with many faces, we begin to wake. "When we look outside that on which we depend we do not know that we are one, like faces which are many on the outside but have one head inside" (*Ennead* V.5 [23].7; see also *Ennead* VI.7 [38].15, 25–34) — the isolated state from which Athena, in Plotinus's story, rescues us.

Or else perhaps it is God in another guise that we must hopefully invoke. On the Christian account it is Christ who is "the image of the invisible God, the firstborn of every creature" (Col 1:15), and it is through sharing in His life that we shall be changed "into the same image from glory to glory, even as by the Spirit of the Lord" (2 Cor 3:18). The later Christian tradition at any rate has linked the doctrine of *theosis*, divinization, entirely to the Incarnate Word. Christ, and not now Adam, is the image of God, by union with whom we may also grow "like" God. Humanity has been taken into the Godhead — not that we thereby have any greater "rights" than other creatures, but that we may begin to share the divine life — and by sharing it also convey it onwards. "It was to re-establish the kingship of man, and to give back his lost equilibrium, that the Word was made incarnate, 'to make him share the divine immortality.'"[29]

What are the implications of this orthodox — but also, for most modern Western audiences, unfamiliar — reading of the Christian gospel?[30] There is some truth in the often-repeated charge that Christian and even Hebrew teachings have seemed to leave "the natural world" and its non-human inhabitants without defense and without acknowledged value. By insisting that only human beings are sacred, and that only they have any hope of ever

---

28 William James, *The Principles of Psychology* (New York: Macmillan, 1890), 1:288–89.
29 Meyendorff, *Gregory Palamas*, 142, after Gregory Palamas, *Homilies* 16, col. 204a.
30 On which see, for example, *Theosis: Deification in Christian Theology*, ed. Stephen Finlan and Vladimir Kharlamov (Eugene, OR: Pickwick Publications, 2006), and Coniaris, *Philokalia*.

joining the life of the Blessed Trinity (or what Platonists have called "the dance of immortal love"[31]), we have strangely reversed the real message: which is indeed that God is Love, that He hates nothing that He has made, and that He is made known in the marvelous generosity and splendor of the creation, however marred or misunderstood that is.

> Beloved, now are we the sons of God, and it doth not yet appear what we shall be: but we know that, when he shall appear, we shall be like him; for we shall see him as he is. (1 Jn 3:2)

The likeness will not lie in our reasoning capacities, nor even in our freedom to transcend or ignore our natures. Satan fell from spiritual pride, from the absurd conviction that he was superior to all earthly beings because he was a properly "rational" creature. Humanity is fallen because we have preferred to judge and to condemn than really to love our "enemies." Even if the Hebrew and Christian story were proven to be false as historical record or explanatory hypothesis, it would still be our one best hope for peace.

---

31 Porphyry, *Life of Plotinus* 23.36f., after 22.54ff. The words are not Plotinus's, but still Plotinian.

2

Hume's "Peculiar Privilege"

THE MERITS OF EVOLVED INTELLIGENCE

When David Hume caused his character Philo, in his *Dialogues concerning Natural Religion*, to enquire "what peculiar privilege has this little agitation of the brain which we call thought, that we must thus make it the model of the whole universe?,"[1] he intended the question merely as a rebuke to the easy assumption that the principle and power that made and governed the universe would of course be something like human intelligence. But the question has a wider force. Especially since the theory of evolutionary change through chance mutation and natural selection came to dominate our intellectual landscape we are bound to suspect that we have the organs, tools and habits that we do only because they helped our ancestors survive and breed a little more successfully than any available rivals. It is worth emphasizing that Darwinian selection does not produce what would probably, in the abstract, be "the best" or most successful outcome: the very point of the theory is that the competing variations have been thrown up at random. There may be — there almost certainly are — possible variations which have simply never happened, or which vanished from the lineage (for no fault of their own) before they were fully tested, which would have been far more successful than any existing variation. We are, perhaps, fairly well adapted as wandering primates in and between Ice Ages: how should we expect that our talents are well suited to discovering the powers and principles that rule the world at large? Why should we expect any congruity between those principles and those that govern human thought? "With me the horrid doubt always arises whether the convictions of man's mind, which have been developed from the mind of the lower animals, are of any value or are at all trustworthy. Would anyone trust in the convictions of a

---

1 David Hume, *Dialogues concerning Natural Religion*, ed. J. C. A. Gaskin (Oxford: Oxford University Press, 2008 [1779]), 50.

monkey's mind, if there are any convictions in such a mind?"[2] The point was well developed by Plantinga,[3] and has been vociferously addressed since then — not, I think, with any resolution at once naturalist and realist.[4]

One immediate response may be to discard Darwin's unwarranted disdain for monkeys. They manage their lives, it would seem, as well as any other creature, even if they have no need nor any ability to do whatever it is that we characterize as "reasoning." We might similarly point to the skills with which grey squirrels leap through trees, or circumvent the cunning obstacles that human experimentalists devise for them. Obviously, it might seem, any normal animal can recognize advantage or disadvantage, and work out ways to obtain or to avoid them. Even slime molds can navigate their way through mazes, with the aid of what amounts to a "mental map."[5] So also ants, creating an externalized record of their individual travels for the benefit of all.[6] Such externalized memories are also significant in human culture, as I shall consider later. "Reasoning," perhaps, is only this set of skills applied over a longer time span, and with the conscious cooperation of other creatures prepared to spend a little energy in working out new paths to mutual profit. Monkeys can learn

---

2 Charles Darwin, *The Life and Letters of Charles Darwin*, ed. Francis Darwin (London: Murray, 1887), 1:315–16. Cf. Chesterton: "It is an act of faith to assert that our thoughts have any relation to reality at all. If you are merely a sceptic, you must sooner or later ask yourself the question, 'Why should anything go right; even observation and deduction? Why should good logic not be as misleading as bad logic? They are both movements in the brain of a bewildered ape'" (*Orthodoxy*, 33).

3 Alvin Plantinga, *Warrant and Proper Function* (New York: Oxford University Press, 1993), 216–40; see also N. M. L. Nathan, "Naturalism and Self-Defeat: Plantinga's Version," *Religious Studies* 33.2 (1997): 135–42.

4 It may be that both Plantinga and I first encountered the argument in C. S. Lewis, *Miracles* (London: Fontana, 1960 [1947]), and since there is an apparently ineradicable belief that Anscombe refuted Lewis's argument (and silenced his philosophical efforts for ever), it is worth noting that Anscombe herself denied that story entirely: she quite properly criticized some formulations of the argument against epistemological naturalism, and he rewrote them in the light of that criticism. See G. E. M. Anscombe, *Metaphysics and the Philosophy of Mind* (Oxford: Blackwell, 1981), ix–x.

5 Chris R. Reid, Tanya Latty, Audrey Dussutour and Madeleine Beekman, "Slime mold uses an externalized spatial 'memory,'" *Proceedings of the National Academy of Sciences* 109.43 (2012): 17490–94.

6 I. D. Couzin, "Collective cognition in animal groups," *Trends in Cognitive Sciences* 13 (2009): 36–43.

from their mistakes, and so can people, all the better because we can talk to each other about them.

The ability to talk about our experience, and be understood, is often taken to be the one crucial human innovation—and it is one that offers an even larger gain. We can talk about merely imagined situations, both those constructed from our memories and reminiscences, and those devised as distant extrapolations, exaggerations or elisions of those memories. We can remember our nightly dreams and record them, with variations, in our waking memory. Some of us can even invent new dreams, without the bother of falling fast asleep. We can tell each other stories, and those stories take on a growing life as story teller and auditors interact, applaud or criticize. Sometimes—and perhaps very often—we confuse the stories with our actual experienced lives, as though the invented characters could actually move amongst us, or their histories impinge on our own personal lives. Modern genre writers especially may enjoy playing with "shared worlds," setting new characters and novel events within the framework of another invented world—Barsoom or Middle Earth or the last days of the cosmos. We can apply familiar criteria of consistency and depth of character and plot to these new contributions, or begin to modify the "shared world" in plausible directions as we learn a little more about the actual world on which we all depend.

But what is the status of this "actual world"? The world of our present experience, we could retort, is just such a "shared world" as the genre writers imagine, stretching out on all sides and into imagined pasts and futures, far beyond the lived experience of any individual person. Let us grant, for the moment, that this shared world is larger, older and more detailed than, we presume, the world of any non-human animal, though it should also be acknowledged that the sensory or phenomenal world of an ordinary dog is likely to be immensely richer, in smells, than any human's: "they haven't got no noses, the fallen sons of Eve."[7] But any educated person—even one educated only in the oral tradition of her particular time, place and clan—can draw on far more information than

---

7 G. K. Chesterton, *Collected Poems* (London: Methuen, 1950), 204–5; see also Alexandra Horowitz, *Being a Dog: Following the Dog into a World of Smell* (New York: Simon & Schuster, 2016).

is simply available to her own senses, and from a greater distance even than a dog. Any such educated person recognizes that her own phenomenal world is only a fragment or an echo or a slice of the larger cosmos, and that her feeling for that larger world may be altered or amended in her intercourse with other persons. Sometimes such alteration is a shock: can it really be that Columbus did not "discover the New World," that medieval Europeans did not suppose the world was flat, that the Catholic Church did not suppress Science, and that Huxley did not defeat Bishop Wilberforce?[8] That constantly modified and expanding story of the world at large is as much a product of our storytelling talents as of our scientific discoveries: more so, indeed, as "scientific discoveries" are only interesting as they confirm or modify the larger story, and give us confidence to find or try some novel practice or technique. Otherwise they are no more than amusing anecdotes or minor glitches, not to be taken seriously by anyone with a living to make and a life to lead.

We can, of course, revert to a fairly "low" doctrine of "reason," in line with what we might "reasonably" expect of a social mammal.[9] Commonsensically, people are judged "rational" when they set aside any personal, peculiar, subjective feelings about their situation, so as to think and act as they could advise just anyone to think and act. They are judged "rational" when they take account of the likely effects of what they do before responding carelessly in rage or lust or fear. They are "rational" if they manage not to contradict themselves too often, do not endorse any very novel thesis until there is socially acceptable "evidence" for it, and stand ready to abandon older certainties — when they think it right. "Rational" people distinguish dreams from waking, are suspicious of whatever sounds "too good to be true," and usually prefer to do and think only what has been done and thought before. "Rational" people are mildly suspicious of what gurus, self-styled experts, dictators and most politicians say, but also hesitate before accepting what is said by anonymous critics of the establishment. Sometimes these rough rules of thumb are elevated to more general

---

8 See Ronald L. Numbers, ed., *Galileo and Other Myths about Science and Religion* (Cambridge, MA: Harvard University Press, 2009).

9 The following remarks were further addressed in my paper "Folly to the Greeks: Good Reasons to Give up Reason," *European Journal for Philosophy of Religion* 4 (2012): 93–113.

principles, and begin to sound absurd. Clifford's Rule, for notorious example, that one should never believe anything without sufficient evidence, is both vague, self-refuting (since there is no unquestionable evidence for this strategy) and impractical, since we are doomed always to be acting on inadequate information.[10] Indeed it is difficult to see how we could ever get experimental or theoretical or even anecdotal "proof" of anything without accepting it as at least a working hypothesis long before there was "proof"—and such acceptance has its costs, which are only cheerfully endured by those who "believe," in advance of evidence, that the search will be worthwhile. Nor it is always sensible, or honorable, to disregard our personal feelings, and peculiar loyalties, when deciding who or what to believe. At any rate perennial sceptics and disloyal partners (quick to disbelieve their significant other's protests unless just anyone would "*have to believe them now*") are not well-regarded. Nor need they be less often deceived by life than are more trusting, loving agents.

But the problem remains. The story may itself be fairly persuasive: this is how we have managed to construct both a fictional, imagined world and the artificial worlds of technological progress. We have both the senses and the practical habits we have needed to cope with the natural and the human worlds: we recognize human faces very early on, as well as having appropriate expectations about object-continuity and the like. Babies are momentarily startled and perhaps amused if a toy train, passing behind a barrier, reemerges with a teddy bear on it. They also very rapidly learn whatever human language (spoken or signed) is in use around them, and also learn to babble their own imitation speech. We have over many generations used these inbuilt capacities to explore and imagine a wider world, finding some place in an extended memory for stories our parents and our teachers tell us, and learning that we ourselves are only of slight size and significance in that wider world. But what power has the imagined world to affect the world of our own experience? Does the imagined

---

10 W.K. Clifford, "The Ethics of Belief" (1877), in *Lectures and Essays*, ed. L. Stephen and F. Pollock (London: Macmillan, 1886), 339–63. Cf. William James, *The Will to Believe* (New York: Longmans, Green & Co., 1897), 30: "if we believe that no bell tolls in us to let us know for certain when truth is in our grasp, then it seems a piece of idle fantasticality to preach so solemnly our duty of waiting for the bell."

world approximate a real world, one that preceded, still surpasses and will long outlast our own personal and all human imagination? Why should we expect our imaginings to match the real? We modify our imaginings to fit experience (that is, we check our theories against experience and even against data from controlled experiments), but this is only to say, as is evident in evolutionary history, that our present theories are only the ones that have survived so far: not necessarily the best possible fits even now, and just as likely to be rendered obsolete by changing circumstance as any other biological artifice.

This indeed is often what is claimed by scientists: not that their theories are true, but only that they are the currently best available ways of representing data, enabling predictions and planning for the future. Even if the world of our present experience were to turn out to be a virtual reality created by intelligences outside the sphere of our experience, we must still engage in the same sort of scientifically guided theorizing and practice. Whatever is true metaphysically, it will be the currently best available theories that we rightly and reasonably rely upon, even while agreeing that we may not yet have thought of the better possibilities, or be unable to state them in currently testable ways. We cannot, after all, act on the mere assumption that the future we experience will be so unlike the past as to render all our theories quaint, even if that is, in the long run, almost exactly what we must expect. Taking his cue from the old catchphrase "There'll always be an England," Robert Heinlein declared, in 1941: "We know better. There won't always be an England—nor a Germany, nor a United States, nor a Baptist Church, nor monogamy, nor the Democratic Party, nor the modesty taboo, nor the superiority of the white race, nor airplanes—they will go—nor automobiles—they'll be gone, we'll see them go. Any custom, technique, institution, belief or social structure that we see around us today will change, will pass, and most of them we will see change and pass."[11] Heinlein himself did indeed live to see change and pass many things that had seemed permanent—though not quite all of the above (indeed, hardly any). We shall see more. We shall also see our present scientific theories modified or abandoned, either from their

---

11 Robert Heinlein, "Discovery of the Future" (1941), cited by J. J. Peirce, *Foundations of Science Fiction* (Westport, CT: Greenwood Press, 1987), 186.

internal contradictions, the emergence of new stories, or a simple collapse of interest in such distant matters. The merely Whiggish notion that our history is inherently "progressive" and bound to continue so has little to support it. We may find, or our descendants find, that Aristotle was right to suggest that proverbs and folk-stories are "the remnants of philosophy that perished in the great disasters that have befallen mankind, and were recorded for their brevity and wit."[12] What will remain of our imaginings is only what our descendants will find useful. But in the meantime we need to live our own lives here and now, and that involves our easy acceptance of the current stories unless they are immediately and obviously "wrong" (whether as scientific predictions or political policies).

THE UNREASONABLE EFFECTIVENESS OF MATHEMATICS

But this story so far, however commendable in its modesty, has flaws. Firstly, almost every scientist and philosopher that *professes* to believe it is being insincere. If all that mattered to us was to find the sort of story that enabled us to carry on with ordinary lives, we would judge all novel suggestions by their practical and social consequences. The Roman Church (and others), on these terms, was wise to caution Galileo, just as later critics might be wise to discourage any research into the genetics of intelligence that might uncover more or less intelligent, or sociable, or warlike "races" (that is, more or less genetically isolated tribes). The results of the researches, after all, are never going to be true, in the strong rhetorical sense: to be accepted as reality whether or not they are expectable, consoling, helpful, or even socially destructive. In which case, they should be assessed for their overall social effect, irrespective of the readiness of the researchers, for their own reasons, to accept them. Experimentalists and scholars, whatever they say, are hoping and believing that their conclusions are correct. So do we all.

> The primary and most universal faith of man [is] his inexpugnable realism, his twofold belief that he is on the one hand in the midst

---

12 Aristotle, *On Philosophy*, fr. 8 Rose, in W. D. Ross, ed., *Works of Aristotle*, volume 12: *Select Fragments* (London: Oxford University Press, 1952), 77 [fr. 10]. Everything has already been discovered, and forgotten, an infinite — or at least an indefinite — number of times: see *De Caelo* 270b19-20, *Meteorologica* 339b27-28, *Politics* 7.1329b25-26.

of realities which are not himself nor mere obsequious shadows of himself, a world which transcends the narrow confines of his own transient being; and on the other hand that he can himself somehow read beyond those confines and bring those external existences within the compass of his own life yet without annulment of their transcendence.[13]

Richard Rorty's declaration that this faith is absurd[14] is itself absurd: obviously, Rorty wishes to say that Lovejoy was simply wrong to believe that there were truths we did not and do not engineer and yet can partly grasp, but he can only manage this rebuttal if indeed there are.

The second problem with the story is that it undermines itself. If we are not equipped to uncover real truths, what is the status of the story from which we infer the conclusion? Darwin was concerned that creatures that had evolved alongside apes and monkeys from some common ape-like ancestor could not reasonably be expected to have the resources to discover that they were indeed the product of that evolution. Others have—not unreasonably—doubted that lately evolved primates on the third rock from a minor sun, with barely five thousand years of written history behind them, could form reliable conclusions about a cosmos many million years old, and many million light-years wide, even if we can manage to survive, more or less equably, here-now.

> Darwin's theory makes the testable prediction that whenever we use technology to glimpse reality beyond the human scale, our evolved intuition should break down.[15]

Tegmark exempts mathematical reasoning about the ultimate nature of things from the breakdown, despite its obvious equal dependence upon "intuition," and perhaps for good reason: he is himself a Platonist and so

---

13 A. O. Lovejoy, *The Revolt against Dualism: An Inquiry concerning the Existence of Ideas* (La Salle, IL: Open Court, 1930), 14.
14 R. M. Rorty, *Philosophy and the Mirror of Nature* (Oxford: Blackwell, 1980), 52n.
15 Max Tegmark, *Our Mathematical Universe: My Quest for the Ultimate Nature of Reality* (London: Allen Lane, 2014), 5.

entitled to appeal past merely "naturalistic" powers. Those materialists who instead make their appeal to "science," as if this were somehow exempt from the Darwinian doubt, have less excuse. But of course that self-destructive theory of the cosmos, and of terrestrial history, is exactly what we are now constrained to doubt. Much the same obstacle is in the way of a recent, otherwise weirdly persuasive argument, that we are increasingly likely ourselves to be players in a complex simulation:[16] the reason for believing this lies in the expectably increasing number of such simulations, so that almost all experiences of 21st century Britain (say) are actually simulated rather than original. But once we doubt the veracity or verisimilitude of our present lives, the very evidence that we are probably "dreaming" has been erased. At least we have little reason to suppose that the makers of the simulation are anything like the people we seem to see: once we entertain the notion that we are inhabiting an invented world, whose apparently vast extent and lifespan is illusory, we may as well suspect that the inventers are entirely alien (the hive intelligences of the End Time, maybe?) or are actually simply angels. Correspondingly, if the evolutionary story diminishes our confidence in our own veracity, we have less reason to believe the story, and to suspect that we might instead have confidence in what we feel and think here-now. Chesterton's account of what sanity requires has some — though not necessarily final — force:

> Every sane man believes that the world around him and the people in it are real, and not his own delusion or dream. No man starts burning London in the belief that his servant will soon wake him for breakfast. But that I, at any given moment, am not in a dream, is unproved and unprovable. That anything exists except myself is unproved and unprovable.
>
> All sane men believe that this world not only exists, but matters. Every man believes there is a sort of obligation on us to interest ourselves in this vision or panorama of life. He would think a man wrong who said, "I did not ask for this farce and it bores me. I am aware that an old lady is being murdered downstairs, but I am

---

16 Nick Bostrom, "Are you living in a computer simulation?," *Philosophical Quarterly* 53 (2003): 243–55.

going to sleep." That there is any such duty to improve the things we did not make is a thing unproved and unprovable.

All sane men believe that there is such a thing as a self, or ego, which is continuous. There is no inch of my brain matter the same as it was ten years ago. But if I have saved a man in battle ten years ago, I am proud; if I have run away, I am ashamed. That there is such a paramount "I" is unproved and unprovable. But it is more than unproved and unprovable; it is definitely disputed by many metaphysicians.

Lastly, most sane men believe, and all sane men in practice assume, that they have a power of choice and responsibility for action.[17]

These unprovable axioms are also the only context in which the scientific and scholarly enterprise can ever be carried out. What their truth (or their undeniability) implies will concern me later. They are not, on their own, quite enough to validate our belief in the larger story about the cosmos and the past of terrestrial life.

But the chief defect in the merely "pragmatic" story I have been telling lies in "the unreasonable effectiveness of mathematics."[18] Wigner's point is that our mathematical intuitions and arguments allow us to describe the universe at large, and must therefore be attuned to principles that govern all things.[19] So also Benedict XVI: "the objective structure of the universe and the intellectual structure of the human being coincide; the subjective reason and the objectified reason in nature are identical. In the end it is 'one' reason that links both and invites us to look to a unique

---

[17] G. K. Chesterton, "Philosophy for the School Room," *Daily News*, June 22, 1907: a reference I owe to Martin Ward and his collection of Chesterton texts: see www.gkc.org.uk/gkc/books/philosophy.html (accessed May 14, 2019).

[18] Eugene P. Wigner, "The Unreasonable Effectiveness of Mathematics in the Natural Sciences," *Communications in Pure and Applied Mathematics* 13 (1960): 1–14.

[19] So also Bett, *Erigena*, 114, after John Eriugena: "We cannot think at all without assuming that our thoughts are to be trusted to bring us into contact with reality, and that the universe is such that we shall not be 'put to permanent intellectual confusion' [quoting Balfour Stewart and Peter Guthrie Tait, *The Unseen Universe, or Physical Speculations on a Future State* (London: Macmillan, 1879), 87, 91]. Now this is purely an act of faith in the reasonableness of the universe, and that is only another way of saying that it is an act of faith in God."

creative Intelligence."[20] The putative success of "science," so far from diminishing the authority of religious theism, is really its vindication: such success is enormously more likely on the theistic hypothesis that the universe is made to be understood (within some limits) than on the merely materialistic hypothesis that any congruence between our thought and the cosmos is a happy accident.

> Far from undermining the credibility of theism, the remarkable success of science in modern times is a remarkable confirmation of the truth of theism. It was from the perspective of Judeo-Christian theism — and from that perspective alone — that it was predictable that science would have succeeded as it has. Without the faith in the rational intelligibility of the world and the divine vocation of human beings to master it, modern science would never have been possible, and, even today, the continued rationality of the enterprise of science depends on convictions that can be reasonably grounded only in theistic metaphysics.[21]

So also Plantinga:

> The traditional theist... has no corresponding reason for doubting that it is a purpose of our cognitive systems to produce true beliefs, nor any reason for thinking that $P(R/(N\&E\&C))$ is low, nor any reason for thinking the probability of a belief's being true, given that it is a product of his cognitive faculties, is no better than in the neighborhood of ½. He may indeed endorse some form of evolution; but if he does, it will be a form of evolution guided and orchestrated by God. And *qua* traditional theist — *qua* Jewish, Moslem, or Christian theist — he believes that God is the premier knower and has created us human beings in his image, an important

---

20 Benedict XVI, Message to Archbishop Rino Fisichella on the Occasion of the International Congress "From Galileo's Telescope to Evolutionary Cosmology. Science, Philosophy and Theology in Dialogue" (2009).

21 Robert C. Koons, "Science and Theism: Concord not Conflict," in *The Rationality of Theism*, ed. Paul Copan and Paul Moser (London: Taylor & Francis, 2003), 72–89.

part of which involves his endowing them with a reflection of his powers as a knower.[22]

To this some may reply once more that the fact that the story we tell about the universe is couched in terms familiar to human mathematicians does not establish any real correspondence, any more than the fact that we can describe the universe in English (or Spanish or Mandarin or whatever) proves that the English (or any other human) language "carves reality at the joints" (as Plato put it: *Phaedrus* 265e; *Statesman* 287c). This is indeed "as if someone were to buy several copies of the morning newspaper to assure himself that what it said was true."[23] A second riposte would be that the accuracy of our mathematical extrapolations is in any case in question: our goal is often to fit the phenomenal evidence to the mathematical prediction, by postulating otherwise imperceptible somewhats to make the equations work! Modern cosmological speculation has resorted to the Original Singularity or Big Bang (where all predictions or retrodictions break down), Dark Matter, Dark Energy and the Multiverse. We may feel affection for these artefacts of our imagination — some would say — but we cannot at the moment confirm their real existence so as to "save the equations." Once again: the whole story may be made up, whether by us or by the makers of our simulation.

But even if this is true, the effectiveness of mathematics must remain a problem: not that our equations enable us to manage lunar landings, or calculate the chemical nature of immensely distant stars, but that mathematics itself, the glorious array of numbers (rational, irrational, imaginary, complex and the rest), forms an interrelated whole. We cannot finally demonstrate that our mathematics forms a consistent whole, but there is enough convergence to show that we are at least dealing with something real, and independent of our own thoughts about it. There are philosophers who would dispute the claim, suggesting instead that numbers and their relationships are fictional, and that many mathematical postulates as yet unproven are, precisely, neither

---

22 Plantinga, *Warrant and Proper Function*, 236.
23 Ludwig von Wittgenstein, *Philosophical Investigations* (4th ed.), ed. P. M. S. Hacker and Joachim Schulte, trans. G. E. M. Anscombe, P. M. S. Hacker and Joachim Schulte (Oxford: Wiley-Blackwell, 2009), 100–101, §265. The context of his remark is different.

Hume's "Peculiar Privilege"

true nor false as yet. All and only what has so far been proved is true; what is not yet proved is neither true nor false. Once again, this is not in practice how mathematicians behave: they may believe a mathematical postulate (that is, they think it true in fact) long before it can be proved. Indeed, it has been shown that there is no finite system in which every mathematical truth can be proved. "The Platonistic view is the only one tenable. Thereby I mean the view that mathematics describes a non-sensual reality, which exists independently of the human mind and is only perceived, and probably perceived very incompletely, by the human mind."[24] Nor is the fictionalist account entirely credible: granted that we cannot prove the system to be consistent (as Gödel himself demonstrated), there is nonetheless a constant confirmation that results achieved in one branch of mathematics also apply in others derived from distinct premises, and with differing terms. We are mapping a preexistent landscape, and can constantly be surprised by discoveries that cannot be merely thought away or redescribed. Consider, for example, "Euler's Identity,"[25] linking e (the base for the natural logarithms, approximating 2.71828 ...), i (the square root of −1) and π (the ratio of a circle's diameter to its circumference: 3.14159 ... : $e^{i\pi} + 1 = 0$. The theorem is widely regarded as a supreme example of mathematical beauty. More to my present point: it demonstrates the unexpected consistency of disparate elements (whether or not the whole system is self-consistent). Π itself turns up so often in mathematics as to be clearly and convincingly a "real thing," despite also being weird (as an irrational number, like the square root of 2, or e itself). There are many aspects of human existence that are indeed mere fictions: structures that are entirely at our disposal if we choose to change them. Some of them — for example the monetary system — may seem more "real" than they are merely because they trade on mathematical relationships. Mathematics itself is not thus at our disposal.

Of course our mathematical explorations are often flawed, and of course the phenomenal world — even the physical world we posit as lying behind

---

24 Kurt Gödel, "Some Basic Theorems on the Foundations of Mathematics and Their Philosophical Implications" (1951), in *Collected Works*, ed. S. Feferman, J. Dawson, W. Goldfarb, C. Parsons, R. Solovay, and J. van Heijenoort (Oxford: Oxford University Press, 1995), 3:304–23.

25 See Paul J. Nahin, *Dr. Euler's Fabulous Formula: Cures Many Mathematical Ills* (Princeton, NJ: Princeton University Press, 2006).

the appearances—is not wholly and finally described by mathematics—or not by any mathematics we can manage now. The question then is: what evolutionary advantage could this insight into the realm of number have? Whether we have any real insight into the depths of space and time may be contested, and our putative success in describing the first few seconds after the "Big Bang" (absurdly so-called[26]) is no guarantee that we have any powers beyond those expected in a transient, terrestrial primate. But our insight into the realm of numbers—or more properly the insight of the mathematically gifted into the realm of numbers—is far less contentious, and even less explicable. Knowing the square root of minus one, the ratio of diameter to circumference, and the base for natural logarithms can do little for our evolutionary success. Therefore there must be something added to the brew, perhaps as Aristotle intended in his suggestion that "intellect" was something added "from outside" (*De Anima* 1.408b20–35; *De Generatione Animalium* 2.736b27–9). This, he also said in an early work, indicates that humanity "has nothing worthy of consideration as being divine or blessed, except what there is in us of reason and wisdom; this alone of our possessions seems to be immortal, this alone to be divine" (*Protrepticus* fr. 10c: Ross, *Selected Fragments*, 42). It is a notion that has had significant effects in Christian and Islamic culture—but perhaps it also needs significant modification, or significant reinterpretation.

REASON, REALITY AND THE MIND OF GOD

Stephen Hawking concluded his *Brief History of Time* with the suggestion that were we to understand why we and the universe existed "it would be the ultimate triumph of human reason—for then we should know the mind of God."[27] He was not claiming, of course, that there was a God

---

26 See Helge Kragh, "Big Bang: The Etymology of a Name," *Astronomy and Geophysics* 54.2 (April 2013): 2.28–2.30 for an account of the gradual triumph of the term, as well as the associated theory. The term is notoriously misleading, as the original Substance did not explode into a previously existing space, nor is there a single center of the explosion. Any observer anywhere would see the distant galaxies flying away from her. The imagined moment marks the beginning (or perhaps the renaissance) of both space and time, and nowhere is more distant from it than anywhere else. The old Egyptian story of Atum's appearance, and the subsequent blossoming, spitting, laughing or ejaculating of all the things there are is at least a little more obviously metaphorical!

27 Stephen Hawking, *A Brief History of Time* (London: Bantam, 1988), 193.

to know, but only that we would then achieve what the imagined person "God" was already supposed to know. "God," in effect, stood only for the supreme and final science. Those future wise men would be what God was supposed to be: effectively all-knowing and all-powerful, as knowing the reason why. Hawking did acknowledge that "even if there is only one possible unified theory, it is just a set of rules and equations," and asked (rhetorically) what it was "that breathes fire into the equations and makes a universe for them to describe?"[28] Later he seems to have decided that those rules themselves can somehow compel the existence of the stuff whose motion they describe[29] — which seems to make little sense. But my concern here is not with cosmological argument for or against the existence of a supreme Creator God. Rather the issue is what it is that "the mind" or "the life of God" amounts to, and what the notion suggests about the nature and vocation of humanity.

That only human beings can "have the mind of God," that only they are "rational," is of course an ancient notion, as I have already indicated. Gods and human beings alone, according to Stoic philosophers, are citizens of the world-city, "because of their participation in reason, which is natural law, and everything else is created for their sake" (SVF 2.528).[30] "Is it not a fearful piece of violence to grant reason to creatures that have no inherent knowledge of God?," enquires Odysseus in Plutarch's *Gryllus* (992e6–7),[31] and gets a barbed reminder of his own atheistical father. In earlier ages those who said so might openly acknowledge that only a few human beings, the wise, could really share God's reason. The rest of us are limited in our vision, our capacities and virtues, so that we can barely do more than lumber slowly from premises to conclusions — which we hurriedly discount when they don't fit our needs. Most of us aren't reasoning beings at all, in the sense that older philosophers intended, since

---

28 Hawking, *Brief History*, 174.

29 Stephen Hawking and Leonard Mlodinow, *The Grand Design* (London: Bantam Press, 2010).

30 *The Hellenistic Philosophers*, ed. A. A. Long and David N. Sedley (Cambridge: Cambridge University Press, 1987), 1:431 [67L]. SVF stands for *Stoicorum Veterum Fragmenta*, an older compendium of the fragmentary remains of Stoic thought.

31 Plutarch of Chaeronia, *Moralia*, vol. 12, trans. Harold Cherniss, Loeb Classical Library (Cambridge, MA: Harvard University Press, 1936), 531 [992E].

we cannot put our personal wishes and unfounded prejudice aside for more than a moment. It is not physicists but philosophers in the ancient sense that might possibly have the mind of God—and the ancients knew that many who professed the title were not to be admired.

> You are a poor cold lump of prejudice, consisting of mere phrases, on which you hang as by a hair. You should preserve yourself firm and practical, remembering that you are to deal with real things. In what manner do you hear,—I will not say that your child is dead, for how could you possibly bear that?—but that your oil is spilled, your wine consumed? Would that someone, while you are bawling, would only say this: "Philosopher, you talk quite otherwise when in the schools. Why do you deceive us? Why, when you are a worm, do you call yourself a man?"[32]

Having the mind of God, in brief, is accepting the apparent will of God, and living without complaint and without attachment to any particular thing or person, knowing ourselves to be but fragments of a larger whole in which there are no privileged times, places, scales or persons. Not merely without complaint: the cosmos was to be welcomed with a sort of joy. Whether it is sensible to set ourselves this ideal, while knowing very well that we are far more likely to crumble, may be moot. Certainly Stephen Hawking may have had more right than many to hope for such an outcome, and may even have achieved it as well as any. But the point is that the wish to live "by intellect" or "in the mind of God" is not to encourage "intellectuals." When Aristotle identified the best life of all with *theoria* (*Nicomachean Ethics* 10.1177a12–18) he did not intend, as worthy scholars and scientists have sometimes assumed, to praise a life dedicated to abstract reasoning. Our task is rather, I suggest, "to love and serve the Lord," *ton theon theorein kai therapeuein* (*Eudemian Ethics* 8.1249b20).[33]

---

32 Epictetus, *Discourses*, vol. 2, trans. W. A. Oldfather, Loeb Classical Library (Cambridge, MA: Harvard University Press, 1959 [1925]), 293 [4.141–43]; see also 1:263 [2.9.20–22].

33 See my "Therapy and Theory Reconstructed."

Hume's "Peculiar Privilege"

I shall address the *moral* or *ethical* issues later. The question here is rather to identify what feature of humanity was originally thought "divine." We may call it "reason" or "intellect," but this was expressly distinguished by ancient classical philosophers from calculating or rationalizing our conclusions. *Nous* is rather the entity, or perhaps the faculty, required for *theoria*: which is to say, for the enjoyment of eternal truth — an enjoyment which we cannot ourselves experience for more than a little time, but which God has always — "for that is God" (Aristotle, *Metaphysics* 12.1072b25–31). This is the "spark of the divine" that philosophers and theologians have sketched, and judged unique to humanity, among all terrestrial beings.

But there are at least two questions to address more carefully. First, what does this spark amount to, and what is it to "theorize"? Second, what reason have we to suppose that only human beings have any share in this divinity? The two questions are entangled: all too often, we have sought to answer the first by seeking to locate whatever it is that human beings do not share with animals. But that would be a tedious question unless we are supposed to share the feature with the authors of our being, with gods or God or whatever other power rules the worlds. The merely commonsensical account of human "rationality," with its strongly social and epistemically modest air, does not have the same effect as a "high" doctrine of Reason, as the faculty or virtue that makes us equal, at least in potential, with the gods. The point is not that we can, with appropriately cautious labor, find out enough about our circumstances and have sufficient sympathy with our human neighbors as to live a modestly productive life: so also, *mutatis mutandis*, could any social animal, without any pretensions to a universal science, or any cosmic importance. Common sense, indeed, may strongly suspect that *pretensions* are what we should above all renounce. "Is my mind my own possession? That parent of false conjectures, that purveyor of delusion, the delirious, the fatuous, and in frenzy or senility proved to be the very negation of mind."[34]

John Wilmot, Earl of Rochester (1647–1680), put the case against us even more vehemently in his "Satire against Reason and Mankind":

---

34 Philo of Alexandria, *Collected Works*, trans. F. H. Colson, G. H. Whitaker, et al., Loeb Classical Library (Cambridge, MA: Harvard University Press, 1929), vol. 2, 77: *On Cherubim* 114–15.

Can We Believe in People?

Were I (who to my cost already am
One of those strange, prodigious creatures, man)
A spirit free to choose, for my own share
What case of flesh and blood I pleased to wear,
I'd be a dog, a monkey, or a bear,
Or anything but that vain animal,
Who is so proud of being rational.

The senses are too gross, and he'll contrive
A sixth, to contradict the other five,
And before certain instinct, will prefer
Reason, which fifty times for one does err;
Reason, an *ignis fatuus* of the mind,
Which, leaving light of nature, sense, behind,
Pathless and dangerous wand'ring ways it takes
Through error's fenny bogs and thorny brakes;
Whilst the misguided follower climbs with pain
Mountains of whimseys, heaped in his own brain;
Stumbling from thought to thought, falls headlong down
Into doubt's boundless sea where, like to drown,
Books bear him up awhile, and make him try
To swim with bladders of philosophy;
In hopes still to o'ertake th' escaping light;
The vapour dances in his dazzling sight
Till, spent, it leaves him to eternal night.
Then old age and experience, hand in hand,
Lead him to death, and make him understand,
After a search so painful and so long,
That all his life he has been in the wrong.
Huddled in dirt the reasoning engine lies,
Who was so proud, so witty, and so wise.[35]

---

35 John Wilmot, *Selected Poems*, ed. Paul Davis (Oxford: Oxford University Press, 2013), 52–53.

Hume's "Peculiar Privilege"

If we are to avoid this conclusion—which Plutarch anticipated in his *Gryllus*—we must still interrogate the notion that "reason" stands for something godlike, whether or not there are gods to share it with. Can it be adequately grasped as Stoic philosophers would wish, merely as a commitment to accept the world, to acknowledge our own smallness and dependence, and so, by an intellectual twist, transcend our own condition as merely social mammals? The commitment, on Stoic terms, is doubtless a little odd, as we have no choice: what we cannot *accept* we must still, perforce, endure. The only result must seem to be that we abandon any wish to rise above the world, and above our station. And how, in that case, does our station and our prospect differ from any other animal's? It seems after all that we should take lessons from our "lesser" kin. At least we should stop despising them. The Skeptical philosopher Pyrrho, according to Diogenes Laertius's *Lives* 9.68, pointed to a pig's indifference to the threat of shipwreck as a good example of serenity in action, and an explanation of his own lack of panic. So also Lev Shestov: "the summit of human existence, say the philosophers, is spiritual serenity, *aequanimitas*. But in that case the animals should be our ideal, for in the matter of imperturbability they leave nothing to be desired."[36]

If this is not to be the conclusion, then perhaps we should take the notion of "escape" more seriously. "Reason," as at least some philosophers intended it, is our route out from being "animal": not merely and commonsensically that we can, to some extent and sometimes, delay our passionate responses, and consider how we would appear to others in doing so and so. So also can other creatures. Aristotle urged us not to follow the advice to consider only what befits a mortal human creature, but "as far as possible to *immortalize* ourselves, and do everything to live by what is best and greatest in us" (*Nicomachean Ethics* 10.1177b21–4). And that best, he thought, was *Nous*. Plotinus reaffirmed the claim: *Nous* is king, "but we too are kings (*basileuomen*), when we are in accord with it; we can be in accord with it in two ways, either by having something like its writing written in us like laws, or by being as if filled with it and able to see it and be aware of it as present" (*Ennead* V.3 [49].4, 1–4).

That vision, by Platonic standards, is the enjoyment of an eternal beauty realized in all the manifold forms of being—an enjoyment likely always, for

---

36 Lev Shestov, *All Things Are Possible*, trans. Bernard Martin (Athens, GA: Ohio University Press, 1977), 54.

us, to be transient, as we are lured or compelled back into the concerns of mortal, bodily existence in the world here-now. Our *memory* of the vision is, as it were, an image stamped in our souls, or as if we were inhabited by another, diviner, spirit (see *Ennead* V.8 [31].10, 39–45). If we cannot recall this, or cannot ever experience it, then we have less reason to believe that we are ever "in touch" (the expression is also Plotinian) with any real world beyond the present phenomena. If we can recall it, or at least imagine something of what the philosophers intended, then we may find the Plotinian description apt:

> Intellect... has one power for thinking, by which it looks at the things in itself, and one by which it looks at what transcends it by a direct awareness and reception, by which also before it saw only, and by seeing acquired intellect and is one. And that first one is the contemplation of Intellect in its right mind, and the other is Intellect in love, when it goes out of its mind "drunk with the nectar"; then it falls in love, simplified into happiness (*haplotheis eis eupatheian*) by having its fill, and it is better for it to be drunk with a drunkenness like this than to be more respectably sober. (*Ennead* VI.7 [38].35, 20–28)

This is the life of gods—and godlike humans. But the question must now arise, what actual reason have we to insist that only humans, of all terrestrial creatures, can experience what, admittedly, is a *wordless* communion with the divine? Maybe only human beings can "speak" (or speak a humanly intelligible language), but how is that a relevant consideration, except to suggest that our *much speaking* may get in the way of "reason"? Maybe there are times when we should envy not merely the beasts' equanimity, but their—partial—silence. Maybe we do not become "godlike" by mastering the world, but by acknowledging that we are not masters. "Let *this* mind be in you, that was in Christ Jesus, who being in the form of God did not think equality with God a thing to be grasped, but emptied himself, by taking the form of a servant, being born in the likeness of men" (Phil 2:5–7).

3

Moral Realism

LIFE'S WORK AND SYMBIOSES

The folk-biological picture has a further element, to which I have already gestured. For there to be a living world there need to be all sorts of creatures working together (however little they know they are) to produce it. Soil itself is very much more than dirt: it is a living system, full of prokaryotic and eukaryotic life. The air we breathe has been created and must be sustained by living things (so that we have no need to visit Mars to know that there is no longer any life on its surface).[1] The trace elements we need in our diets are produced and disseminated by creatures of whom most of us have never heard. All of us depend on the continued being of the prokaryotic population, otherwise called eubacteria and archaea.[2] The eubacterial population, though we divide it up into species very much as we divide more familiar plants and animals, is really a single population, in which genetic information is widely shared between what seem to us to be different sorts of bacteria. There are of course pragmatic and transient reasons to treat different bacterial forms rather differently: some of them digest our food for us, and others spread toxins in their wake. But those distinctions are transient, and unreliable. The very bacteria that once caused diseases in a virgin population may develop into symbiotic helpers — or of course vice versa.

Some philosophers, notably those with Stoic sympathies, have concluded that a creature's *ergon* is not only to do what preserves it in its

---

[1] See James Lovelock, *Gaia: A New Look at Life on Earth*, 3rd ed. (Oxford: Oxford University Press, 2000 [1979]).

[2] Archaebacteria are a distinct kingdom — as distant from eubacteria as the latter are from eukaryotes such as plants, animals and fungi. Both sorts of prokaryote are vital to global — and our own — survival. Eukaryotes may have originated in an alliance between strains of archaebacteria and eubacteria. See Lynn Margulis and Dorion Sagan, *Microcosmos: Four Billion Years of Microbial Evolution*, 2nd edition (Berkeley: University of California Press, 1997).

own characteristic activity but also to serve the larger good. What a dog does, its *ergon*, is not merely to preserve *itself*, but to help preserve its pack—and also the larger world in which predator and prey are mutually dependent. Individual organisms, as much as individual organs, exist within a larger and more complex whole. The question to ask of any particular organism, or any particular sort of organism, is not merely how its various limbs, organs and behavior patterns serve that organism's own survival, but what good it does in the larger world (whether or not it means to). "The endeavor (*conatus*) wherewith each thing endeavors to persist in its own being is nothing more than the actual essence of the thing itself" (Spinoza, *Ethics* 3.7). But no individual thing can thus persist merely by itself: it needs an entire world to sustain it, and particularly the local, living world. A creature that damages that larger world does damage to itself. Other philosophers have been unwilling to consider any such external functions: organisms aren't organs, and human beings, especially, aren't tools. It makes sense to say of eyes, ears, lungs, heart, liver, legs and so on that they wouldn't exist at all if they didn't—in general—do some good to their possessors (or at least enabled them to reproduce). It also makes sense to say that dogs, sheep, cattle and so on wouldn't exist—at least in their domesticated forms—if they didn't do people any good. But it does not seem that creatures "in the wild" wouldn't exist unless they did some larger good.

Anthropocentrists have traditionally responded that all such creatures do nonetheless exist to do us good: even bedbugs, according to Chrysippus, help to get us out of bed![3] Less anthropocentric theorists have preferred to say that the world is not organized simply for *our* good, but for the beauty and integrity of the whole. If there were no wolves, crocodiles, cassowaries, mosquitoes and the like the world would be distinctly worse, aesthetically or even practically. The whole would be less varied and inclusive, and soon there would be far too many herbivores even for their own comfort. If existing predators were suddenly removed from the system, it would not be long—geologically speaking—before other predators emerged from hitherto herbivorous lines—which is as

---

3 Plutarch, *Moralia*, vol. 13, trans. Harold Cherniss, Loeb Classical Library (Cambridge, MA: Harvard University Press, 1976), 503: *On Stoic Self-contradictions* 21.1044d.

Moral Realism

much as to say that there is a stable pattern to which the living world is drawn. Correspondingly, the reintroduction of such predators as wolves has a valuable "trophic cascade" effect on the whole local environment.[4]

But this is not enough to validate the earlier synthesis, expressed by William Kirby as follows:

> In our ascent from the most minute and least animated parts of that Kingdom to man himself, we have seen in every department that nothing was left to chance, or the rule of circumstances, but every thing was adapted by its structure and organization for the situation in which it was to be placed, and the functions it was to discharge; that though every being, or group of beings, had separate interests, and wants, all were made to subserve to [sic] a common purpose, and to promote a common object; and that though there was a general and unceasing conflict between the members of this sphere of beings, introducing apparently death and destruction into every part of it, yet that by this great mass of seeming evil pervading the whole circuit of the animal creation, the renewed health and vigour of the entire system was maintained. A part suffers for the benefit and salvation of the whole; so that the doctrine of the sufferings of one creature, by the will of God, being necessary to promote the welfare of another, is irrefragably established by every thing we see in nature; and further, that there is an unseen hand directing all to accomplish this great object, and taking care that the destruction shall in no case exceed the necessity.[5]

Maybe there is an unseen hand, but the story nowadays seems neither plausible nor ethically uncontroversial. Far more of our history is down to chance, and to the choices of individual organisms than Kirby supposed.

What does this change about the way we should evaluate individual

---

4 Amaroq E. Weiss, Timm Kroeger, J. Christopher Haney and Nina Fascione, "Social and Ecological Benefits of Restored Wolf Populations," *Transactions of the 72nd North American Wildlife and Natural Resources Conference* 2007 (Washington, DC), 297–319.

5 William Kirby, *On the Power, Wisdom and Goodness of God as Manifested in the Creation of Animals and in their History, Habits and Instincts* (Cambridge: Chadwyck Healey, 1998 [1835]), 2:526.

organisms? Domesticated plants and animals exist both as natural organisms and as means to humanly determined ends. A good dog or a good cereal crop both perform as we wish them to, for purposes we or our masters have selected (and is that also the criterion our masters use for us?). But none of our domesticated servants are only and entirely human artefacts: they are indeed natural organisms, with their own inchoate purposes and their own "functions" in the larger world—functions, *erga*, that most of them would take up again without delay once we were gone. Even wild creatures are often subsumed into the human enterprise. Game birds, deer, and (in the past at any rate) large carnivores have been preserved in order to be hunted. McKibben has a point: "by domesticating the earth, even though we have done it badly, we've domesticated all that lives on it. Bears hold more or less the same place as a golden retriever,"[6] though it might be as well not to act on this assumption when you next encounter a bear. But in those cases we remember much more easily that they do indeed have their own purposes, and some of them may look on us as food. Sometimes we may even see them as something wonderful and beautiful, significant elements of the wider world on which we still depend and which we—sometimes—love.

> The Torah laws that safeguard the health and humanity of society as a whole deal with justice in the broadest sense, not only for the poor but also for the land. This is especially true for the laws of *Sh'mitah*, the sabbatical year (often spelled *Shmita*), and *Yovel*, the Jubilee year. According to the Levitical section on *Sh'mitah*, when the rights of the land conflict with the needs of people, the rights of the land take precedence (Lev 26:34, 43). Not only that, but wild animals have the right in the *Sh'mitah* year to forage freely on land that would normally be cultivated (Lev 25:7). The Torah is explicit that our moral frame of reference must extend beyond the human world. (The latter rule also suggests that *Sh'mitah* is a kind of return to Eden, where all the creatures shared the same food supply.) Even from the perspective of human needs—most

---

6 Bill McKibben, *The End of Nature* (Harmondsworth: Penguin, 1990), 78.

especially the need for justice—we must not put on moral blinders that prevent us from empathizing with the more-than-human creatures and ecosystems around us. Justice can never be complete without justice for the land.⁷

The wider world is imagined, in effect, as a great work of art, constructed out of themes and variations. Whether a particular variant is an allowable, even a welcome, variation or a fault will always be a matter of judgment. The more traditional view will often see faults where others might see lucky accidents, or the beginning of an unfamiliar theme. What we admire, or tolerate, or condemn will depend on our conception of some *proper* form, and there may be a sudden shift in attitude when the object we are assessing slips in our thought from one imagined paradigm to another (whether that paradigm is a real biological attractor or merely a human image). What do we expect of dogs? As long as we hold the image of Faithful Hound any deviation from that loyalty will mark the animal as a "bad dog." If we recall instead the image of Intelligent Wolf we may have less reason to be surprised that the dog seeks his own maturity, and companions of his kind. Crudely, domestic dogs are what wolves would be if they did not grow up. What do we think of snakes? As long as we imagine the stereotypical enemy of other, warm-blooded life, we may find snakes, just as such, unappealing. Imagining them instead as images of wisdom, or still better simply as reptilian organisms with as long an evolutionary past as ours, may allow us to see—as Aristotle advised—something wonderful and beautiful in them as also in the smallest and commonest of things. Snakes aren't simply "legless," any more than seals are "deformed quadrupeds." Or rather, their "deformity" or "lack" is relative only to a form, an *eidos* that is not wholly theirs. People have often found apes (or the other apes?) alarming just because they are both like and unlike people: *apes* of humanity. To see them straight requires that we stop judging them to be deformed. Might not the same apply within our own kind? In the common view, to be blind, deaf, rather stupid, dyslexic, autistic, dwarfish, ugly or overly emotional are all variously "defects." Oddly, we generally care

---

7 Seidenberg, *Kabbalah and Ecology*, 127.

less — or rather academics writing on these topics care rather less — about physical clumsiness, lack of stamina, myopia, innumeracy, ambition and personal conceit (which are, rationally speaking, just as much defects)! Might we not wonder instead whether there are some other ideals in action than the ones we insist are "really human"?

> Suppose he [that is, a particular "backward" child] did remain more like a child than the rest of us. Is there anything particularly horrible about a child? Do you shudder when you think of your dog, merely because he's happy and fond of you and yet can't do the forty-eighth proposition of Euclid? Being a dog is not a disease. Being a child is not a disease. Even remaining a child is not a disease.[8]

THE ATHEISTICAL PARADOX

Mathematical realism may be the default assumption of working mathematicians, and this may — in the end — require some form of metaphysical theism to provide a place for such seemingly abstract objects as numbers, sets, ratios and the like. At least, the attempt to do without such realism is awkward and usually inconsistent. But is there a larger problem with *moral* realism? How can it be that there are "real" (causally significant) norms of behavior, whether in a merely material cosmos or in one devised by superior intelligence? How can we believe that humane values have any large effect, or that they will in the end be vindicated? How can we suppose that the world is arranged, even over the very long run, for the good of human beings, in anything like the sense that we appreciate?

The twofold atheistical charge against "religion" is that any Creator of such a world as this appears to be would be unworthy of worship (and so could not be God), and that "religious believers" are often guilty of great evil. But for these to be powerful arguments some form of moral realism is required: there must be immediate moral truths that we can know, although most modern atheists will also usually insist that our moral sentiments and principles are only those embedded in us by Darwinian selection. I propose

---

8 G. K. Chesterton, *Four Faultless Felons* (London: Cassell, 1930), 39.

that neither Darwinian Naturalism (of a sort endorsed by H. G. Wells), nor the more liberal Naturalism now generally preferred, nor Quasi-Realism (in which "moral truths" are merely social facts devised by cultured humans) can provide a solid basis for the moral judgments made against God and against "believers." Moral and other absolute truths are best conceived as unified within an eternal, creative, non-material intellect: only theists, that is, have good grounds for condemning either the "religious" or whatever lesser gods once formed this world.

It is hardly surprising that atheists may also be moral realists: how else can the charge against a putative Creator God and more especially against His devotees be supported? But that conjunction is nonetheless contentious. What sort of moral realism can support the charges against either "the religious" or an imagined God? What force can the charges have *without* firm moral judgments? And how could an atheistical cosmos include firm moral truths?

That there really are atheists who are also moral realists is confirmed in a recent survey of philosophers' opinions about standard philosophical issues. This revealed that while only 14.6% of those targeted claimed to be or to be inclined to be theists, 56.4% declared themselves moral realists and 65.7% moral cognitivists.[9] Far more philosophers, that is, apparently accepted that there were moral truths discernible by reason than that there was an eternal guarantor of moral truth. It is probable that some atheistical philosophers have abandoned classical theism merely because of doubts about the conceptual integrity of such notions as omnipotence, omniscience, omnipresence and the like. But much the strongest and most immediately recognizable argument against classical theism is constituted in the so-called "problem of evil." How can such a world as this be created or even permitted by any decent deity? How can religious believers be trusted when they are themselves often guilty of great evil? My argument will be that these charges are only significant if there are indeed substantive moral truths — and that the basis for such truths must lie in some form of theism. The resolution of this seeming paradox is made easier by examining past ethical and metaphysical philosophies — notably Stoic, Epicurean and Platonist.

[9] David Bourget and David J. Chalmers, "What Do Philosophers Believe?," *Philosophical Studies* 170 (2014): 465–500.

Can We Believe in People?

To return to the survey of opinion: it seems likely (at least in this age of the world) that a majority of those moral realists, in addition to being atheists, accept the truth of evolutionary naturalism — and so of the conclusion that our moral inhibitions and priorities, as well as our more general rational capacities, are the result of Darwinian selection. On this account we have them, as we have other stable features of our characters, not because they are *true* or likely to be accepted by just any "rational" intelligence of whatever stock (if "rational" identifies a real character rather than a guddle of shared practices and assumptions) but solely because in the long run, and so far, accepting (or at least professing) them gave our ancestors a slight reproductive edge over the available alternatives. There need be no reason to expect our moral views to form a coherent set, nor to be universal in our species (though some might be), nor yet to be exclusively human. "Human behavior — like the deepest capacities for emotional response which drive and guide it — is the circuitous technique by which human genetic material has been and will be kept intact. Morality has no other demonstrable function"[10] — that is, or so Wilson declares, there is nothing else that it consistently does, and that explains the particular shape it takes (if it takes any). Neither claim — that it has this effect consistently and that there are no other possible explanations for its form — is beyond dispute. Even if they are true, it does not follow, of course (though Wilson almost seems to think it does) that we would therefore have good reason to *amend* our moral code to help preserve that material. Who are "we"? And what could count as "reason"? "When ancient opinions and rules of life are taken away, the loss cannot possibly be estimated. From that moment we have no compass to govern us; nor can we know distinctly to what port we steer."[11] Nor can we expect our successors to respect *our* aims, especially if we have taught them to disrespect tradition! We may seek to suppress or to control an appetite for sugar, but only because we are *not* suppressing an appetite for good teeth, and a long and healthy life. If neither appetite is grounded in anything but past reproductive success, neither has any definite priority.

10 E. O. Wilson, *On Human Nature* (Cambridge, MA: Harvard University Press, 1978), 167.
11 Edmund Burke, *Reflections on the Revolution in France*, ed. Conor Cruise O'Brien (Harmondsworth: Penguin, 1968), 172; see also 129–31.

Moral Realism

There have been moralists who openly equated moral good with natural success, and perhaps that would be the excuse of atheistical realists of the sort uncovered in the survey: dissatisfied with existing codes and convinced of Darwinian theory, H. G. Wells, for example, insisted that "if the universe is non-ethical by our present standards, we must reconsider those standards and reconstruct our ethics."[12] He drew the conclusion that we should cooperate with the Darwinian process, and thence that we should eliminate all inferior or inconvenient forms (which he was sure he could recognize).

> The insoluble problems of pain and death, gaunt, incomprehensible facts as they were, fall into place in the gigantic order that evolution unfolds. All things are integral in the mighty scheme, the slain builds up the slayer, the wolf grooms the horse into swiftness, and the tiger calls for wisdom and courage out of man. All things are integral, but it has been left for men to be consciously integral, to take, at last, a share in the process, to have wills that have caught a harmony with the universal will, as sand grains flash into splendour under the blaze of the sun.... The old ethical principles, the principle of equivalents or justice, the principle of self-sacrifice, the various vague and arbitrary ideas of purity, chastity and sexual "sin," came like rays out of the theological and philosophical lanterns men carried in the darkness.... But now there has come a new view of man's place in the scheme of time and space, a new illumination, dawn.... The act of faith is no longer to follow your lantern, but to put it down.[13]

The notion that we should, in some way, live "in harmony with nature" is an ancient one, and had always carried the implications both that we should be aware how small a part of nature we really were, and that we should acknowledge the law written in our hearts and history—the laws, amongst other things, of justice, modesty and charity.[14] Wells and his New Republicans ("the scientifically trained middle class") chose instead

---

12 H. G. Wells, *Anticipations* [1903] *and Other Works* (London: Fisher Unwin, 1924), 248.
13 Wells, *Anticipations*, 253–54.
14 See C. S. Lewis, *The Abolition of Man* (London: Geoffrey Bles, 1946).

Can We Believe in People?

to model their lives on "nature," conceived as a constant struggle to "succeed," a "universal will" directed only to survival. Everything is integral, but some things ("weak and silly and pointless things") serve only by being destroyed. The New Republicans will have no pity for such "contemptible and silly creatures," and "to make life convenient for the breeding of such people will seem to them not the most virtuous and amiable thing in the world... but an exceedingly abominable proceeding.... The procreation of children who by the circumstances of their parentage, *must* be diseased bodily or mentally... is absolutely the most loathsome of all conceivable sins."[15] The notorious Scopes Trial, in 1925, it is ironical now to remember, concerned a textbook written from the heights of American Eugenicism,[16] which contained such gems as this:

> Parasitism and its Cost to Society. — Hundreds of families such as those described above exist today, spreading disease, immorality, and crime to all parts of this country. The cost to society of such families is very severe. Just as certain animals or plants become parasitic on other plants or animals, these families have become parasitic on society. They not only do harm to others by corrupting, stealing, or spreading disease, but they are actually protected and cared for by the state out of public money. Largely for them the poorhouse and the asylum exist. They take from society, but they give nothing in return. They are true parasites. The Remedy. — If such people were lower animals, we would probably kill them off to prevent them from spreading. Humanity will not allow this, but we do have the remedy of separating the sexes in asylums or other places and in various ways preventing intermarriage and the possibilities of perpetuating such a low and degenerate race. Remedies of this sort have been tried successfully in Europe and are now meeting with some success in this country.[17]

---

15 Wells, *Anticipations*, 257–58.

16 See Edwin Black, *War against the Weak: Eugenics and America's Campaign to Create a Master Race* (New York: Four Walls Eight Windows, 2003) for a detailed account of the "experts" who imprisoned, sterilized and castrated people they deemed "unfit," in defiance of law, the American Constitution and ordinary decency.

17 George William Hunter, *A Civic Biology: Presented in Problems* (New York: American

Moral Realism

My guess is that rather few of those who proclaim themselves both moral realists and atheists would now regard these policies with respect. The irony is that they would almost all insist on banning Hunter's book (and probably firing the teacher), as outraging their moral sense. Indeed, as I observed before, the most convincing reason that modern atheists usually offer for their atheism is a moral one — that the imagined Creator of a world like this must be a villain, who *ought not* to exist. The oddity of that covert argument is obvious: only if something like theism is correct can there be any reason to limit our ontology by our ethics, and only if some things, some actions, some events are wholly impermissible can we have reason, from our limited perspective, to decide that nothing could ever justify or excuse the pains and evils of creation. As George Berkeley remarked: "he who undertakes to measure without knowing either [the measure or the thing to be measured] can be no more exact than he is modest, . . . who having neither an abstract idea of moral fitness nor an adequate idea of the divine economy shall yet pretend to measure the one by the other."[18] Not knowing what a putative Creator intends, nor how best that intention may be globally realized, nor even whether those aims are in fact already realized in the universe at large, we are in no position to judge Its work — unless what we already know about this world here is *essentially* at odds with some *absolute* standard, irrespective of all consequentialist calculations. If all we know is that much of it makes us uncomfortable, or is not what we ourselves (or so we think) would choose (without knowing the eventual outcome, nor what might have been done instead), there is no *moral* case to be made against the Creator (nor even against those, like Wells or — maybe — Wilson, who prefer to go along with what they conceive to be the inescapable way things are). Our only choice would be the one defined for us by the Stoics. We are much like

---

Book Co., 1914), 263. See Edward J. Larson, *Summer for the Gods: The Scopes Trial and America's Continuing Debate over Science and Religion* (Cambridge, MA: Harvard University Press, 1998) for an account of the political and economic context of the trial; Stephen J. Gould, *Rocks of Ages: Science and Religion in the Fullness of Life* (London: Jonathan Cape, 1999) describes William Jennings Bryan's humanitarian motives (Bryan being Clarence Darrow's adversary in the Trial). The play *Inherit the Wind* (1955; filmed in 1960) misrepresents Bryan, Darrow and the point at issue.

18 George Berkeley, *Alciphron, or The Minute Philosopher* [1732], in *Works*, vol. 3, ed. A. A. Luce and T. E. Jessop (Edinburgh: Thomas Nelson, 1950), 251–52.

a dog tied to a moving cart: we may run willingly behind it or else resist, but move we will. Better (perhaps) go quietly.[19]

In selecting Wells as a spokesman for a purely "naturalistic" ethic, rather than the softer and more agreeable versions of evolutionary ethics that seek to suggest that a more "humane" sensibility, emphasizing care for the weak, loyalty to the tribe and family and courage in adversity, will reliably emerge, I may seem to have stacked the case against naturalism. Maybe any intelligent animals will come to value cooperation over competition, and have some care for others. Even non-human primates show some signs of valuing fairness above their individual profit. But all such signs of a "liberal humanity" are balanced by other emergent habits: greed, xenophobia, disgust, negligence and the lust to dominate. Human beings characteristically develop societies discriminatory in regard to caste and gender, plan war and genocide, and ignore the long-term consequences of all they like to do, at least as often as they construct liberal democracies. The latter, indeed, are rarer, and readily subverted. If we are to wait until the very end to discover which values have survived Darwinnowing, we cannot easily be sure that the "liberal" ones will win. That the "meek" will inherit the earth, let alone the cosmos, does not seem, naturalistically, likely.

So the atheistical cases against God and against "religion" must chiefly be founded on moral indignation of a kind that only makes sense if there indisputably are Absolute Moral Norms which we can at once discern, which are more than maxims drawing their strength from the likely consequences of obeying or disobeying them, and if things could, somehow or other, be otherwise. If the moral worth of the cosmos will be discernible only at its end, and only by one capable of assessing all possible alternate histories, we have no way to judge it, and so no way of judging its putative Creator. Some things, some actions, some events — we must suppose — are already visibly and unalterably bad or good, whatever happens next. But what sort of things can these Norms be? If they are only our projected preferences, then the best that we could say is that the world is not to our current taste, and that there is no reason why it should be: no reason, that is, either to suppose that it ever will be, or that it really *should* be. We may *want* humanity to

---

19 Hippolytus, *Refutation of All Heresies* 1.21, in Long and Sedley, *Hellenistic Philosophers*, 1:386 [62A].

Moral Realism

last forever, both as our own lineage and as an imagined ideal of personal, "humane" living (an ideal very different, we must admit, from most actual human life). But it seems more likely—within a naturalistic framework of the sort that modern atheists prefer—that no form of life will last, and that the final outcome will be only "that calm Sunday that goes on and on, when even lovers find their peace at last, and Earth is but a star, that once had shone."[20] Even if we let ourselves imagine a far future when some unified living purpose controls all remaining stuff, it is far likelier that eusocial insects or distributed computer programs will be the nearer analogue in our experience of the eventual lords.[21] And if we are living in a universe where those lords are already active (how would we tell?), there seems to be no point *condemning* them, nor yet—as far as we yet know—propitiating them either (or at least not yet). What moral effect should we allow these thoughts? Either humanity, as a lineage and an ideal, will be lost in an unmeaning wilderness, as Bertrand Russell grandiloquently imagined,[22] or else the "final meaning" will be no human one. What merit is there then in seeking and failing to preserve "humanity"—as either a lineage or an ideal? Russell himself sought to maintain an "heroic" pose:

> It remains only to cherish, ere yet the blow falls, the lofty thoughts that ennoble his little day; disdaining the coward terrors of the slave of Fate, to worship at the shrine that his own hands have built; undismayed by the empire of chance, to preserve a mind free from

---

20 James Elroy Flecker, "The Golden Road to Samarkand," in *Collected Poems* (London: Martin Secker, 1916), 145.

21 See Freeman Dyson, "Time without End: Physics and Biology in an Open Universe," *Reviews of Modern Physics* 51.3 (1979), reprinted in *Selected Papers of Freeman Dyson* (Providence, RI: American Mathematical Society, 1996), 529–42.

22 "That Man is the product of causes which had no prevision of the end they were achieving; that his origin, his growth, his hopes and fears, his loves and his beliefs, are but the outcome of accidental collocations of atoms; that no fire, no heroism, no intensity of thought and feeling, can preserve an individual life beyond the grave; that all the labours of the ages, all the devotion, all the inspiration, all the noonday brightness of human genius, are destined to extinction in the vast death of the solar system, and that the whole temple of Man's achievement must inevitably be buried beneath the debris of a universe in ruins—all these things, if not quite beyond dispute, are yet so nearly certain, that no philosophy which rejects them can hope to stand" (Bertrand Russell, "The Free Man's Worship" [1903], in *Mysticism and Logic* [London: Allen & Unwin, 1918], 46–57; 47–48).

the wanton tyranny that rules his outward life; proudly defiant of the irresistible forces that tolerate, for a moment, his knowledge and his condemnation, to sustain alone, a weary but unyielding Atlas, the world that his own ideals have fashioned despite the trampling march of unconscious power.[23]

"By Jove," as Logan Pearsall Smith remarked, "that *is* a stunt."[24]

Mild mockery aside, the heroic stance may strike us admirable—the only way we have of affirming values that we deeply feel, even in the face of a universal failure. How well it can survive the universal acid of a Darwinian account of how we came to admire such heroism—especially in others—may be moot. And how shall we "worship" the temples or the idols our own hands have made?[25] There can hardly be "anything more wretched than for a man to be in thrall to what he himself has made."[26] Must not this creed, in any case, contain its own destruction? If we denounce the world and its offspring, how can we still affirm even those heroic emotions, which are, after all, as much a product of mindless evolutionary processes (or inhuman engineering work) as any of the moralities that Wells and Russell despised? "What beauty can be found in a moral system, formed, and governed by chance, fate or any other blind, unthinking principle?"[27]

A QUASI-REALIST ALTERNATIVE

Strong Moral Realism of the sort that modern atheists seem to need, and do sometimes profess, dictates that there are real Norms, of an absolute and recognizable sort. Our trust in them can qualify as cognitive because it is they that *cause* us to believe: that is, they have sufficient causal power to influence at any rate our feelings and beliefs, even if they do not *directly*

---

23 Russell, *Mysticism and Logic*, 56–57.

24 Logan Pearsall Smith, *All Trivia* (New York: Harcourt, Brace, 1945), 91.

25 See the prophet Isaiah, mocking those who cut down a tree and shape it for different aims: "some of it he takes and warms himself, some he kindles and bakes bread on it, and some he makes into a god and prostrates himself, shaping it into an idol and bowing down before it" (44:15–16).

26 Augustine, *City of God*, trans. R. W. Dyson (Cambridge: Cambridge University Press, 1998), 347 [8.23].

27 Berkeley, *Alciphron*, 128.

Moral Realism

influence any larger sphere. They also constitute a consistent set, obedience to which is always *possible* (even if often painful). In brief, they form the substance of at least a partially influential godhead — one God rather than many disparate values whose power lies only in our belief in them. This was the moral and metaphysical synthesis accepted by our predecessors, especially in the Platonic School. But before examining its implications, I should consider again a possible alternative.

Quasi-Realists take seriously the suggestion — implicit in Russell's rhetoric — that we have built our shrines ourselves, and that we are subject to a variety of *nomoi* rather than *thesmoi*: tacit or explicit agreements of much the same sort as lie behind other institutions, such as property, money, marriage, rather than commands from any higher authority.[28] There are "social" facts as well as "natural" ones, as our Greek predecessors recognized, and only a few of us can ever imagine leaving the social entirely behind, either by living, literally, in the wilderness or by ignoring all merely social differences and merely social artefacts (including human language). Such absolute renouncers may be beasts or gods (as Aristotle proposed: *Politics* 1.1253a1–30), but most of us non-renouncers suspect that their lives will not be long. Even beasts, of course, have their own social or species-specific universe, and they respond not merely to the material nature that they encounter but to the very detailed discriminations that their ancestry and individual experience have created. "Before soul it was a dead body, earth and water, or rather the darkness of matter and non-existence, and 'what the gods hate,' as a poet says" (Plotinus, *Ennead* V.1 [10].2, 13–23, 26–28).[29] That is, until there are living things to mark a real difference between here and there, then and now, one "thing" and another, there is nothing orderly or beautiful. But it would be foolish (surely?) to insist that nothing is really orderly or beautiful "now." We earthly organisms live in the world we have created over many million years, and especially — at least for our own species — during the millennia of human exploration and narration. Variations and revisionings are possible within that world, and we humans can even imagine or faintly

---

28 See Martin Ostwald, *Nomos and the Beginnings of the Athenian Democracy* (Oxford: Clarendon Press, 1969).

29 Plotinus is quoting the Homeric description of Hades in *Iliad* 20.65.

discern quite other worlds (for example, the worlds of eusocial insects), or startlingly horrid changes in our own. We may also recognize that our world is transient: that it may change beyond our recognition, or expire entirely, sooner than we hope. Its transience is not a final reason to abandon it in favor of—allegedly—more lasting dreams.

So perhaps the atheistical realists and cognitivists, and especially those who have a rooted "moral" objection to God and to religion, can be conceived as "quasi-realists" rather than strict realists. As such, they may plausibly claim to "know" whether or not someone is lawfully married, who won the last election, what the current value of a dollar is in sterling, that Rembrandt is a great painter, and how wicked it is to rape a five-year-old. The values they variously discern are products of "our" lives together, and had no influence in the beginning. By the same argument, of course, the gods and God Himself are quasi-real, as much pervasive features of the human mindscape as marriage, money, argument and art, as Epicureans seem to have supposed.[30] We may be moved by them and by what represents or even constitutes them (music, art, narrative and theology) without insisting that they exist outside the human frame—except so far as visibly and obviously the greatest of them (sex, hunger, anger, fear) do also influence the non-human. "Our preconception of them will be a genuine piece of *moral* knowledge, an accurate intuition of man's natural good"[31]—though Long and Sedley here give too much credit to the notion of a "natural" good, for reasons spelt out before. The only proper question is whether the stories and the images are helpful ones: do they serve our continuing human life, as we have come to conceive it? What moral examples are implicit in the stories, what standards of "moral beauty"? In criticizing some elements of our shared stories we are relying on other elements: when Plato attacked the poets for suggesting that "godly" behavior includes incest, patricide, kidnapping, deception and murder he was relying on other stereotypes of good behavior: respect for kinship ties and protective care of the weaker, in particular (Plato, *Republic* 2.377d–383c). Olympian Zeus, as the sculptor Pheidias represented him, was a greater

---

30 So Long and Sedley, *Hellenistic Philosophers*, 1:145: "gods, like giants, are thought-constructs."

31 Long and Sedley, *Hellenistic Philosophers*, 1:147.

Moral Realism

creation, the very image, so admirers said, of how Zeus would appear in human form (Cicero, *Orator* II.8–9; Plotinus, *Ennead* V.8 [31]). Molded in gold and ivory, cypress and citron-wood, in the late 5th century BC and stationed in Olympia, it represented Zeus in majesty:

> The god sits on a throne, and he is made of gold and ivory. On his head lies a garland which is a copy of olive shoots. In his right hand he carries a Victory, which, like the statue, is of ivory and gold; she wears a ribbon and — on her head — a garland. In the left hand of the god is a sceptre, ornamented with every kind of metal, and the bird sitting on the sceptre is the eagle. The sandals also of the god are of gold, as is likewise his robe. On the robe are embroidered figures of animals and the flowers of the lily.[32]

The throne was further surrounded by Victories, Graces and Seasons, together with images of athletic contests, war, murder and assault. The Roman general Aemilius Paulus "was moved to his soul, as if he had seen the god in person" (Livy, *History of Rome* 45.28.5: *Iovem velut praesentem intuens motus animo est*),[33] and according to Plutarch was the first to declare that Pheidias had molded the Zeus of Homer, presumably with reference to *Iliad* 1.528–30.[34] According to Dio Chrysostom (40–115 AD) three centuries later (or at least according to an account he chose to offer — and subsequently deconstruct a little),

> Even the irrational brute creation would be so struck with awe if they could catch merely a glimpse of yonder statue, not only the bulls which are being continually led to the altar, so that they would willingly submit themselves to the priests who perform the rites of sacrifice, if so they would be giving some pleasure to

---

32 Pausanias, *Description of Greece*, trans. W. H. S. Jones and H. A. Ormerod, Loeb Classical Library (London: Heinemann, 1926), 437 [5.11.1].

33 Plutarch's *Life* is widely reported as the source of this remark — even, unfortunately, by me: *Plotinus: Myth, Metaphor and Philosophical Practice* (Chicago: University of Chicago Press, 2016), 200.

34 Plutarch of Chaeronia, *Lives*, vol. 6, trans. Bernadotte Perrin, Loeb Classical Library (London: Heinemann, 1918), 429 [*Aemilius Paulus* 270, ch. 28].

the god, but eagles too, and horses and lions, so that they would subdue their untamed and savage spirits and preserve perfect quiet, delighted by the vision; and of men, whoever is sore distressed in soul, having in the course of his life drained the cup of many misfortunes and griefs, nor ever winning sweet sleep—even this man, methinks, if he stood before this image, would forget all the terrors and hardships that fall to our human lot. Such a wondrous vision did you devise and fashion, one in very truth a "charmer of grief and anger, that from men all the remembrance of their ills could loose!" So great the radiance and so great the charm with which your art has clothed it.[35]

The "first conception of God" as Chrysostom represented it amounts to the elevation of human mind and judgment over the "brute beasts" of despair, passion and disorder—an elevation that has often been employed also to fight with foreigners, and defend imperial control of recalcitrant *human* populations. But the main import of his speech is to suggest that Pheidias displayed in art the proper conception of God, the proper ideal for all good rulers:

> His sovereignty and kingship are intended to be shown by the strength in the image and its grandeur; his fatherhood and his solicitude by its gentleness and kindliness; the "Protector of Cities" and "Upholder of the Law" by its majesty and severity; the kinship between gods and men, I presume, by the mere similarity in shape, being already in use as a symbol; the "God of Friends, Suppliants, Strangers, Refugees," and all such qualities in short, by the benevolence and gentleness and goodness appearing in his countenance. The "God of Wealth" and the "Giver of Increase" are represented by the simplicity and grandeur shown by the figure, for the god does in very truth seem like one who is giving and bestowing blessings.[36]

---

35 Dio Chrysostom, "On Man's First Conception of God," in *Discourses*, trans. J. H. Cohoon, Loeb Classical Library (London: Heinemann, 1939), 57 [12.51], citing Homer, *Odyssey* 4.221. He was speaking at Olympia, in 97 AD.

36 Dio Chrysostom, *Discourses*, 79–81 [12.77].

Moral Realism

The chief moral of Dio's discourse is his recognition that great artists like Pheidias may fix an image for all those who follow after.

> In times past, because we had no clear knowledge, we formed each his different idea, and each person, according to his capacity and nature, conceived a likeness for every divine manifestation and fashioned such likenesses in his dreams; and if we do perchance collect any small and insignificant likenesses made by the earlier artists, we do not trust them very much nor pay them very much attention. But [Pheidias] by the power of [his] art first conquered and united Hellas and then all others by means of this wondrous presentment, showing forth so marvellous and dazzling a conception, that none of those who have beheld it could any longer easily form a different one.[37]

Statues, stories, music represent a dream — of justice, majesty, generosity and other virtues. We make these up, individually and collectively, and live among them, drawing inspiration rather than explanation from them all.

> The believer who has communicated with his god is not merely a man who sees new truths of which the unbeliever is ignorant; he is a man who is stronger. He feels within him more force, either to endure the trials of existence, or to conquer them. It is as though he were raised above the miseries of the world, because he is raised above his condition as a mere man; he believes that he is saved from evil, under whatever form he may conceive this evil. The first article in every creed is the belief in salvation by faith.[38]

Inspiration rather than explanation is the point of much religious art and practice, and the world that it delineates is not offered as a neutral *description*

---

[37] Dio Chrysostom, *Discourses*, 58 [12.43]. Cf. Libby Purves, *Holy Smoke: Religion and Roots* (London: Hodder & Stoughton, 1998), 19: "Sculpture, like music, has a peculiar power to start communicating at the place where logic and experience have to stop. Great statues, like music, speak to small children with a directness not to be underestimated."

[38] Emile Durkheim, *The Elementary Forms of the Religious Life: A Study in Religious Sociology*, trans. J. Swain (London: Allen & Unwin, 1915), 416–17.

of the "way things actually are," but as a dream. "Religion is the sigh of the oppressed creature, the heart of a heartless world, and the soul of soulless conditions. It is the opium of the people"[39] — not because it drugs the people quiet but because it keeps their dream alive, and gives them strength to endure. Marx hoped of course that the dream could be made reality if only we stopped depending on the fantasy of an external savior, but that hope too has seemed to others to be profoundly unrealistic.

The problem lies when the dream becomes a nightmare of competing drives. As a later Platonist observed:

> Visions of these eternal principles or characters of human life appear to poets, in all ages; the Grecian gods were the ancient Cherubim of Phoenicia; but the Greeks, and since them the Moderns, have neglected to subdue the gods of Priam. These gods are visions of the eternal attributes, or divine names, which, when erected into gods, become destructive of humanity. They ought to be the servants, and not the masters of man, or of society. They ought to be made to sacrifice to Man, and not man compelled to sacrifice to them; for when separated from man or humanity, who is Jesus the Saviour, the vine of eternity, they are thieves and rebels, they are destroyers.[40]

Consider this "humanistic," quasi-realist morality and religion more closely. The ideals and stories by which we guide our lives, the characters we internalize, are all, confessedly, dreams. Some of those dreams, sometimes, are nightmares, and we may reasonably hope to wake from them, to put aside the demons that distress us, the false goals that oppress us, and so at length to see all things "new," "pure," "uncontaminated" by false beliefs and fears. That dream of awakening, taken in its strongest form, is the hope that we may find "the Truth," and the Truth shall make us free — but this must of its nature have a *realist* interpretation. Despairing of a truth that is at once

---

39 Karl Marx, "Contribution to the Critique of Hegel's *Philosophy of Right*," in *Critique of Hegel's Philosophy of Right*, trans. Annette Joplin and Joseph O'Malley, ed. Joseph O'Malley (Cambridge: Cambridge University Press, 1970 [1843–44]), 129–42; 131.

40 William Blake, "A Descriptive Catalogue" (1809), in *Complete Writings*, ed. Geoffrey Keynes (London: Oxford University Press, 1966), 571.

Moral Realism

accessible and hopeful we may admit instead that we are only wishing to rid ourselves of nightmares in the name of a "better" dream: so Plato, *Theaetetus* 167b, in the voice of an imagined Protagoras:

> I believe that a man who, on account of a bad condition of soul, thinks thoughts akin to that condition, is made by a good condition of soul to think correspondingly good thoughts; and some men, through inexperience, call these appearances true, whereas I call them better than the others, but in no wise truer.

We may still use words like "truth" and "reason," but mean something less by them. The only truth that we could mind about, is "what it is better for us to believe, rather than the accurate representation of reality."[41] And that judgment will in turn be made on the basis of what it is we love, not on the results of any controlled experiment:

> Bacchanals did not say, "Let us discover whether there is a god of wine." They enjoyed wine so much that they cried out naturally to the god of it. Christians did not say, "A few experiments will show us whether there is a god of goodness." They loved good so much that they knew that it was a god. Moreover, all the great religions always loved passionately and poetically the symbols and machinery by which they worked — the temple, the coloured robes, the altar, the symbolic flowers, or the sacrificial fire. It made these things beautiful: it laid itself open to the charge of idolatry.[42]

What is there to choose between the Zeus of Pheidias's vision and the Christ of Chesterton's? What is there to choose between *traditional* dreams in

---

41 Rorty, *Philosophy and the Mirror*, 10. Cf. William James, *Pragmatism* (London: Longmans, Green, 1907), 77: "Ought we ever not to believe what it is *better for us* to believe? And can we then keep the notion of what is better for us, and what is true for us, permanently apart?" The end result of this strategy is unfortunately obvious: in practice it hands the power to determine what is to be believed to those with the strongest grip on popular opinion. See my "Orwell and the Anti-Realists," *Philosophy* 67 (1992): 141–54.

42 G. K. Chesterton, "Skepticism and Spiritualism," *Illustrated London News*, April 14, 1906 (http://www.cse.dmu.ac.uk/~mward/gkc/books/skeptic.html, accessed 4th April 2018).

general and modernist "enlightenment"? Thomas Sprat, in his proleptic *History of the Royal Society*, declared his faith in the "Real Philosophy" that had the power to banish fantasies:

> The poets of old to make all things look more venerable than they were devised a thousand false Chimaeras; on every Field, River, Grove and Cave they bestowed a Fantasm of their own making: With these they amazed the world.... And in the modern Ages these Fantastical Forms were reviv'd and possessed Christendom.... All which abuses if those acute Philosophers did not promote, yet they were never able to overcome; nay, not even so much as King Oberon and his invisible Army. But from the time in which the Real Philosophy has appear'd there is scarce any whisper remaining of such horrors.... The cours of things goes quietly along, in its own true channel of Natural Causes and Effects. For this we are beholden to Experiments; which though they have not yet completed the discovery of the true world, yet they have already vanquished those wild inhabitants of the false world, that us'd to astonish the minds of men.[43]

Consciously or otherwise (my guess is that he knew quite well what he was doing), he drew on the passage of St. Athanasius that I cited earlier.[44]

Athanasius and Thomas Sprat alike were strong realists, persuaded that it was their opponents only who were immersed in fantasy, and that there was an eternal Word which could dispel the phantoms. But if our moral and aesthetic purposes, at least, are merely those that happen to have survived, and have no more than "quasi-realist" status, the same must be true of both the Christian and the Scientistic dreams. It is a dispute, as it were, between the fans of *Star Wars* and *Star Trek*. Which dream shall we prefer? The modern would-be-atheistical answer is that it is "religion" that most often causes "evil"—but this is only to say that those devoted to a different dream sometimes behave in ways that other dreamers hate. The same retort can be made to those who think that "Realism" itself, or the conviction

---

[43] Thomas Sprat, *History of the Royal Society* (New York: Elibron, 2005 [1722]), 213.
[44] Athanasius, *On the Incarnation*, ch. 8, par. 47, quoted above on p. 17.

that there is a single Truth we all ought to acknowledge, is the source of authoritarian evil.⁴⁵ The reverse may be as plausible: realists, after all, have no real need to persuade or to compel — the World is as it is, and no deceits will in the end prevail. Quasi-realists, by contrast, know that only their own persistence will maintain the dream they wish, that they must drown the opposition or else it will drown them. The sad truth (if even this much is *realistically* the case) is probably only that we are ready to distort whatever dream and use it to excuse whatever we currently fancy. "I will even own," said Berkeley's Crito,

> that the Gospel and the Christian religion have often been the pretexts for [feuds, factions, massacres and wars]; but it will not thence follow they were the cause. On the contrary, it is plain they could not be the real proper cause of these evils; because a rebellious, proud, revengeful, quarrelsome spirit is directly opposite to the whole tenor and most express precepts of Christianity.... And secondly, because all those evils... were as frequent, nay, much more frequent, before the Christian religion was known in the world.⁴⁶

Rhetorically, at least, both Sprat and Athanasius were advancing a change of heart, a happy liberation from past fantasy by internalizing what was conceived as "Reason" or the Word. In both cases, we were to give up the search for a particular meaning in natural happenings. In both cases, indeed, this rested on a belief that God's ways were not ours, that we had no access to His plans beyond the mere conviction that He did not mean

---

45 What is most odd about attacks on a Divine Command Morality that raise the question, "would you agree to torture or kill if God commanded it?," is that just the same question can be directed against all Moral Realists: "would you agree to torture or kill if it turned out that this was *in fact* the right thing to do?" God at least, as theistically conceived, is likelier to be both stable and consistent: if "moral facts" are just what "happens" to be the case, it is much easier to suppose that they might change, or be entirely other than our own firmest views. T. D. Perry, in *Moral Reasoning and Truth: An Essay in Philosophy and Jurisprudence* (Oxford: Clarendon Press, 1976), treated this as an argument against moral realism: if moral truths are not fixed by "us," we might turn out to be entirely *wrong* even about our most fundamental moral judgments. To which we should perhaps reply that the beginning of wisdom is the realization that we might indeed be wrong!

46 Berkeley, *Alciphron*, 190.

us to be defenseless in a world of shadows, and that there were patterns we could come to see and partly rely upon. There may be little difference in visible practice between realist and quasi-realist: in either case their readings of sacred texts, their company with the like-minded, their performance of significant rituals all serve to maintain the proper spirit. And this applies as well to scientific practice and atheistic materialism as to any other creeds.

But there is one significant difference, acknowledged by William James:

> The subjectivist in morals, when his moral feelings are at war with the facts about him, is always free to seek harmony by toning down the sensitiveness of the feelings. Being mere data, neither good nor evil in themselves, he may pervert them or lull them to sleep by any means at his command. Truckling, compromise, time-serving, capitulations of conscience, are conventionally opprobrious names for what, if successfully carried out, would be on his principles by far the easiest and most praiseworthy mode of bringing about that harmony between inner and outer relations which is all that he means by good. The absolute moralist, on the other hand, when his interests clash with the world, is not free to gain harmony by sacrificing the ideal interests. According to him, these latter should be as they are and not otherwise. Resistance then, poverty, martyrdom if need be, tragedy in a word, — such are the solemn feasts of his inward faith. Not that the contradiction between the two men occurs every day; in commonplace matters all moral schools agree. It is only in the lonely emergencies of life that our creed is tested: then routine maxims fail, and we fall back on our gods.[47]

Quasi-realists can only, rationally, go along with whatever social ideals and practices have currently the upper hand: pointless opposition is, exactly, pointless.

---

47 William James, "Rationality, Activity and Faith," *Princeton Review* 2 (1882): 58–86, 82; reprinted as part of "The Sentiment of Rationality" in James, *Will to Believe*, 63–110.

Moral Realism

THE ETERNAL

On the one possibility, moral judgments are no more than our continually changing agreements (*nomoi*), and their strength over us and over the world in general is only the strength of our "convictions." On another, moral judgment is confined by Darwinian processes: the overriding value is just survival value—and not even "our own" survival, but that of our unimaginable future lineage.

> On then! Value means survival-
> Value. If our progeny
> Spreads and spawns and licks each rival,
> That will prove its deity
> (Far from pleasant, by our present,
> Standards, though it may well be).[48]

When Lewis described the planetary angel Malacandra's conversation with the corrupt scientist Weston, in his interplanetary fantasy, he can hardly have imagined that anyone would so readily admit the charge:

> "You do not love any one of your race.... You do not love the mind of your race, nor the body. Any kind of creature will please you if only it is begotten by your kind as they are now. It seems to me... that what you really love is no completed creature but the very seed itself; for that is all that is left."

Weston retorts by appealing to "a man's [fundamental] loyalty to humanity," and the angel continues:

> "I see now how the lord of the silent world has bent you. There are laws that all hnau know, of pity and straight dealing and shame and the like, and one of these is the love of kindred. He has taught you to break all of them except this one, which is not one of the greatest laws; this one he has bent till it becomes folly and has set

---

48 C. S. Lewis, *Poems*, ed. Walter Hooper (San Diego: Harcourt, 1964), 55.

it up, thus bent, to be a little, blind Oyarsa in your brain. And now you can do nothing but obey it, though if we ask you why it is a law you can give no other reason for it than for all the other and greater laws which it drives you to disobey."[49]

But neither quasi-realism nor evolutionary moralism grounds any convincing atheistical criticism of whatever powers (once conceptualized as Titans or rebellious spirits) may rule the world. That requires us to have a real insight into genuine moral norms that have at least this much power, that we believe in them precisely because they are real norms. It also requires us to believe that our criticisms and complaints are not caused entirely by the powers of which we complain. To put the point mythologically (that is, in narrative style: *Ennead* III.5 [50].9, 24–29), whatever designed and built the world also designed its critics, and may be getting some amusement from its puppets' misotheistic rants: "it is as if a poet in his plays wrote a part for an actor insulting and depreciating the author of the play" (Plotinus, *Ennead* III.2 [47].16, 8–11). In denouncing the Creator, it may be, we are doing exactly what that Creator wants! The very values that we most mind about are those the mischievous Creator has instilled in us, perhaps to make life yet more difficult. Detesting that imagined Creator we must also dismiss Its lures (and what to do after that, who knows). The more coherent position at any rate is that there is a creative value lying beyond the world of conflict and confusion, and that it is in *that* Name that we can pass judgment on the earthly powers. Pheidias's Zeus, perhaps, will not have quite that authority, whether as the (quasi-realist) expression of an Hellenic dream or as a (strong realist) description of an everlasting god demanding worship.

Both modern atheistical materialists and more ancient Gnostics wish to be able to reject the values of this world, and hang on to the ungrounded but psychologically helpful hope that the world or our experience might yet be transformed. We might, as Richard Dawkins oddly hopes, defy our selfish genes. More Stoical materialists persuade themselves that all is already for the best, or at least that the best that *we* can manage is Submit. The one

---

49 C. S. Lewis, *Out of the Silent Planet* (London: Pan Books, 1952 [1938]), 163. *Hnau* means "rational animal"; *Oyarsa* is the title of a planetary ruler in Lewis's mythology.

Moral Realism

further option that I have been describing by omission is the Platonic. We and the world together are corrupted, but there is nonetheless a real Pure Land discernible by insight or revelation.

> Let us fly to our dear country. What then is our way of escape, and how are we to find it? We shall put out to sea, as Odysseus did, from the witch Circe or Calypso—as the poet says (I think with a hidden meaning)—and was not content to stay though he had delights of the eyes and lived among much beauty of sense. Our country from which we came is there, our Father is there. How shall we travel to it, where is our way of escape? We cannot get there on foot; for our feet only carry us everywhere in this world, from one country to another. You must not get ready a carriage, either, or a boat. Let all these things go, and do not look. Shut your eyes, and change to and wake another way of seeing, which everyone has but few use. (*Ennead* I.6 [1].8, 16–28)[50]

The start of that awakening will often—and maybe always—be a puzzle. Iamblichus of Calchis put more trust in the effects of religious ritual, "theurgy," than in the reflections of philosophers, "theology." He did nonetheless approve of dialectic, insisting that Apollo is the inspiration of philosophers not because he speaks "rationally" and "clearly," but because he poses riddles: dialectic is dealing with ambiguity and homonymy, "and the ferreting out of any double meaning." It is conducted in play and disputatious dialogue—which is why Hermes carries, so Iamblichus lightheartedly remarks, a staff with two snakes looking toward each other, poised to test themselves against each other! The goal is "the purification of the intellect through refutation."[51] Refutation is possible, as is demonstration, because there is a real truth to be discovered, once we have found our way through paradox.

---

50 Odysseus, by an allegorizing interpretation, chose neither to be beast (with Circe) nor god (with Calypso), but instead to return to a sort of domesticity: see also Plato, *Republic* 10.620cd.

51 Iamblichus, *Letters: Writings from the Greco-Roman World*, trans. John M. Dillon and Wolfgang Pelleichtner (Atlanta: Society of Biblical Literature, 2009), 15 [*Letter* 5: Stobaeus, *Anthologia* 2.2.5].

> Since, then, there exists soul which reasons about what is right and good, and discursive reasoning which enquires about the rightness (*dikaion*) and goodness (*kalon*) of this or that particular thing, there must be some further permanent rightness from which arises the discursive reasoning in the realm of soul. Or how else would it manage to reason? And if soul sometimes reasons about the right and good and sometimes does not, there must be in us Intellect which does not reason discursively but always possesses the right, and there must be also the principle and cause and God of Intellect. He is not divided, but abides, and as he does not abide in place he is contemplated in many beings, in each and every one of those capable of receiving him as another self, just as the center of a circle exists by itself, but every one of the radii has its point in the center and the lines bring their individuality to it. For it is with something of this sort in ourselves that we are in contact with God and are with him and depend upon him, and those of us who converge towards him are firmly established in him. (*Ennead* V.1 [10].11)

The truth of things — in both the moral and the mathematical spheres — depends on there being a place for them to be, distinct from the present corruption of our senses and of competing bodies. If that is a dream, it is one borne out of "memory." We cannot merely *hope* for a world where our norms reign supreme, for the very reasons that Russell gave: namely that our personal and racial powers are bound to be overpowered by the complex processes that constitute our present material and time-bound world. Even Dyson's speculations about a future cosmos wholly controlled by Mind don't exorcise that vision:[52] why should that Mind — if it ever happens — be anything like ours, or recognizably "Mind" at all? Some fantasists have suggested that It would have reason to reconstruct the earlier days of the cosmos (and our primitive minds within it) and that it is most likely, therefore, that our present experience is indeed a dream, a merely virtual reality, a construct by the End Time Powers. But would it follow that It/

---

52 Dyson, "Time without End."

Moral Realism

They meant us well, or even that they allowed us any glimpse of the truth at all? Any hope we have in It derives, consciously or otherwise, from older religious stories — and in that case, might it not be easier and more honest to accept the older versions for what they are?

We are sitting, Plato suggested, like ants or frogs around a pond, in the muddy crannies of Reality (*Phaedo* 109b). If we can criticize our surroundings, or hope for a better future, it must be because we retain an image of that larger, brighter world. That "memory," so to call it, is what animates our moral and epistemological conviction. It is because we retain some "fragment" or "mirrored image" of the divine that we can afford to trust even our "scientific" vision, and the reputed success of our "scientific" investigations gives weight, as I have already observed, to a traditional theism.

That our *moral* convictions are to be trusted is even more clearly dependent on some form of theistic Platonism: even atheistical attacks on a putative Creator and on the iniquities of the "religious" must be grounded in our knowledge of a *moral* truth, of how the world *should* be but often isn't. In their last despair, the Last Men of Olaf Stapledon's fantasy — many million years in an imagined future and on another planet — speak of the

> many million, million selves; ephemeridae, each to itself, the universe's one quick point, the crux of all cosmical endeavour. And all defeated! It is forgotten. It leaves only a darkness, deepened by blind recollection of past light. Soon, a greater darkness! Man, a moth sucked into a furnace, vanishes; and then the furnace also, since it is but a spark islanded in the wide, the everlasting darkness. If there is a meaning, it is no human meaning. Yet one thing in all this welter stands apart, unassailable, fair, the blind recollection of past light.[53]

Stapledon meant more than that we could console ourselves, a very little, by the ordinary memory of past domestic comforts. He really did mean that we "remembered" our first Home, the world of real beings united in a

---

53 Olaf Stapledon, *Last and First Men* [1930] and *Last Men in London* [1932] (London: Penguin, 1972), 605.

single comprehensive vision, the company of the holy ones,[54] the dance of immortal love (Porphyry, *Life of Plotinus* 23.36–7).

Pagan and Abrahamic Platonists alike can agree that the world of our present experience is a *fallen* world, and that we deal daily with spirits of anger, greed and sloth that separate us from the forms of beauty that we also, somehow and sometimes, intuit. Without that glimpse of eternal beauty, we have no good grounds for condemning even the most outrageous fantasies either of what is or should be, or the expectably bad behavior of both believers and unbelievers. Only theists can afford to challenge God! Or rather, it is in the name of that One God that they can challenge the present Powers.[55]

---

54 Immanuel Kant, *Kant's Political Writings*, ed. Hans Reiss (Cambridge: Cambridge University Press, 1970), 107. Kant was quoting Francisco Orazio della Penna (an eighteenth-century Capuchin friar who settled in Lhasa) on how Tibetan lamas had defined God for him.

55 See Walter Wink, *Naming the Powers: The Language of Power in the New Testament* (Minneapolis: Fortress Press, 1984).

4

Is Humankind a Natural Kind?

THE PROBLEM OF DARWINIAN SPECIES

I shall return to the notion of Platonic norms and Forms, but there is a further problem to be addressed. What force can such norms and forms have in an evolutionary history understood in Darwinian terms? Darwin's own explicit claim was to have replaced Platonic *archetypes* by *ancestors*: we resemble each other—members of any biological taxon resemble each other—because they share a common descent.[1]

> Nothing can be more hopeless than to attempt to explain this similarity of pattern in members of the same class, by utility or by the doctrine of final causes. The hopelessness of the attempt has been expressly admitted by [Richard] Owen in his most interesting work on the "Nature of Limbs." On the ordinary view of the independent creation of each being, we can only say that so it is;—that it has so pleased the Creator to construct each animal and plant. The explanation is manifest on the theory of the natural selection of successive slight modifications,—each modification being profitable in some way to the modified form, but often affecting by correlation of growth other parts of the organisation. In changes of this nature, there will be little or no tendency to modify the original pattern, or to transpose parts. The bones of a limb might be shortened and widened to any extent, and become gradually enveloped in thick membrane, so as to serve as a fin; or a webbed foot might have all its bones, or certain bones, lengthened

---

1 See Adrian J. Desmond, *Archetypes and Ancestors: Palaeontology in Victorian London 1850–1875* (Chicago: University of Chicago Press, 1982). Plotinus, *Ennead* VI.1 [42].3, 1–7, anticipated the idea: the Heraclids are a unity not because they share a single essence, but because they have one ancestor.

to any extent, and the membrane connecting them increased to any extent, so as to serve as a wing: yet in all this great amount of modification there will be no tendency to alter the framework of bones or the relative connexion of the several parts. If we suppose that the ancient progenitor, the archetype as it may be called, of all mammals, had its limbs constructed on the existing general pattern, for whatever purpose they served, we can at once perceive the plain signification of the homologous construction of the limbs throughout the whole class.[2]

Darwin also distanced himself from *catastrophist* interpretations of evolutionary history: change over generations was always gradual, barely to be noticed for many thousand or even million years. Attempts by anti-Darwinian theorists to distinguish "microevolution" from "macroevolution," the mere variation of features within a species from a real difference "in kind," are beside the point: all such "differences in kind," on Darwinian terms, are merely the result of accumulated differences, unconstrained by any natural barrier. And it is this feature of Darwinian theory that Chesterton identified as a special problem:

> If evolution simply means that a positive thing called an ape turned very slowly into a positive thing called a man, then it is stingless for the most orthodox; for a personal God might just as well do things slowly as quickly, especially if, like the Christian God, he were outside time. But if it means anything more, it means that there is no such thing as an ape to change, and no such thing as a man for him to change into.[3]

Neo-Darwinian theory—formed through the rediscovery of Mendel's work—is more open than the original Darwinian to the possibility of relatively sudden change in a lineage, but this does not mean that entirely new species emerge in a single step, a single generation. Nor are members of

---

[2] Charles Darwin, *On the Origin of Species by Means of Natural Selection, or the Preservation of Favoured Races in the Struggle for Life* (London: John Murray, 1859), 435.

[3] G. K. Chesterton, *The Everlasting Man* (London: Hodder & Stoughton, 1925), 17.

Is Humankind a Natural Kind?

one species all essentially distinct from members of another sister species: the difference between such species is rather that the range of characters displayed across one species is slightly different from the range displayed in another, to the point where those species are — mostly — divided. A species, biologically, is a set of interbreeding populations, such that there is little transfer of genetic information from one such set to another. These barriers are not rigid: there may be some limited crossbreeding, and there may also be transfers via viral or bacterial infection. Perhaps we need not be greatly concerned that there need be no essential or significant distinction between different animal species. Perhaps we need not be concerned that neither plants, fungi, nor prokaryotes are easily divided into distinct, reproductively isolated species. But whether humankind is a "natural kind" may be of more importance, as Chesterton observed. There were no literal "First Humans," essentially distinct from their non-human parents. The current characters of human populations are no more fixed than those of any non-human population. Humankind may yet be divided into distinct biological species — and there is in any case good reason to suspect that there were once many more-or-less human species, and our own descent is from one of many such hominin twigs within primate evolution. What effect does this suggestion have on notions of "human dignity" or "human rights"? Is it necessarily true that nothing "human" is ever "alien" to us? Are there genuine norms for all of us, human and non-human alike? And if so, what are they?

SPECIES-SPECIFIC PERFECTIONS[4]

Taxonomy is the art of classifying entities, and its principal use has been to draw up lists of living organisms, whether by their form or function, their meaning in the social and ceremonial life of the classifiers, or their genealogical relations. The pre-Darwinian biological synthesis assumed that there were distinct types of living organism, which could — as types — be ranked by their "perfection" (in effect, their similarity to the human form), and — as

---

4 The following sections are drawn, with appropriate revisions, from Stephen R. L. Clark, "The Ethics of Taxonomy: A Neo-Aristotelian Synthesis," in *Animal Ethics: Past and Present Perspectives*, ed. Evangelos D. Protopapadakis (Berlin: Logos Verlag), 38–58, with the permission of the editor.

individuals — by how well they performed their supposed function in the world. Each sort of living thing had its own "*telos*," whose completion served the overarching goal of "nature." This synthesis helped explain particular features of each type, and identified human beings as that for which the whole of terrestrial nature was organized: "we" (that is, we humans) were thought to be "lords of creation."

This was not, as some have supposed, an *Aristotelian* theory, though some fragmentary thoughts of Aristotle were caught up in it. Aristotle's own theory was closer to the Darwinian synthesis: individual organisms have the features that they do because of their ancestry, and those features chiefly help sustain them in the form of life they characteristically follow. All such organisms have something wonderful and beautiful to show us (Aristotle, *De Partibus Animalium* 1.645a15f.), and — insofar as there is a settled form of life for human beings — it is best shown in admiring and understanding those beauties. The second-best form of life consists in acting virtuously in a world that is often far from beautiful. Aristotle does seem to endorse the notion that the human form is that from which others deviate, but this very notion also suggests that there is a genealogical connection between all earthly organisms, and that it is from such apparently flawed deviations that new possibilities emerge.[5] Even the production of a female offspring is, in a way, a "lucky accident."

The post-Darwinian synthesis (though proponents do often still unconsciously rank organisms by their similarity to the human) is both more egalitarian and less inclined to draw strict boundaries between one kind of creature and another. All contemporary earthly living organisms are related, all are equally "evolved," and the divisions between biological *taxa* are always permeable (not least because every eukaryotic organism is itself an alliance between different lineages). It is *useful*, as Aristotle saw, to classify organisms according to their overall similarities, but this is not to show that one species, family or phylum is radically other than another: all are phenotypical expressions of an underlying unity. Once this is fully realized, it is clear that *ethical* distinctions between one sort and another can never be other than pragmatic decisions: differences between individuals and types

---

5 See Clark, *Aristotle's Man*, 28–47.

Is Humankind a Natural Kind?

matter for some purposes, but not for all. All of us are as correctly described as eukaryotes, vertebrates, mammals, and primates, as well as human beings. All of us have the problem of how to live peaceably and productively with creatures of many other species, families and phyla than "our own."

But this thesis, to be intelligible, now needs expanding.

The older biological synthesis, which still influences popular thought in the West, proposed that biological species were natural kinds: that is to say that conspecifics share a distinct, distinctive nature which both serves to explain much or most of what they do, and serves as a standard against which their individual characters and achievements can be assessed. To be, for example, a dog, *Canis familiaris*, is to be governed by the very same form that governs all others of that kind. Dogs may differ from each other, but those differences, unless they are merely accidental, serve only to rank them by how close they come to "the ideal dog." Dogs alone and only beget dogs: neither their ancestors nor their descendants can be anything but dogs, however much they vary from the ideal, the true, the really doggy dog. Alternatively, dogs might instead be classified as wolves—and their domestic features would then be considered merely accidental, and fairly easily subverted: if they were released from human domination, they would "revert to type," and even in a human household their real identities may sometimes triumph over the conventional. Either way, their being *dogs* (or wolves) is at once a matter of fact (that they are of a certain natural kind, grounded in a shared form and nature), and a value judgment (that their virtues are the ones that enable them—fortune permitting—to live as *good* dogs or wolves, and so fulfil their "natural destiny"). The less they live up to their type, the fewer virtues they have, the less they are anything at all, as their form does less and less to unify and manage the mere matter of which they are composed. To determine what those virtues are, what it is to be a good dog, we must identify what dogs are, and what it is they do: their *eidos*, their *ergon*, and their *telos*.

These latter terms, though they are Aristotelian or Platonic in their origin, do not accurately represent either Aristotle's or Plato's actual thoughts about living creatures. Their use rather reflects a widely distributed folk-biological understanding. Different species of living creature are distinguished not merely by how they look, but by how they characteristically behave. But a dog can't become a cat merely by behaving like a cat, nor by being disguised as one. The underlying nature of the creature, so we assume, is constant, even if it is not immediately apparent. The very fact that a disguised dog's offspring will be *dogs* reveals that its *eidos*, its controlling form, is canine. And actually whatever the dog does will be something that *dogs* do (and nothing else, at least in quite the same way): a dog's *ergon* is (probably) to cooperate with his human-dominated pack in hunting or herding, guiding or consoling. The dog's development, from puppy to mature adult, is directed towards the realization of his potential as, exactly, an adult dog, playing a proper part within the pack: that is his *telos*. Failure to achieve that goal—by premature death, disease or disability—is a failure only because there is such a *telos*, such a proper fulfilment of the dog's given nature. And if they are really wolves, domestication also is an injury (on a par with enslavement).

In the dog's case, of course, such failures are not *moral* failures (or at any rate, we don't usually suppose they are). The dog has not deliberately betrayed his calling—though his human master may have done (that is, betrayed both the dog's calling, and his own). Human beings, it is traditional to suppose, may play an active role in their own failure to live up to the human paradigm. The very nature of humanity is that we have to decide what to do with ourselves: our choices reflect and embody our personal conception of the better life. It is of course possible that someone may have no such conception, but rather drift from one occasion to the next, at the mercy of her own transient desires and fears. Maybe that is the best she could imagine for herself, though she does not *choose* such a life with any set purpose, or with any wish to recommend it to another. But only "natural slaves" and children live like that: mature humans, even if they are sometimes distracted by transient desires and fears, live as they do because that's how they think it right to live. Any advice to human beings—who are the only creatures who will ever ask for it—on how to live, must therefore begin by suggesting that we should discover what we need in order to be able to make good choices. "The best life for human beings is a life lived in accordance with virtues, and if there is more than one such virtue, in accordance with the best and most complete" (Aristotle, *Nicomachean Ethics* 1.1098a16–18). And this in turn requires us to have some grasp of the world in which we live, and of the obvious truth that we are not alone in it.

Is Humankind a Natural Kind?

Neither Plato nor Aristotle quite endorsed the system that I have described. Plato seems to have considered that there was a single, unchanging *eidos* for every real collection of individuals, but it does not follow that every individual belongs wholly and inescapably to a single such collection. On the contrary, it is because individuals are not wholly, inescapably and only reflections of a single *eidos* that he can think them less than wholly real. No individual dog (as we call it) is only and entirely canine: every such organism may be pulled, as it were, in several directions. The sensible world (that is, the world displayed through our senses, which seems to consist of physical particulars arranged in three dimensions of space, and one of time) is not wholly obedient to the eternal pattern of *eide*, which later Platonists explicitly identified as ideas in the mind of God. Aristotle too, though he saw no need to suppose that *eide* had any existence separate from the sensible world, would agree that sensible things are not perfectly and entirely ruled by them. Accidents happen, and genetic variations, because the father's *eidos*, transmitted through seminal fluid, does not perfectly master the matter provided by the mother.[6] It is indeed unusual for offspring to look exactly like their father (and one well-known mare was known as Honest Lady precisely because her colts did resemble their fathers).[7] Plato's *eide* constitute ideals to which living things are drawn, and have an intelligible existence, as a coherent system, in the mind of God. Aristotle too supposed that all things were drawn towards "the Unmoved Mover," and later commentators drew the conclusion that this Mover was eternally united to intelligible reality. Everything has its proper place, in principle, within an Aristotelian cosmos, just in that there is somewhere, or some condition, that each thing tends towards, such that it takes a definite effort for it *not* to stay there, once it has arrived. But it does not follow that the cosmos as a whole tends towards a static condition, with the elements exactly distinguished: on the contrary, everything is always being stirred up and kept away from stasis, by the revolution of the heavens in their own effort to persist in as much of the divine life, the Unmoved Mover, as they can manage. The cosmos,

---

6 See D. M. Balme, "Aristotle's Biology was not Essentialist," *Archiv für Geschichte der Philosophie* 62 (1980): 1–12.

7 Aristotle, *Politics* 2.1262a; see further Devin Henry, "Aristotle on the Mechanism of Inheritance," *Journal of the History of Biology* 39 (2006): 425–55.

almost all Greek philosophers concluded, is eternal, but it does not follow that it is unchanging: there are global catastrophes, as well as local ones, and even if there must always be something like plants and animals in a living world, it does not follow that there must always have been exactly the same ones, nor that all lineages are uniform.

In brief, the classical Greek philosophers were much more open, in principle, to the thought that one creature can change into another, or beget creatures of another sort than itself, than is usually supposed. There are different styles of living, different ideal forms, and even if no other creature than the human consciously *chooses* which style or form to follow, it is possible for individual organisms to deviate from what had been customary in their kind, and possible for whole lineages to change their way of life, and so in the end their physiology. In the modern post-Darwinian synthesis, this latter transformation depends on chance variations within the line which then prove to have a reproductive advantage in their particular context: there is no expectation that favorable changes will occur more often when individuals take to a new way of life, but only that different variations will be "selected" than would have been before. Whether this is true or not is much more contentious than popular presentations of neo-Darwinian theory suggest. It may be instead that a change of life awakens potentialities of which there had been no need before, or that by changing their way of life the creatures find themselves within the influence of another *eidos*, a different "biological attractor," so that favorable variations occur more often than they would "by chance." But that is another story.

CLADES AND CLASSES

The discovery that there had been other sorts of creature in the past confirmed one long-held suspicion, that there had been other worlds before our own, divided from us by catastrophe. At the same time it seemed to confirm that something like the same abiding forms, or biological attractors, had been at work in different circumstances. There had been almost-trees, almost-birds, almost-carnivora in the long ago, and God or Nature had swept them aside to make way for what were—to us—more natural-seeming creatures. As fossil evidence accumulated, the suspicion grew that these long-lost creatures

Is Humankind a Natural Kind?

were, somehow, related to the more modern sort. The new worlds did not simply replace the old: they grew from the old. This did not of itself prove anything against the notion that living creatures variously embodied or copied the ideal forms, *eide*. Embodied forms might look different under different conditions, founded on different material, and not all the possible forms of life need be present contemporaneously. If there were no dinosaurs nowadays it might still be true that being-a-dinosaur is an eternal possibility, a coherent form of life (or rather a set of such lives) within the larger vertebrate scheme. Dinosaurs weren't defective, but magnificent examples of reptilian life, even if they had to be removed to make way for another sort.[8] Richard Owen, sometime Director of the British Museum, and inventor of the term "dinosaur," remained adamant throughout his life that the forms of earthly life reflected those ideals, and that variations within their lineages were occasions when they were moved by a different attractor. Darwin, as I noted above, replaced archetypes with ancestors.

But before Charles Darwin's innovation — an idea that Richard Owen rather ungraciously described as "no very profound or recondite surmise," but that lacked, at the time, any clear empirical basis[9] — there had been another suggestion. In 1833 Charles Babbage constructed a small portion of the calculating engine he had devised, the Difference Engine, and set it to list the integers. It counted up from 1 to 2 to 3 to every number up to 100,000,001. We might reasonably expect that it would continue "in like fashion," adding 1 to each succeeding number — yet the numbers that followed were 100,010,002; 100,030,003; 100,060,004; 100,100,005; 100,150,006 "and so on" until the 2672nd term, when the rule seemed to change again (and yet again after 1430 terms, and again after 950, and so on).[10]

> Now it must be remarked, that the law that each number presented by the Engine is greater by unity than the preceding number, which

---

8 So Adam Sedgwick in his "Objections to Mr. Darwin's Theory of the Origin of Species" of April 7, 1860, reprinted in David Hull, ed., *Darwin and His Critics* (Chicago: University of Chicago Press, 1983), 159–66: "the reptilian fauna of the Mesozoic period is the grandest and highest that ever lived" (ibid., 162–63).

9 Hull, *Darwin's Critics*, 195.

10 Charles Babbage, *The Ninth Bridgwater Treatise: A Fragment* (London: Frank Cass, 1967 [1838]), 34–37.

Can We Believe in People?

law the observer had deduced from an induction of a hundred million instances, was not the true law that regulated its action; and that the occurrence of the number 100,010,002 at the 100,000,002d term was as necessary a consequence of the original adjustment, and might have been as fully foreknown at the commencement, as was the regular succession of any one of the intermediate numbers to its immediate antecedent. The same remark applies to the next apparent deviation from the new law, which was founded on an induction of 2761 terms, and to all the succeeding laws; with this limitation only that whilst their consecutive introduction at various definite intervals is a necessary consequence of the mechanical structure of the engine, our knowledge of analysis does not yet enable us to predict the periods at which the more distant laws will be introduced.[11]

A less alert investigator, of course, might simply have concluded that the engine was defective, even if he could not tell how. Babbage's own insight was that the fossil record revealed just such "sudden changes," "programmed in" (as we would say) from the beginning.[12] Robert Chambers amplified the claim: the very same inherited rules can produce apparently dissimilar phenotypes in differing circumstances as a response to those changed circumstances: birds are what dinosaurs beget when the proper moment comes.[13]

Babbage's challenge to all inductive science was mostly ignored.[14] Chambers's explicit application of the notion to evolutionary history was mercilessly attacked, by Thomas Huxley (later to be Darwin's bulldog) amongst others. The chief complaint was that this hypothesis was not empirically confirmed: no lineage within our experience had given the

---

11 Babbage's larger Difference Engine was not completed till 1991, and seems to be able to return expectable results up to 31 digits. His imagined "Analytical Engine" has not so far been completed—except that all modern computers are its descendants.

12 Babbage, *Bridgwater Treatise*, 44–46.

13 Robert Chambers, *Vestiges of the Natural History of Creation* (Leicester: Leicester University Press, 1969 [1845]).

14 Though see Stewart and Tait, *Unseen Universe*, 90–91, who choose to put their trust in God's not choosing so to confuse His creatures.

appearance of such sudden change (which is hardly a good argument against the possibility). Darwin's thesis was instead that the changes were very small ones of a kind that we do notice here and now, accumulating over many million years, that they weren't *responses* to environmental change, and that they were programmed from the beginning only in the sense that the mechanisms of inheritance, whatever they were, allowed for many unguided variations. The later, neo-Darwinian synthesis has been more hospitable to catastrophic changes — in the environment and in the lineages themselves — than Darwin, and has also acknowledged that some genotypes, as Chambers supposed, have several different phenotypic manifestations, under different conditions.[15] The modern synthesis is also much *less* sympathetic than Darwin was to the inheritance of acquired characteristics, preferring to suppose that what is strictly inherited through the germ-line is insulated from any of the responses individual organisms make. Strictly, this separation is not complete: mothers may pass antibodies to their offspring, and even eukaryotes can pick up novel genetic information by retroviral infection. There is no need for evolutionary theorists to be ideologically opposed to all the other, superficially non-Darwinian, hypotheses about evolutionary change. Even Owen's biological attractors may be manifested in convergent evolution: plesiosaurs, whales, dolphins, manatees, seals, otters may all be guided by or towards a common form — and maybe rational humanity is also such

---

15 See A. Bergfeld, R. Bergmann and P. V. Sengbusch, "Phenotypic and Genetic Variation; Ecotypes": *Botany Online* 1996–2004, http://www1.biologie.uni-hamburg.de/b-online/e37/37b.htm (accessed June 11, 2019): "*Hieracium umbellatum* [leafy hawkweed], for example, occurs at the Swedish west coast in two different ecotypes. One ecotype is a bushy plant with broad leaves and expanded inflorescences growing on rocky cliffs at the sea. The other is a prostrate plant with narrow leaves and small inflorescences, that grows on sand dunes. As the rocky cliffs and the sand dunes alternate along the coast, so does *Hieracium umbellatum* giving rise alternatively to its corresponding ecotypes. The plants keep their habitat-specific appearance under standardized experimental conditions. If, however, plants from one habitat were moved to the other type of habitat, they changed their appearance and adapted to the new environment. These experiments demonstrate the profound selective advantage of different genotypes in different habitats. Furthermore, they show, that a given genotype has enough flexibility to produce phenotypes that are optimally adapted to the actual environmental conditions through modification." Rather more radically, the implication of Chambers's hypothesis is that birds — were they to be removed to a Jurassic environment — would begin to hatch dinosaurs instead.

an attractor, as Conway Morris has proposed.[16] And ancestral programs may reemerge after many generations: Pax6, the master gene for eyes, seems to have been invented only once, back in the pre-Cambrian, but not every creature still containing that gene has eyes. Pax6 is necessary, but not sufficient, and where there is no need for eyes, that gene may seem to be surplus. Inferentially, what we consider "junk DNA," not currently expressed, may be stockpiled against some possible future emergency.

What all these evolutionary ideas have in common, however, is that species boundaries — crudely — are unreal.[17] Whether dogs are a different *species* than wolves may once have depended on whether they were of different natural kinds. Nowadays they are a single species insofar as they can breed together — and Chihuahuas and Irish wolfhounds would *not* count as a single species were it not that there is a range of dog breeds in between (as it were) the small and large. Darwin himself supposed that humankind was on the brink of speciation: "the Negro and the European are so distinct that, if specimens had been brought to a naturalist without any further information, they would undoubtedly have been considered by him as good and true species."[18] He also thought that there would one day be an even greater gap than now between human and non-human, "for it will intervene between man in a more civilized state, as we may hope, than the Caucasian, and some ape as low as a baboon, instead of as at present between the Negro or Australian and the gorilla"[19] — because both gorillas and native Australians would be extinct. The barriers against interbreeding (that is, against combining otherwise separate gene lines into hybrid offspring) may be merely geographical, or behavioral, or physiological, or biochemical. And even thoroughly separate species may still share genetic information, by retroviral infection. Species are distinct only in the way

---

16 Simon Conway Morris, *Life's Solution: Inevitable Humans in a Lonely Universe* (New York: Cambridge University Press, 2003); see also idem, ed., *The Deep Structure of Biology: Is Convergence Sufficiently Ubiquitous to Give a Directional Signal?* (West Conshohocken, PA: Templeton Foundation Press, 2008).

17 "Perhaps a less elegant but more apposite title for Darwin's book would have been *On the Unreality of Species as Shown by Natural Selection*": Elliot Sober, *The Philosophy of Biology* (Boulder, CO: Westview Press, 1993), 143.

18 Charles Darwin, *The Descent of Man* (London: John Murray, 1871), 2:388.

19 Darwin, *Descent of Man*, 1:201.

that different streams of water are distinct: those streams may divide and reunite, and never *needed* to trace exactly the path they did. There is even some reason to suspect that the separate lineages that led to chimpanzees and hominins merged again before their final (so far) separation.[20]

There was never a first *human* couple, different in nature from their immediate parents. Instead, the lineage grew more human (that is, more like us) only by degrees — and some of our contemporaries, it was easy to suggest, were still less human than ourselves. Slightly less complacent thinkers might agree that modern, Western humanity was only a bridge between the sub-human and the super-human. But even they had no doubt of their own superiority over their contemporaries, and no doubt that the super-human would be just like them, only better. Very few drew the other conclusion, that even those we categorize as non-human are our close cousins, just as highly evolved and just as deserving of our care and admiration.

This thesis, that life forms a continuum in which any apparently separate sorts are historical accidents or maybe even merely specious or fashionable divisions, is not without precedent. Aristotle himself suggested as much (*De Partibus Animalium* 4.681a12f.). It is convenient to group creatures together by their resemblances, but there will always be creatures that seem to belong in more than one class, and there will always be underlying unities even between creatures that are not superficially similar. There are even some signs that he thought some creatures resembled each other chiefly because they shared an ancestor: whereas Plato's system allows for unrelated creatures nonetheless to reflect or embody one and the same form, Aristotle proposed that form was transmitted only procreatively, from father to offspring. There would have been a better fit with the phenomena he describes if he had not assumed that mothers only provide the matter on which that form can be

---

20 See news.bbc.co.uk/2/hi/science/nature/4991470.stm, reporting N. Patterson, D. J. Richter, S. Gnerre, E. S. Lander, D. Reich, "Genetic evidence for complex speciation of humans and chimpanzees," in *Nature* 441:1103–8 (June 29, 2006; published online May 17, 2006): "Our analysis also shows that human-chimpanzee speciation occurred less than 6.3 million years ago and probably more recently, conflicting with some interpretations of ancient fossils. Most strikingly, chromosome X shows an extremely young genetic divergence time, close to the genome minimum along nearly its entire length. These unexpected features would be explained if the human and chimpanzee lineages initially diverged, then later exchanged genes before separating permanently" (www.nature.com/nature/journal/v441/n7097/abs/nature04789.html, accessed June 11, 2019).

impressed: strictly both parents pass the information on. Indeed, insofar as it is up to the cells that grow from the maternal ovum to decide which part of the DNA they should read and act upon, it might be better to emphasize maternal ancestry. Either way, the conclusion is that we are all related, all descended from a common stock, all reading from the same genetic pages. One way of bringing this point home is to imagine how the present human population itself might, over time, expand to fill the ecological niches vacated by all the creatures eliminated in the Sixth Extinction. In that imaginable future — rather like the future sketched by Olaf Stapledon in *Last and First Men* — our descendants could be anything from super-humans to sea squirts. And each of those apparently separate lines could still contain the potential for a further flowering.

Folk-taxonomy still relies on *classes*, whether these are defined by phenotype or genotype, the visible characteristics or the hidden, inherited, codes. This isn't necessarily any more of an error than is speaking of "sunrise" and "sunset" even though we know very well that it is the earth that revolves, and not the sun that rises and falls through the heavens. Even biologists make use of many different concepts of *a species*.[21] It is sometimes important to distinguish vipers (*Vipera berus*) and grass snakes (*Natrix natrix*) just because it is vipers that are very much more likely to be venomous. But the reality, from a longer point of view, is that creatures classed as vipers and grass snakes are all members of a particular *clade*,[22] a line of descent (*Serpentes*), which does not necessarily retain any particular distinct character, visible or genetic, through all its generations.

> Since species evolve ... they should be treated not as classes whose members satisfy some fixed set of conditions — not even a vague cluster of them — but as lineages, lines of descent, strings of imperfect copies of predecessors, among which there may not even be

---

21 Richard A. Richards, *The Species Problem: A Philosophical Analysis* (Cambridge: Cambridge University Press, 2010).

22 A clade is defined as the descendants of a common ancestor: how far back that ancestor is to be found determines in practice what level of biological taxon (kingdom, phylum, class, order, family, genus, species) is in question. See Henry Gee, *Deep Time: Cladistics, the Revolution in Evolution* (London: Fourth Estate, 2001).

the manifestations of a set of central and distinctive, let alone necessary and sufficient common properties.[23]

This point is especially evident when we try to identify fossil species. It is not merely that we don't now *know* where to put the lines between, for example, *Homo erectus, habilis, heidelbergensis, antecessor, neanderthalensis, sapiens* and so on — but that there is nothing actually to know. All these hominins (and how easy is it to distinguish hominins from other primates?) are descended, probably, from some fairly recent single primate population, just as all modern humans, however various they seem, are descended from a small band of hominins somewhere, probably, in northeast Africa. Once upon a time (and not that long ago) there were many contemporaneous more-or-less human kinds. Even now there are many distinct populations of *Homo sapiens*: the common idea that evolution has somehow halted is a political and not a scientific thesis.[24] And all primates are likewise descended from a single mammalian population, contemporaneous with the downfall of the dinosaurs. All of them — indeed all living creatures in the world — carry the same core genes, and all are rivulets, as it were, from a single spring. Different clades may carry different selections from the ancestral genome, or accumulate significant variations in their relative isolation. Those differences may be expressed in many different phenotypes, which may also converge upon especially useful forms, so that it will not be immediately evident whether some shared phenotypical character indicates a recent common ancestor, or merely a common situation. Crocodiles are more closely related to birds than they are to lizards. Oak trees are closer genealogically to daisies than they are to pines.

THEME AND VARIATION

Biological taxa aren't natural kinds. But it might still be true that each individual organism has a definite nature, determining what it can do and suffer. It is possible that each such organism has a unique nature, requiring

---

23 A. Rosenberg, *Sociobiology and the Pre-emption of Social Science* (Baltimore: Johns Hopkins Press, 1980), 122–23.

24 See Gregory Cochran and Henry Harpending, *The 10,000 Year Explosion* (New York: Basic Books, 2009).

precisely engineered conditions for its best survival. That indeed may be the current biomedical future: medications designed precisely for each individual gene set, as that is expressed through nurture and the environment. But it is likelier that we will settle, even there, for a cut-price version, in which drugs, diet and mode of life are recommended on the basis of the individual's membership of a finite set of classes: male, sedentary, elderly Caucasians will get different treatment than female, athletic, youthful Aboriginals (and only occasionally will this be the wrong bet). Even though elephants can swim (and some of their descendants, like their cousins, may someday be marine mammals — or creatures for which we have no present label), present-day elephants mostly live on land. So even though biological taxa don't have quite the weight that folk-taxonomy has given them, they may still be important to decisions about how to treat different creatures, and what a good life might be like for creatures of one sort or another.

But despite these concessions to the merits of folk-taxonomy, it is still worth examining the more radical suggestion that all living creatures are variations on a single theme, inheritors of a single genome, companions in a single enterprise. The moral revolution that gave us humanism as an ideal was founded on the recognition of a common nature, a common inheritance, in human beings of widely differing appearances and capabilities. A similar change in outlook is required for a better-informed biocentrism. Humanism is compatible with the understanding that most adult human beings are lactose-intolerant: the variation that allows most adult Caucasians to drink cow's milk is not widely shared. Biocentrism is also compatible with understanding that most animals live commonsensically within their own immediate surroundings: the variation that allows most modern humans (and probably other, extinct hominins as well as, possibly, extinct creatures of quite another line) to construct and share dream-worlds (so that we live not only in our immediate sense-world but in an *imagined* world, whether that is inhabited by gods and ghosts or by more "scientific" entities) may be responsible for our present dominance (and may be responsible also for our sometime extinction).

Was Chesterton right to be alarmed? He saw in Darwinian theory (as he also might in Chambers's theory) the threat that humanity itself was not a natural kind, and therefore not a kind to be preserved or honored.

Is Humankind a Natural Kind?

Not only was there no clear break between the human and non-human (as there may be no clear break between day and night), the human was not even a single, stable thing (as if daytime itself could not be counted on). "Human nature" turns out to be simply a ragbag of once-useful adaptations and not-too-harmful oddities, and the ease with which we recognize "the human" across the globe, from English villagers to Amazonian tribes, is simply a reminder that our common ancestors were very recent. The fact that European explorers have sometimes thought non-Europeans more alien than they are[25] should not prevent our seeing that sometimes the different human tribes are already much more alien to each other than good liberals prefer. And in that rests a danger.

> The subconscious popular instinct against Darwinism was . . . that when once one begins to think of man as a shifting and alterable thing, it is always easy for the strong and crafty to twist him into new shapes for all kinds of unnatural purposes. The popular instinct sees in such developments the possibility of backs bowed and hunch-backed for their burden, or limbs twisted for their task. It has a very well-grounded guess that whatever is done swiftly and systematically will mostly be done by a successful class and almost solely in their interests. It has therefore a vision of unhuman hybrids and half-human experiments much in the style of Mr. Wells's Island of Dr. Moreau. . . . The rich man may come to be breeding a tribe of dwarfs to be his jockeys, and a tribe of giants to be his hall-porters.[26]

It was not a fear without foundation, and insofar as evolutionary theory is still taken to have such implications, it is understandable that many would rather it wasn't true. This is especially so when Darwin's own theory of natural selection was wrongly interpreted:

> Among the innumerable muddles, which mere materialistic fashion made out of the famous theory, there was in many quarters a

---

25 See John L. Baker, *Race* (Oxford: Oxford University Press, 1974).
26 G. K. Chesterton, *What's Wrong with the World* (Cassell & Co: London, 1910), 259.

queer idea that the Struggle for Existence was of necessity an actual struggle between the candidates for survival; literally a cut-throat competition. There was a vague idea that the strongest creature violently crushed the others. And the notion that this was the one method of improvement came everywhere as good news to bad men; to bad rulers, to bad employers, to swindlers and sweaters and the rest. The brisk owner of a bucket-shop compared himself modestly to a mammoth, trampling down other mammoths in the primeval jungle. The business man destroyed other business men, under the extraordinary delusion that the eohippic horse had devoured other eohippic horses. The rich man suddenly discovered that it was not only convenient but cosmic to starve or pillage the poor, because pterodactyls may have used their little hands to tear each other's eyes. Science, that nameless being, declared that the weakest must go to the wall; especially in Wall Street. There was a rapid decline and degradation in the sense of responsibility in the rich, from the merely rationalistic eighteenth century to the purely scientific nineteenth. The great Jefferson, when he reluctantly legalised slavery, said he trembled for his country, knowing that God is just. The profiteer of later times, when he legalised usury or financial trickery, was satisfied with himself; knowing that Nature is unjust.[27]

But as Chesterton recognized, this interpretation of Darwinian theory was mistaken: the race is not to the swift, and certainly not to the tyrannical. And we may suspect that the supposed effects of believing in a biological continuum would also rest on a mistake. Those who accept that there are no rigid boundaries in nature, and that nearly the same gene set which maintains our own bodily being might, in different circumstances, have had a very different outcome, don't have to believe that we, as individuals, are indefinitely malleable, nor that it would be right to engineer particular outcomes to suit the interests of the rich and powerful. On the contrary, we may both relish the actual outcomes, and remember that there is one

---

27 G. K. Chesterton, *The Well and the Shallows* (London: Sheed & Ward, 1935), 43.

Is Humankind a Natural Kind?

and the same nature at work in all of us—from super-humans to sea squirts. Nor do we have to *imagine* what people who think like this would do: Platonists and Pythagoreans were the ones who more often insisted on respect for other creatures, however little "like us" they might at first appear, while also supposing that the same soul, the same life, was at work in all of them. That is another and still longer story. It is enough for now to understand the dangers, and embrace the opportunities, of a biologically educated biocentrism.

There is a danger that we interpret difference as dangerous, and therefore either humanely deny the differences or more aggressively destroy them—but both responses are paying homage to monoculture. There is also a danger, identified by Chesterton, that we might welcome difference, but only where it serves our ends (or our masters'). But this too pays homage to monoculture—a conviction that all is for the best when it is organized toward a single goal. There is a better response, and one that is more in tune with the actual history, so far as we can see, of the living earth. Differences are desirable, in the living earth as much as in human society, since it is only such differences that allow us to survive at all. They are desirable also in that—as we recognize—it is the more varied, colorful world that is the more beautiful, the more worth our respect. Differences are not diseases. And variations are always on a theme.

5

Human Dignity

FAMILY DISPUTES

Differences need not be defects, and there is no one right way of being human (or canine or what you will). Members of one species need not all share any single feature which is not also shared with members of another, and the borders between all species are more porous than we have in the past supposed. It may still be true that all modern human beings share many distinctive features, but that is rather because we have common ancestors, not very long ago. Common ancestry, in fact, has often been acknowledged as the source of human fellowship.

Thus, for example, in 1625, the philosopher Nathanael Carpenter in his *Geography* maintained that Moses' motivation, in writing his genealogical lists, was so that all people would understand themselves to be descended from the same original "then which there is no greater meanes to conciliate and ioyne mens affections for mutuall amitie and conversation" (*Geography Delineated Forth in Two Books* [Oxford, 1625], 2:207). Similarly, in 1656, the year of La Peyrère's *Men before Adam*, John White remarked in his commentary on *Genesis* that the reason for God's having created only one couple was to unite all men in love to one another so that "we cannot shut up our bowels of compassion from any man, of what Nation or Kindred soever he be" (*A Commentary upon the Three First Chapters of Genesis* [London, 1656], 1:111). Some forty years later, Richard Kidder, Bishop of Bath and Wells, suggested that the origin of all people was from one man to ensure that claims of racial superiority could not arise, that "men might not boast and vaunt of their extraction and original . . . and that they might think themselves under an obligation to love and assist each other as proceeding from the same original and common parent" (*A Commentary on the Five Books of Moses* [London, 1694], 1:6).[1]

This was also the chief reason for the widespread belief that there were no habitable lands on the other side of the world: the earth, undoubtedly, was a globe, but the other side, being inaccessible because of the trackless ocean and the impassable heats of the equator, could not have been colonized by our human ancestors. We had better suppose, according to Gregory Palamas (1296–1359), that there was only landless ocean there, rather than run the risk of encountering "people" unrelated to ourselves.[2] Augustine had the same problem.[3] The discovery that tropic heats and the wastes of water are not after all impassable, and that we have human cousins of the same stock on the other side of the world, has resolved that issue — though nowadays we wonder instead about the possibility of encountering "people" of a sort on *other* worlds.

Different branches of the human family may still have somewhat different characters, and it may still be possible for that family to speciate. But the fact or fable of common descent still has some force, and some advantages: even if the human beings we encounter elsewhere *look* uncouth or unfamiliar, they are still our cousins, and for the moment at least we may also share descendants. It may even be that those imagined mongrel descendants will strike us all as closer to an ideal human form: amalgamated photographs of different human faces, at any rate, display an almost unearthly beauty.[4] That latter point, reverting to pre-Darwinian perspective, will concern me later: the practice, sadly, was begun by Galton in his pursuit of the essentially "criminal face." "It will be observed," he said, "that the features of the composites are much better looking than those of the components. The special villainous irregularities in

---

1 Philip Almond, "Adam, Pre-Adamites, and Extra-Terrestrial Beings in Early Modern Europe," *Journal of Religious History* 30.2 (2006): 163–74; 168–69.

2 Gregory Palamas, *The 150 Chapters*, trans. Robert E. Sinkewicz (Toronto: Pontifical Institute of Mediaeval Studies, 1988), 9–14.

3 Augustine, *City of God*, trans. R. W. Dyson (Cambridge: Cambridge University Press, 1998), 664 [16.9].

4 Judith H. Langlois, Lori A. Roggman and Lisa Musselman, "What is Average and What is Not Average about Attractive Faces," *Psychological Science* 5.4 (1994): 214–20.

the latter have disappeared and the common humanity that underlies them has prevailed."⁵

Both the fact of common ancestry and the suggestion of a common ideal form only variously realized in different clades have some effect on our moral sensibilities. But neither need be powerful enough to compensate for the thought that "man is a shifting and alterable thing," a mere moment in a much longer line, a mere sample of hominin or primate vitality.⁶ Talk of "missing links" between ancestral species and the present day tended to suggest that certain creatures—and in the end *all* creatures—are no more than a passing phase, rather than creatures "in their own right" (though it is likely that those who said so also believed that they themselves were at least precursors of the Coming Race). Those who thought that there were once "partially human" people were all too likely to think that there are still such "partial humans"; those, like Chesterton, who believed that all human beings were *people*, preferred to believe that humanity—and maybe other creaturely kinds—appeared abruptly.⁷

Chesterton recognized another danger, already evident in the writings of "progressive" Darwinists. H. G. Wells, and others, thought that evolution happened quickly. "We can realize now, as no one in the past was ever able to realize it, that man is a creature changing very rapidly from the life of a rare and solitary ape to the life of a social and economic animal."⁸ He accepted Arthur Keith's estimate that there had been changes in the face

---

5 Francis Galton, "Composite Portraits," *Journal of the Anthropological Institute of Great Britain and Ireland* 8 (1878): 132–42; 135.

6 "'I was a fish and I shall be a crow,' said Tancred": Benjamin Disraeli, *Tancred, or The New Crusade* (London: Henry Colburn, 1847), 1:227. Disraeli was satirizing Robert Chambers's evolutionary ideas, or rather the "progressive" interpretation commonly given them.

7 See G. K. Chesterton, *The Everlasting Man* (London: Hodder & Stoughton, 1925), 47: "I shall waste no further space on these speculations on the nature of man before he became man. His body may have been evolved from the brutes; but we know nothing of any such transition that throws the smallest light upon his soul as it has shown itself in history."

8 H. G. Wells, *Mr. Belloc Objects to "The Outline of History"* (London: Methuen, 1926), 53. Wells's claim is simply mistaken: our ancestors, even if they were more like modern apes than we are, were certainly not solitary. See Wiktor Stoczkowski, *Explaining Human Origins: Myth, Imagination and Conjecture*, trans. Mary Turton (Cambridge: Cambridge University Press, 2002) for a good account of the mythological origins of much popular and even "scientific" speculation about prehistory.

and skull within the last five thousand years.⁹ From which, as Chesterton had observed, it follows that

> The employer need not mind sending a Kaffir underground; he will soon become an underground animal, like a mole.... Men need not trouble to alter conditions; conditions will so soon alter men. The head can be beaten small enough to fit the hat. Do not knock the fetters off the slave; knock the slave until he forgets the fetters.¹⁰

It is by these techniques after all that we have bred domestic beasts to servitude, because we have been bold enough to kill or castrate "poor stock." As Hunter said, "if such people were lower animals, we would probably kill them off to prevent them from spreading."¹¹ And what *counts* as poor stock will depend on the uses that we have for them.

Wells's contempt at "the spectacle of a mean-spirited, under-sized, diseased little man, quite incapable of earning a decent living even for himself, married to a some underfed, ignorant, ill-shaped, plain and diseased little woman, and guilty of the lives of ten or twelve ugly ailing children"¹² could be conjoined with happy admiration of some other human animals, adapted to their station. What he looks forward to, it seems, is an imitation of the form of life achieved by the social insects or the denizens of his Moon.¹³ In fairness to Wells, it should be noted that in an essay written a few years later than the first edition of *Anticipations* (1904), he denounced the attitude that says "when the convict tramps past us — 'There goes another sort of animal that is differentiating from my species and which I would gladly see exterminated'"¹⁴—but it is not clear why he denounced it. Perhaps it is merely that the *convict*, after all, may only have been guilty by the older

---

9 Wells, *Mr. Belloc Objects*, 30–31, citing Arthur Keith at the Royal Society of Medicine, November 16, 1925. Some evolutionary changes do indeed seem to happen more quickly than Darwin himself supposed, especially in the bacterial realm, and so also, by infection, in the eukaryotic.

10 Chesterton, *What's Wrong*, 22.

11 Hunter, *Civic Biology*, 263.

12 Wells, *Anticipations*, 264.

13 H. G. Wells, *The First Men in the Moon* (London: George Newnes, 1901).

14 Wells, *Anticipations*, 322.

standards, and may actually be brighter and braver than the dull citizens who watch him go. What should it matter if he stole or killed? Those are the acts, after all, that Wells said were appropriate (he was gentlemanly enough not to approve of rape or assault—but why?).

The older biological synthesis, it is true, might also think of idiots (and women) as "defective," or judge all creatures by their closeness to the "human" (which is usually to say, the adult, rational, male) form. But it was also open to believers to acknowledge every real existent, and specifically every human child, as equally a child of God, not to be judged "defective" in comparison with Us. The new doctrine proposed that we were all material in more than a metaphysical sense: we were material for others' purposes.

It was a doctrine that the ruling classes have chosen, it seems, to impose upon the public. "In the lower classes the schoolmaster does not work for the parent but against the parent. Modern education means handing down the customs of the minority, and rooting out the customs of the majority."[15] Specifically, it has often meant instructing children to despise everything their parents thought and felt, including any residual respect for justice. The issue is only marginally about a scientific theory—the theory, that is, of gradual change through differential reproduction. It was and is about the implications of that theory as it has been expounded by men ignorant of the actual theory. The problem was originally made worse because Darwinians, even Darwin himself, had no clear notion of *inheritance*, nor of "genes." Children inherit many things from their parents, not all of them by way of DNA, and the features which were usually identified as disabilities or diseases were, to other eyes, socially rather than biologically engendered.

Two inferences were open to Darwinians of this stamp. The first and simplest was to conclude, with Wells:

> It has become apparent that whole masses of the human population are as a whole inferior in their claim upon the future to other masses, that they cannot be given opportunities or trusted with power as the superior peoples are trusted, that their characteristic

---

15 Chesterton, *What's Wrong*, 258.

weaknesses are contagious and detrimental in the civilizing fabric, and their range of incapacity tempts and demoralises the strong. To give them equality is to sink to their level, to protect and cherish them is to be swamped in their fecundity.[16]

So his New Republicans will sterilize and kill (perhaps "put down" or "put to sleep" would be the appropriate term) all those considered surplus to requirements. They may control them by "scientific" torture,[17] but will usually find it easier to kill offenders. "They will contrive a land legislation that will keep the black or yellow or mean-white squatter on the move" to prevent their procreating.[18] It was Wells's expectation (and incidentally, Darwin's) that "the inferior races," including "mean-white" trash, would be extinguished unless they could prove useful. At least we should stop *preserving* these "inferior" specimens:

> There is reason to believe that vaccination has preserved thousands, who from a weak constitution would formerly have succumbed to smallpox. Thus the weak members of civilized societies propagate their kind. No one who has attended to the breeding of domestic animals will doubt that this must be highly injurious to the race of man. It is surprising how soon a want of care, or care wrongly directed, leads to the degeneration of a domestic race; but excepting in the case of man himself, hardly anyone is so ignorant as to allow his worst animals to breed.[19]

An alternative inference, founded in a suspicion that perhaps not all inherited characteristics are inherited "through the seed," was to remove children from their parents and their peers, to rear them under proper "scientific" guidance, or at least — as above — to break down parental influence. As Chesterton said, "nobody could pretend that the affectionate mother of a rather backward child *deserves* to be punished by having all the happiness

---

16   Wells, *Anticipations*, 250.
17   Ibid., 259.
18   Ibid., 263.
19   Darwin, *Descent of Man*, 1:168.

taken out of her life. But anyone can pretend that the act is needed for the happiness of the community"[20] — or the imagined "health" of the race.

In either case, of course, it will be the *poor* that are the chief victims of a supposedly "scientific" assessment of their character and prospects. Chesterton's comment on those attempting to discover "criminality" in the shape of the skull or face, and how to remedy that "fault," is unfortunately apt:

> In a popular magazine there is one of the usual articles about criminology; about whether wicked men could be made good if their heads were taken to pieces. As by far the wickedest men I know of are much too rich and powerful ever to submit to the process, the speculation leaves me cold. I always notice with pain, however, a curious absence of the portraits of living millionaires from such galleries of awful examples; most of the portraits in which we are called upon to remark the line of the nose or the curve of the forehead appear to be the portraits of ordinary sad men, who stole because they were hungry or killed because they were in a rage. The physical peculiarity seems to vary infinitely; sometimes it is the remarkable square head, sometimes it is the unmistakable round head; sometimes the learned draw attention to the abnormal development, sometimes to the striking deficiency of the back of the head. I have tried to discover what is the invariable factor, the one permanent mark of the scientific criminal type; after exhaustive classification I have to come to the conclusion that it consists in being poor.[21]

PRESERVING HUMAN DIGNITY IN AN EVOLUTIONARY COSMOS

The human species — like others — is very various, and we all resemble each other chiefly because we are all descended from a relatively small and relatively homogeneous population. Our differences equip us to meet many different challenges, and offer many different advantages to the communities we form. That variation, and that variability, unfortunately also make us variously manipulable, and — especially when the manipulators

---

20 G. K. Chesterton, *Fancies versus Fads* (London: Methuen, 1923), 91.
21 Chesterton, *What's Wrong*, 41.

also believe, quite inconsistently, that there is after all a superior form of humanity (namely, their own) — the results may be, and often have been, as bad as Chesterton suggested. Human beings, it seems, easily fall into the bad habit of caste division, and, in effect, seek to breed people to fit the roles that best serve the masters. The full rigors of such caste systems may sometimes be alleviated by the thought or fancy that we shall all be born again into whatever form of life we most deserve.

> There is no accident in a man's becoming a slave, nor is he taken prisoner in war by chance, nor is outrage done on his body without due cause, but he was once the doer of that which he now suffers; and a man who made away with his mother will be made away with by a son when he has become a woman, and one who has raped a woman will be a woman in order to be raped. (Plotinus, *Ennead* III.2 [47].13, 11–15)

Whether this thought encourages us *not* to outrage others, or else not to complain when others are outraged (as perhaps they really deserve it) may be moot, but at least the story helps us to conceive our fundamental unity. Even without these dire possibilities, we may be saved from the very worst by the thought that each of us, no matter what our character and circumstances, whatever our words or actions, is indeed a member of the human family, a close relative whose feelings we cannot afford always to ignore or violate.

The older biological and moral synthesis which Chesterton defended (at least in part) insisted that humankind was something different in kind from all other forms of life. "Cruelty to animals is cruelty and a vile thing," remember, "but cruelty to a man is not cruelty, it is treason. Tyranny over a man is not tyranny, it is rebellion, for man is royal." *Each* human being, that is, is royal, and to be treated as an image of the Creator God (male or female, Hebrew or gentile, freeborn or slave, and so on). To repeat the Rabbinic gloss:

> A man stamps many coins with one seal, and they are all identical, but the King of the kings of kings stamped every man with the seal

Human Dignity

of the first man, and none is identical with his fellow. Therefore it is the duty of every one to say: For my sake the world was created.[22]

That unity, in the older synthesis, may be symbolized by our common descent from Adam, but it is possible in principle for that same seal to be stamped elsewhere than in the strictly Adamite lineage. If there are recognizably "human" or "humane" beings elsewhere in the cosmos, we cannot reasonably deny them the same claim—to life, liberty and the pursuit of happiness—merely because they are not "of our blood." It is after all a primary claim of Christians both that one and the same Logos makes creatures "*logikoi*" and that "to all who have yielded him their allegiance he gave the right to become children of God, not born of any human stock, or by the fleshly desire of any human father, but the offspring of God himself" (Jn 1:12–13).[23] Biological relationships are not the primary sort—just as Jesus insisted that whoever did the will of God was his "mother and sister and brother" (Mt 12:48–50). *Friendship*, or at any rate a friendship founded in the love of God, trumped Family—as both Buddhists and Epicureans also claimed.[24]

I hinted that there might be "human" or "humane" creatures elsewhere in the cosmos with whom we might hope and expect to have some "humane" relationship, acknowledging their rights and dignity. What possible other forms of life might also claim to be "in the image and likeness of God" I shall consider later. But whether there are such entities or not elsewhere, we need to consider more carefully whether there are such entities already here. Chesterton—and much of the Western tradition—may be right to say that all and only human beings have the status that they claim, and

---

22 *Mishnah: Sanhedrin* 4.5, in Urbach, *The Sages*, 217; see also Mt 22:21.

23 See Giuseppe Tanzella-Nitti, "Jesus Christ, Incarnation and Doctrine of Logos" [DOI:10.17421/2037-2329-2008-GT-2], in *Interdisciplinary Encyclopedia of Religion and Science*, ed. idem, I. Colagé, and A. Strumia (Interdisciplinary Documentation on Religion and Science, Rome, 2008) for a scholarly account of the trope.

24 See Stephen R. L. Clark, *Ancient Mediterranean Philosophy* (London: Continuum, 2013), 151–56: Epicureans were essentially, and perhaps historically, a Buddhist sect, convinced that all is *dukkha* (transient), and that we could "escape" by acknowledging our own non-entity, and extinguishing or disciplining our desires. They took refuge in their inspiration (Epicurus), their Society of Friends, their doctrine (that is to say: the Buddha or enlightened one), the *sangha*, and the *dharma*.

that all other creatures with whom we have to do are (at best) to be treated kindly, but with no special reverence or care. To accommodate this idea we have had to claim that there is indeed an extra Something that breaks into our biological descent, a spirit or an intellect literally "from outside." That something may not manifest itself until the human animal is of some certain age — when it begins to chatter, or to take responsibility, or to acknowledge its Creator — but it has been there from the entity's beginning. "Thou it was who didst fashion my inward parts; thou didst knit me together in my mother's womb" (Ps 139:13).

But suppose instead that there is no such single abrupt intrusion, in phylogeny or ontogeny, either in the beginning of the human species or the single human individuals. If there were an *intrusion* in an embryo's development, then the embryo, until that "quickening," was only an "animal organism" — and the very people who are most inclined to resist the notion that human beings are a certain sort of animal, a particular twig within the primate lineage, will also resist the idea that human embryos aren't properly human till some — seemingly arbitrary — moment (in the ancient Mediterranean that moment would most likely have been when the child's father accepted it as his: till then it was fit for exposure). The process of real becoming is very rarely abrupt, and even changes that mark a sudden shift depend on underlying much more gradual movements: water boils and freezes at well-defined temperatures, but still cools or warms up "by degrees." It may be, by remote analogy, that some primates were suddenly human, as the effect of many slow, subtle alterations — but the case would be clearer if we had a clearer notion of what that "sudden humanity" amounted to: infants now don't "suddenly" speak their mother tongue, but acquire their competence at different speeds, with different slips and idiolects. Some never quite manage to speak — and are still considered worth consideration. John Paul II, in *Evangelium Vitae*, makes the point, while still asserting an absolute distinction between human and other beings:

> The theory of human rights is based precisely on the affirmation that the human person, unlike animals and things, cannot be subjected to domination by others. We must also mention the mentality which tends to equate personal dignity with the capacity for verbal

Human Dignity

and explicit, or at least perceptible, communication. It is clear that on the basis of these presuppositions there is no place in the world for anyone who, like the unborn or the dying, is a weak element in the social structure, or for anyone who appears completely at the mercy of others and radically dependent on them, and can only communicate through the silent language of a profound sharing of affection. In this case it is force which becomes the criterion for choice and action in interpersonal relations and in social life. But this is the exact opposite of what a State ruled by law, as a community in which the "reasons of force" are replaced by the "force of reason," historically intended to affirm.[25]

But why does the "silent language of a profound sharing of affection" apply only to the purportedly *human*? And why is it that "animals and things" can be subjected to domination by others, though human beings "cannot" be? John Paul cannot mean that human beings literally *cannot* be thus dominated: the sad history of our kind shows clearly that they can, and can even be persuaded that this is the natural order. Many non-human beings, contrariwise, cannot in fact be dominated, however much we would like this outcome: "Canst thou draw out Leviathan with a hook?" (Job 41:1). The claim is rather that those other creatures are somehow "made" to be our property, as other human beings never are, and have only such rights as mirror our duties of care toward them — which duties, to be sure, are more extensive than we ordinarily remember. "A righteous man regardeth the life of his beast: but the tender mercies of the wicked are cruel" (Prov 12:10): such mercies nowadays include debeaking chickens so as to minimize the harm overcrowded and stressed birds may do each other.

Human characteristics are not necessarily confined within our species — indeed we can already be sure that there were many hominin species once, with whom our ancestors communicated, and probably interbred. Whether we are *remembering* those long-gone hominins, with stories of elves, dwarves and giants, is uncertain: the memories, if they are veridical, are from very long ago, and probably much changed to suit the later

---

25 John Paul II, *Evangelium Vitae: On the Value and Inviolability of Human Life* (London: Catholic Truth Society, 1995), §19.

generations' needs. We may instead have been making up the stories, perhaps on the basis of discovered relics, as we also made up stories of dragons from old bones. Or perhaps we simply made the stories up entirely, to sketch alternative ideas from which to form an idea of ourselves. At the same time, our ancestors were confident that there were many truly non-human tribes around with whom they were well acquainted: wolves, eagles, lizards, fishes—even trees and grasses. Nowadays we moderns prefer to think that "primitive peoples," our ancestors or our contemporaries, are simply, foolishly mistaken. Of course the other creatures with whom we share the world are dumb. Of course they have no plans for life, nor any need, it seems, to think about what they're doing. Of course all stories to the contrary are only "anthropomorphic." This same notion, which derives its strength from the older notion that human beings are of another kind entirely, is still adopted by the very scientists and scholars most likely to insist on the truth of the Darwinian story. On the one hand, all non-humans are our cousins, and on the other they are only things required for our own benefit: they are "given" to us even if there is no Giver. It is to Richard Dawkins's credit that he acknowledged, and pressed, the proper implication of Darwinian theory: if human beings are not an utterly different sort of creature, we are all related through our common ancestor, and all share, in varying degrees, a common set of powers.[26] If human beings are granted "rights" in virtue either of their characters or their consanguinity, then so should be other creatures—though the force of this argument is lessened in a thoroughly Darwinian mindset: why shouldn't we be openly selfish, if we are so confident that every creature, covertly, already is? Must we not confine our morals to those strategies that theory tells us will be "evolutionarily stable"? Can we be altruistic only when it helps our genes survive? Must justice, or self-sacrifice, or chastity, or simple friendliness lose out? Dawkins occasionally suggests that we might be able to "defy" our selfish genes—but how, and why? Must those values not have lost out long ago, and our devotion to them be merely hypocritical? "Scratch an 'altruist' and watch a 'hypocrite' bleed."[27]

26 Richard Dawkins, "Gaps in the Mind," in P. Singer and P. Cavalieri, eds., *The Great Ape Project: Equality Beyond Humanity* (London: Fourth Estate, 1993), 80–87.
27 M. H. Ghiselin, *The Economy of Nature and the Evolution of Sex* (San Francisco: University

Human Dignity

Morality, remember, "has no other demonstrable ultimate function" than "to keep human genetic material intact."[28]

Is there another way of phrasing some more kindly or cooperative ideal? Darwin's theory, in essence, was an application of an Enlightenment doctrine, that we should not trouble to discover final causes. What purpose things in general serve is not for us to say, and good Enlightenment philosophers, for theological as well as scientific reasons, preferred much barer accounts of what was going on. Falling objects did not *seek* the earth. The planets did not offer omens. Pigs did not exist "for" us, as locomotive meals with souls instead of salt (as Stoic philosophers had, jestingly, suggested). This intellectual chastity, refusing the temptation to consider things only in their relationship to us and our employment of them, was a spiritual as well as a scientific practice. Unfortunately, it could be read in at least two ways.

By the first and better reading, this was just to say that we should view things not as means but themselves as ends.

> The egg only exists to produce the chicken. But the chicken does not exist only to produce another egg. He [sic] may also exist to amuse himself, to praise God, and even to suggest ideas to a French dramatist. Being a conscious life, he is, or may be, valuable in himself.[29]

Every really existent thing stands out from emptiness. "There is a primeval light in which all stones are precious stones; a primeval darkness against which all flowers are as vivid as fireworks."[30] Real science — as distinct from mere technology — is founded in that wonder at the being of things, the wish to see them clearly "as they are," to waken from the delirium of normal life, in which we only see pets or pests, dirt, vermin, weeds and useful crops. If we open our eyes, we can agree with MacIntyre:

---

of California Press, 1978), 247.
28 Wilson, *Human Nature*, 167.
29 Chesterton, *What's Wrong*, 9.
30 Chesterton, *Fancies*, 149.

Different as they are from language-using human beings, they [that is, other animals] are able to form relationships not only with members of their own species, but also with human beings, while giving expression to their own intentions and purposes. So that the relationships are far more clearly analogous to human relationships than some of the philosophical theorizing that I have discussed would allow. Some human beings indeed and some nonhuman animals pursue their respective goods in company with and in cooperation with each other. And what we mean by "goods" in saying this is precisely the same, whether we are speaking of human or dolphin or gorilla.[31]

The very *differences* between ourselves and others, and between those others and each other, should be an occasion for delight. "Each creature possesses its own particular goodness and perfection.... Each of the various creatures, willed in its own being, reflects in its own way a ray of God's infinite wisdom and goodness. Man must therefore respect the particular goodness of every creature, to avoid any disordered use of things."[32] Once again, it is not clear that the full implications of this concession have been realized. At any rate it seems that most Christian pastors and theologians, even if they pay lip-service to such sentiments, continue to eat their factory-reared meat, their cousins, with undiminished appetite, and without even the excuse of being poor. The Catholic *Catechism* "firmly states that human power has limits and that 'it is contrary to human dignity to cause animals to suffer or die needlessly.'"[33] What counts as "need," in practice, seems endlessly extendible.[34]

---

[31] Alasdair MacIntyre, *Dependent Rational Animals* (Chicago: Open Court, 1999), 61; see also Marc Bekoff, "Wild Justice and Fair Play: Cooperation, Forgiveness, and Morality in Animals," *Biology and Philosophy* 19 (2004): 489–520.

[32] *Catechism of the Catholic Church*, 339, cited by Francis, *Laudato Si'*, §69.

[33] Francis, *Laudato Si'*, §130, citing *Catechism* 2418.

[34] The *Catechism*, without blinking, also says that "God entrusted animals to the stewardship of those whom he created in his own image. Hence [sic] it is legitimate to use animals for food and clothing. They may be domesticated to help man in his work and leisure. Medical and scientific experimentation on animals is a morally acceptable practice, if it remains within reasonable limits and contributes to caring for or saving human lives. It is contrary to human dignity to cause animals to suffer or die needlessly. It is likewise unworthy to spend money on them that should as a priority go to the relief of human misery. One can love animals; one should not direct to them the affection due only to persons" (2417–18).

Human Dignity

The drastic alternative is to empty the world of any significance *except* its usefulness to us (which is to say, we happy few, we rulers). That is the "dreadful dry light" that "must at last wither up the moral mysteries as illusions."[35] This is the core of uncaring vivisection. It is true that many experimentalists regret their tasks, and seek to mitigate the effects of their experiments. There are many who sincerely seek to refine, reduce and replace "animal experiments," but still think them necessary if we are ever to cure ills that afflict both animals and humans. But there are also some who honestly see no obstacle in using "animals" entirely as they wish. It is a matter of unhappy record that some see no obstacle in using *humans,* or what they call sub-humans, as they wish, if only the law allowed them (as sometimes it has). The ethical effect of this is obvious. The epistemological effect should also not be forgotten. "The suppression of sympathies, that waving away of intuitions or guesswork, which make a man preternaturally clever in dealing with the stomach of a spider, will make him preternaturally stupid in dealing with the heart of man."[36] Some scientists have seemed to operate as if our scientific understanding is wholly separate from empirical and empathetic understanding, when the truth is rather that they could not even understand their own case-notes or another's scientific papers without relying on tacit understanding of intention, context, logic and good sense. The stomach of spiders can perhaps be viewed almost mechanically, without importing sympathies or antipathies, but even of a spider it is absurd to think it "only a spider." Even of a fish it is blasphemous to say it is *only* a fish.[37]

The principal point is not to offer explanations of a suitably familiar "human" sort for animal behavior or for other natural happenings. Our confrontation with the Other is more mysterious than that.

> Possibly the most pathetic of all the delusions of the modern students of primitive belief is the notion they have about the thing they call anthropomorphism. They believe that primitive men attributed phenomena to a god in human form in order to explain them,

---

35 G. K. Chesterton, *The Poet and the Lunatics* (London: Darwen Finlayson, 1962 [1929]), 70.
36 G. K. Chesterton, *Heretics* (New York: John Lane, 1905), 143.
37 Chesterton, *The Poet and the Lunatics*, 58.

because his mind in its sullen limitation could not reach any further than his own clownish existence. The thunder was called the voice of a man, the lightning the eyes of a man, because by this explanation they were made more reasonable and comfortable. The final cure for all this kind of philosophy is to walk down a lane at night. Anyone who does so will discover very quickly that men pictured something semi-human at the back of all things, not because such a thought was natural, but because it was supernatural; not because it made things more comprehensible, but because it made them a hundred times more incomprehensible and mysterious. For a man walking down a lane at night can see the conspicuous fact that as long as nature keeps to her own course, she has no power with us at all. As long as a tree is a tree, it is a top-heavy monster with a hundred arms, a thousand tongues, and only one leg. But so long as a tree is a tree, it does not frighten us at all. It begins to be something alien, to be something strange, only when it looks like ourselves. When a tree really looks like a man our knees knock under us. And when the whole universe looks like a man we fall on our faces.[38]

This sudden confrontation, the moment when we recognize Another and—perforce—admit that Other into our own experience, is at the root of Martin Buber's account of the I/Thou relationship, which he did not confine to merely human relations.

> The tree is no impression, no play of my imagination, no aspect of a mood; it confronts me bodily and has to deal with me as I must deal with it—only differently. One should not try to dilute the meaning of the relation: relation is reciprocity. Does the tree then have consciousness, similar to our own? I have no experience of that. But thinking that you have brought this off in your own case, must you again divide the indivisible? What I encounter is neither the soul of a tree nor a dryad, but the tree itself.[39]

---

38   Chesterton, *Heretics*, 63.
39   Martin Buber, *I and Thou*, trans. Walter Kaufmann (New York: Simon & Schuster, 1996 [1923]), 58–59.

Human Dignity

Is there a contradiction here, between my earlier deconstruction of the existence of distinct species and individuals and this forceful encounter with a genuine Other? On the contrary: the encounter shows us that our imperial pretensions, our sense of ourselves as masters of a world of objects, are mistaken. Anyone may be such an Other. Suddenly, we are reminded of the underlying truth: our former perception of things is no more than a dream and a delirium, a distortion even of the sort of *Umwelt* that we had patronizingly ascribed to merely animal experience. The world, in the shape of dog or tree, is suddenly looking back at us, reminding us that we are all travelers together in what Aldo Leopold called "the odyssey of evolution,"[40] and Platonists have called "the dance of immortal love" (Porphyry, *Life of Plotinus* 23.36). So also Henry Beston:

> They are not brethren, they are not underlings; they are other nations, caught with ourselves in the net of life and time, fellow prisoners of the splendour and the travail of the earth.[41]

Suddenly we are no longer "in control," no longer an aloof intelligence considering a world entirely outside us. Really to appreciate and experience this is a revelation. To remember it may require a novel narrative. "Looking like a man," as Chesterton puts it, is in this context perhaps a misleading phrase. Dog, tree and the universe don't have the shape or even the character of *men*, nor do they look "like ourselves" (certainly not as we had supposed ourselves to be). The point is that they are *subjects*—but not *our* subjects—as well as objects: alive and constantly communicating.[42] Theologians acknowledge this experience, of encountering something that is more than we can say, in the case of other *human* creatures:

> A person is a mystery, never totally circumscribed by a definition, that is, as an essence or a "what." A person is not a "what" but a

---

40 Aldo Leopold, *A Sand County Almanac and Sketches Here and There* (New York: Oxford University Press, 1968 [1949]), 109.

41 Henry Beston, *The Outermost House: A Year of Life on the Great Beach of Cape Cod* (New York: Henry Holt & Co., 1988 [1928]), 25.

42 See Val Plumwood, "Nature in the Active Voice," in *Handbook of Contemporary Animism*, ed. Graham Harvey (Durham: Acumen, 2013), 441–53.

"who," and "who" you are, just as Who God is, is ultimately indefinable, undetermined, and of infinite depth. To say "what" something is, is to circumscribe that something in terms of essence or essential definition; to say "who" is to speak, not of some "thing" which can be defined in terms of its essence, but of some "one," an ultimately uncircumscribable and indefinable "who."[43]

The claim is constantly repeated, even by authors who also admit the significance of other creatures:

> Human beings, even if we postulate a process of evolution, also possess a uniqueness which cannot be fully explained by the evolution of other open systems. Each of us has his or her own personal identity and is capable of entering into dialogue with others and with God himself. Our capacity to reason, to develop arguments, to be inventive, to interpret reality and to create art, along with other not yet discovered capacities, are signs of a uniqueness which transcends the spheres of physics and biology. The sheer novelty involved in the emergence of a personal being within a material universe presupposes a direct action of God and a particular call to life and to relationship on the part of a "Thou" who addresses himself to another "thou." The biblical accounts of creation invite us to see each human being as a subject who can never be reduced to the status of an object.[44]

Can *any* creature be thus reduced without loss or error? Why should we not acknowledge the same sort of confrontation and recognition in the company of the non-human? Nor is it only *our* human recognition that is in question.

> If the dog, now, wants something, he wags his tail; impatient of Master's stupidity in not understanding this perfectly distinct and

---

[43] Vincent Rossi, "Presence, Participation, Performance: The Remembrance of God in the Early Hesychast Fathers," in James S. Cutsinger, ed., *Paths to the Heart: Sufism and the Christian East* (Bloomington, IN: World Wisdom, 2004), 64–111; 79.

[44] Francis, *Laudato Si'*, § 81.

expressive speech, he adds a vocal expression—he barks—and finally an expression of attitude—he mimes or makes signs. Here the man is the obtuse one who has not yet learned to talk. Finally something very remarkable happens. When the dog has exhausted every other device to comprehend the various speeches of his master, he suddenly plants himself squarely, and his eye bores into the eye of the human.... Here the dog has become a "judge" of men, looking his opposite straight in the eye and grasping, behind the speech, the speaker.[45]

Animals become our friends, we become their friends, when they look back at us, and we are confronted by the mystery of the Other which is at the root also of our own being. Non-humans aren't, in human terms, as clever as we are, but neither are we, in their terms, as clever as *they* are. Language is not all important, and the boundaries it creates are there to be transcended. We can "communicate through the silent language of a profound sharing of affection." Pythagoras—it is said—objected when a puppy was being thrashed, saying that he recognized a friend, and knew him by his voice.[46] Maybe the story intended a literal belief in metempsychosis, but it need not. We may simply observe that Pythagoras's heart went out to the dog when he heard his yelps: in that moment, he became a friend. It's not the only possible reaction to an animal's complaint. A story is told of the Rabbi Judah that when he heard a calf complaining on the way to slaughter, he rebuked him, saying that it was for this that the calf had been created. For this insensitivity he had toothache for thirteen years until one day he saved a weasel's life, and was pardoned.[47] At least Judah gave the calf an answer. The commonest reaction of all, of course, is simply to ignore the noise, which cannot really be a *complaint*, nor an appeal for justice, nor even a cry for help. Animals, after all, are merely animal.

---

45 Oswald Spengler, *The Decline of the West*, abridged by Helmut Werner and Arthur Helps, trans. C. F. Atkinson (New York: Oxford University Press, 1991 [1924, 1926]), 258.

46 Diogenes Laertius, *Lives of Eminent Philosophers* 8.36.12–15 (21B7DK), in Waterfield, *First Philosophers*, 30 [F20].

47 Richard H. Schwartz, *Judaism and Vegetarianism* (New York: Lantern Books, 2001), 29, citing *Baba Metzia* 85a, *Midrash Genesis Rabbah* 33.3; see also Seidenberg, *Kabbalah*, 146.

THE IMAGE REIMAGINED

What most humanists insist must make us "more than animal" is that we have a choice in what to do and be. Being *human,* as Aristotle insisted long before the existentialists, is being the sort of creature that has to *decide* what it is right to do (*Nicomachean Ethics* 1.1098a3–18) — and may often make mistakes. The mistakes made by the "merely animal" are merely practical or technical: missing a kill, or falling from a branch. Our mistakes are *practical* in the stronger, Aristotelian sense (a *praxis* is something done for a reason, which we can assess as good or bad): we do the wrong thing, thinking it is right, or failing to live by what we have decided. But why should this susceptibility to error be reckoned a mark of our "superior" nature? It seems, on the contrary, to be a failure: a proof that we are not, after all, divine. If other creatures do exactly and entirely what they are meant to do, are they inferior? May they not be a better image, exactly, of what is meant to be? And if we are after all "superior," in being able to transcend our own biology and background so as to give "inferiors" some slight consideration, why don't we?

One of the oddest features of much secular moral philosophy, as well as more theologically inspired enquiry, is the assumption that our *primary* obligations can only be to actually "rational" people: that is, to those with whom we could be expected to have made bargains, and who can themselves acknowledge congruent obligations. This is explicit in most post-Kantian moralizing, drawing on ancient Stoic notions: we can be obliged to do only what all other rational beings can also be obliged to do. Even those who have adopted a more "consequentialist" outlook, for whom our primary duty is to do as much good as possible (sometimes interpreted as ensuring as much pleasure, for as little pain, as possible), think chiefly of their effect on adult, rational beings. Utilitarians may insist, in Bentham's familiar words, that creatures are morally significant because they can *suffer,* and that we should minimize their suffering — but even those who emphasize the "moral considerability" of animals will usually add that most biologically "animal" organisms have no conception of their own continued being, and that their pains and pleasures are therefore transient, and easily to be ignored in favor of the *conscious* enjoyments and torments of the adult human.[48] In both

---

48 See Joan Dunayer, *Speciesism* (Derwood, MD: Ryce Publishing, 2004).

cases, our obligations seem in practice to depend on what "we" can agree between ourselves: *nomoi* rather than *thesmoi*, and we, by definition, are those creatures who can reason our way to conclusions, and remember what we agreed. Those agreements *may* be kindly to our non-human cousins, but they need not be—and mostly aren't.

What is especially strange in this is not so much our neglect of the non-human, even in ages and among peoples who are rationally convinced that there is no clear dividing line between the human and the non-human, as that these moral theories utterly neglect the actual primary *experience* of obligation. It should be obvious that any moral theory which explains our concern for babies, infants, toddlers and so on solely because these creatures are *potentially* adult, rational beings, is missing the point. It should also be obvious that any obligation we may have to obey or to revere *authority* cannot depend either on our having *agreed* to such obedience, or to our current calculation of the eventual consequences of obedience or disobedience. There are, in short, at least two sources of obligation: the pull to care for the young and the defenseless, and the pull to revere those placed "above" us, by their age, experience or obvious virtue (even if they are no longer what they were). Neither pull, of course, is absolute either *de facto* or *de iure*: we are often cruel to or neglectful of the young, and often disdainful of those whose claim on our obedience or reverence is suspect. The latter behavior, at least, is often the better way, but not because it is wrong to reverence age, experience and virtue: on the contrary, it is because such reverence is *right* that we ought not to revere mere make-believe.

When John Paul II spoke of communicating "through the silent language of a profound sharing of affection," he hinted at the proper use of "reason": we are most in accord with *Nous* when we acknowledge the good outside ourselves, and put aside the incessant chatter with which we ordinarily disguise the real. Infants, the very ill, the elderly may all be unable to *speak* or even "reason" (in the sense of calculating outcomes and possibilities), but they are all the proper objects of love and reverence. They are made "in the image of God," and so to be reckoned sacred: any disrespect or injury to them is to be taken as disrespect or injury to God (Mt 25:40; see also Mt 18:6).

John Paul II also acknowledged duties to the non-human, though without—I suspect—fully thinking through the implications of his remarks:

Can We Believe in People?

As one called to till and look after the garden of the world (cf. Gen 2:15), man has a specific responsibility towards the environment in which he lives, towards the creation which God has put at the service of his personal dignity, of his life, not only for the present but also for future generations. It is the ecological question—ranging from the preservation of the natural habitats of the different species of animals and of other forms of life to "human ecology" properly speaking—which finds in the Bible clear and strong ethical direction, leading to a solution which respects the great good of life, of every life. In fact, "the dominion granted to man by the Creator is not an absolute power, nor can one speak of a freedom to 'use and misuse,' or to dispose of things as one pleases. The limitation imposed from the beginning by the Creator himself and expressed symbolically by the prohibition not to 'eat of the fruit of the tree' (cf. Gen 2:16–17) shows clearly enough that, when it comes to the natural world, we are subject not only to biological laws but also to moral ones, which cannot be violated with impunity."[49]

If it is in the defenseless that we are to see the "image of God," irrespective of any ordinary power they have to compel our respect (their power lying only in the demand they make by being), then we must, as I hinted earlier, revise our image of God Himself. God, we are to understand from Dio Chrysostom,[50] is Majesty personified—and perhaps that is not altogether a mistake. But the Christian tradition especially (but not quite uniquely)

---

49 John Paul II, *Evangelium Vitae*, §42, citing an earlier encyclical, *Sollicitudo Rei Socialis* (December 30, 1987), §34. As I remarked earlier of Genesis 9:1–4, "this bond doth give thee here no drop of blood." John Paul mentioned the Noahic covenant in *Evangelium Vitae* §39, but only with regard to the spilling of *human* blood. A little later he suggests that "to celebrate the Gospel of life means to celebrate the God of life, the God who gives life: 'We must celebrate Eternal Life, from which every other life proceeds. From this, in proportion to its capacities, every being which in any way participates in life, receives life. This Divine Life, which is above every other life, gives and preserves life. Every life and every living movement proceed from this Life which transcends all life and every principle of life. It is to this that souls owe their incorruptibility; and because of this all animals and plants live, which receive only the faintest glimmer of life'" (§84, citing Dionysius the Areopagite, *On the Divine Names* 6, 1–3: *PG* 3, 856–57). Why animals and plants should be supposed to have only "a glimmer of life" is unclear even on pre-modern principles.

50 Dio Chrysostom, *Discourses*, 58 [12.43].

offered a different picture. God is to be known in an infant threatened with murder, in a homeless preacher, in an outcast condemned to a humiliating and excruciating death, abandoned even by God as well as by his people.

> My God, my God, why has thou forsaken me and art so far from saving me, from heeding my groans?... I am a worm, not a man, abused by all men, scorned by the people. All who see me jeer at me, make mouths at me and wag their heads. (Ps 22:6–7; see Mt 27:46)

The most familiar pictures of Jesus, whom Christians identify as the very Word of God, are of his infancy in Mary's arms, or on the cross. And yet it is this Jesus who is exalted (Acts 2:22–36; Eph 1:20–23; Phil 2:9). There is a fairly easy reading of the story that has no metaphysical implications: whenever a clear innocent is condemned, especially to death, by the powers and principalities of this world, it is those powers and principalities which are themselves condemned, and lose the moral authority they abused. We owe, or feel we owe, a primary obedience to authority—but that authority is borrowed from a higher source, and can be lost. Those who observe the event can feel themselves released, if not from reasonable fear of what the abusers can do, at least from any sense that the abusers have a right to do it. But the more strongly metaphysical sense of the Christian gospel should not be simply ignored, or allegorized away. The serious claim is being made that it is in the defenseless, the overtly powerless, the pitiable whose only power lies in the love they somehow evoke, that we see what God is like. Deane-Drummond, while offering some support to the traditionally Thomist view that it is *only* human beings, in virtue of their intellectual potential, that can be considered "images of God," adds that "we might want to push th[e] idea [that human image-bearing applies even in those who have, in different circumstances, lost their use of reasoning powers] even further than Aquinas does and suggest that it is when human beings are at their most vulnerable that the veiled grace of God in image-bearing becomes most visible."[51]

---

51 Deane-Drummond, "God's Image and Likeness," 938, referring to Aquinas, *Summa theologiae* I.93.8. Aquinas maintains that the image is more fully perfected according as it enters

Can We Believe in People?

Pagan philosophers might agree that we need to be cured of our usual conviction that health, wealth, bodily beauty, pleasure and the rest are real goods (ones whose possession makes us better people). They might agree that the presently powerful trade on our mistakes to preserve their power. Only those who have realized the insignificance of their own death or bodily wellbeing — and that of their favored others — are immune to bribery and threat. It is on *them* that our freedoms, such as they are, will always depend, in that our tyrants can never be entirely free of fear of them. Slaves who no longer fear the cross and rack, nor need the little comforts of sensual ease and social reputation, can both inspire and assist their unenlightened and unliberated brethren. But by the same logic — precisely because these things didn't *matter* — pagan philosophers did not think it their duty to liberate any slaves from cross and rack. The God of their imagination was always in control, and we might share his life and his felicity by turning away from all those mortal ills. The God of the Christians (and also of other Abrahamists) had set his face against evil and oppression, and was concerned to heal even the little evils that beset us, not by imperial fiat but by drawing us into His ongoing project, His revolt against mere power. Human suffering and unhappiness is too often conceived, not only by those who wish to justify God's ways to man, as the "just" punishment for wickedness, whereas the Christian Gospel is that we are forgiven, and that what happens to us is not *punishment*, but opportunity.

> As he went on his way Jesus saw a man blind from his birth. His disciples put the question, "Rabbi, who sinned, this man or his parent? Why was he born blind?" "It is not that this man or his parents sinned," Jesus answered; "he was born blind so that God's power might be displayed in curing him." (Jn 9:1–3)

The way things currently are is not the way they should be, nor the way they shall be.

---

into actuality; it therefore reaches perfection in the beatific vision, which is granted not to the intelligent but to the charitable.

Human Dignity

> For riseth up against realm and rod,
> A thing forgotten, a thing downtrod,
> The last, lost giant, even God,
> Is risen against the world.[52]

But before the rising comes the catastrophe:

> When the world shook and the sun was wiped out of heaven, it was not at the crucifixion, but at the cry from the cross: the cry which confessed that God was forsaken of God. And now let the revolutionists choose a creed from all the creeds and a god from all the gods of the world, carefully weighing all the gods of the world, carefully weighing all the gods of inevitable recurrence and of unalterable power. They will not find another god who has himself been in revolt. Nay (the matter grows too difficult for human speech), but let the atheists themselves choose a god. They will find only one divinity who ever uttered their isolation; only one religion in which God seemed himself for an instant to be an atheist.[53]

Žižek has suggested that in this cry, or in the record of this cry, the early Christian gospel put aside the whole notion of a *Deus ex machina* (as it were) who would hurry to save us all. This is to repeat, with variations, the account given by Paul Ricoeur in his Bampton lectures (1966):

> This entails that the God that has to pass away is the "moral God who [is] the principle and foundation for an ethics of prohibition and condemnation" (Ricoeur 2004, 447) and "the providential

---

52 G. K. Chesterton, *Collected Poems* (London: Methuen, 1950), 268. Jon D. Levenson similarly pointed out in *Creation and the Persistence of Evil: The Jewish Drama of Divine Omnipotence* (Princeton, NJ: Princeton University Press, 1994 [1985]), xvii, that "the overwhelming tendency of biblical writers as they confront undeserved evil is not to *explain* it away but to call upon God to *blast* it away." That God does not do this instantly may be ascribed to His patience with creation: "God searches for the least excuse to show mercy to His creations" (Ronald L. Eisenberg, *What the Rabbis Said: 250 Topics from the Talmud* [Santa Barbara: Preiger, 2010], 12).

53 Chesterton, *Orthodoxy*, 102; see Slavoj Žižek, *The Puppet and the Dwarf: The Perverse Core of Christianity* (Cambridge, MA: MIT Press, 2003), 13–14, 171.

God"—that is, God both as "the ultimate source of accusation" and as "the ultimate source of protection" (Ricoeur 2004, 455). According to Ricoeur, this "death" of the ethical God enables a transition to new kind of faith, a "tragic faith beyond any assurance or protection," and it is precisely Job who is put forward by Ricoeur as the model for this new faith (Ricoeur 2004, 455–456, 460).[54]

Ricoeur, Žižek and even Chesterton neglect to notice that the cry from the cross is the opening of Psalm 22, which concludes with the promise of vindication.

But the Christian faith was "eschatological" indeed—and that, in Thomas Altizer's words, is "a form of faith that calls the believer out of his old life in history and into a new Reality of grace,"[55] rather than confirming his immediate natural and social status, and requiring him to bow down before the Boss—whether that Boss was a Supernatural Demon or "the Evolutionary Process" reified. The best that even the Cynic philosophers could manage was to endure, and mock the Powers: Christians expected that they would one day "judge angels" (1 Cor 6:3), and that the world would—somehow—be made new (Rev 21:5). Till then, it was the community of the faithful, the body of Christ, that was the seed of a new world growing in the old. How far this could be a credible prediction in the absence of a strongly metaphysical belief in God the Creator may be moot, but it is at least a perspective worth remembering, to avoid the constant resurgence of a merely imperial deism.

---

54 Frederiek Depoortere, "The Faith of Job and the Recovery of Christian Atheism," *Expositions* 4 (2010): 105–13, at 107 (slightly edited), citing Paul Ricoeur, "Religion, Atheism and Faith" [1966], trans. Charles Freilich: *The Conflict of Interpretations: Essays in Hermeneutics*, ed. Don Ihde (Evanston, IL: Northwestern University Press, 2004 [1974]), 436–63.

55 Thomas J. J. Altizer and William Hamilton, *Radical Theology and the Death of God* (Indianapolis: Bobbs-Merrill, 1966), 101.

6

The Roots of Religion

THE REASON WHY

So let us suppose that God is represented to us in the defenseless, evoking our love rather than our fearful submission. The life we are invited to share, the life that is God, is one of compassion rather than of domination. We are to suppose ourselves made as "images of God," standing as God's representatives — but perhaps we might also consider ourselves "images of Creation," a place where all His Creation is brought before the Lord. Chesterton proposed that we might at least be representative mammals!

> We stand as chiefs and champions of a whole section of nature, princes of the house whose cognisance is the backbone, standing for the milk of the individual mother and the courage of the wandering cub, representing the pathetic chivalry of the dog, the humour and perversity of cats, the affection of the tranquil horse, the loneliness of the lion.[1]

Joseph Ashkenazi of Safed (1525–1572) similarly wrote, "when the midrash puts human beings at the center, it is because we include within us, and stand for, all the creatures of the universe, who are altogether called 'Adam.'"[2]

> The primary meaning of the image of God in the human is that we participate in every being and every level of Being. If so, then all the other creatures also participate in us. Each is somehow part of our humanity, just as each is part of God's name. Cutting ourselves off from the other creatures means cutting off these parts

---

1 Chesterton, *What's Wrong*, 264.
2 David M. Seidenberg, "Being Here Now: This Creation Is the Divine Image," *Tikkun* 132.1 (2017): 62–64; 63.

of ourselves, parts of the image of God, just as it means cutting off part of God's name.³

A related point has also been made more recently, in the light of current cosmological research:

> The pursuit of natural science is one of the ways in which man, the child of God, fulfils his distinctive function in the creation. That is how, for example, Francis Bacon at the outset of our modern scientific era understood the work of human science as a form of man's obedience to God. Science properly pursued in this way is a religious duty. Man as scientist can be spoken of as the priest of creation, whose office it is to interpret the books of nature written by the finger of God, to unravel the universe in its marvellous patterns and symmetries, and to bring it all into orderly articulation in such a way that it fulfils its proper end as the vast theatre of glory in which the Creator is worshipped and hymned and praised by his creatures. Without man, nature is dumb, but it is man's part to give it word: to be its mouth through which the whole universe gives voice to the glory and majesty of the living God.⁴

Torrance, in this work, takes his start from evidence of "fine-tuning" in the cosmos as described by Bernard Lovell:

> Why is the universe expanding so near the critical rate to prevent its collapse? If the universe had begun to expand in the first few minutes after the explosion of its original incredibly dense state by a rate minutely slower than it did, it would have collapsed back again relatively quickly. And if the expansion of the universe had been different only by a tiny fraction one way or the other from its actual rate, human existence would evidently have been impossible. "But our measurements," Sir Bernard declared, "narrowly define

---

3 Seidenberg, *Kabbalah*, 254, citing much Kabbalistic meditation.
4 T. E. Torrance, *The Ground and Grammar of Theology: Consonance Between Theology and Science* (Edinburgh: T&T Clark, 2001), 5–6.

one such universe—which had to be that particular universe if it was ever to be known and comprehended by an intelligent being."[5]

This problem—that the cosmos seems arbitrarily well-suited to the emergence of complex life-forms—is typically addressed in one of three ways. The first is simply to deny the problem: we wouldn't be here to consider the cosmos if things had been widely different, and there's an end of it. Anyone who values explanation as an enterprise is likely to be dissatisfied: I wouldn't be here if I had not survived various accidents and surgical interventions, but it still seems sensible for me to ask how it came about, on those occasions, that I did. The second is also to deny that there is a problem, by suggesting that in an infinite multiverse all possible outcomes somewhere happen, and it is therefore no surprise, of course, that we find ourselves in a cosmos that allows for us (though even an infinite array of actual outcomes need not necessarily include *all* possible outcomes). This too is likely to disturb any who sincerely value explanations: if all possible outcomes happen somewhere then there is no need for any special explanation for anything at all, however seemingly odd.[6] Nor does this explain why there is anything at all. The third, which Torrance and other theists have, for obvious reasons, preferred is to conclude that the cosmos is created *to be enjoyed and understood.* One very abrupt codicil, advanced by Torrance and others, is that it is to be understood *by us:* a conclusion that goes beyond even the broadly teleological inference. We might more reasonably wonder what intelligences elsewhere make of things, over a longer time span and with better tools. Even if the cosmos is intended to be enjoyed and understood, we earthbound primates may be marginal byproducts of that plan.

I shall not directly address this revivified cosmological argument: like most such arguments it is at once a plausible conjecture and one more likely to be dismissed, or accepted, for quite other reasons than its possible cogency. My present concern is rather with its effects on our religious sense. Are we, for example, making Richard Owen's error? Owen proposed that the planet

---

5 Torrance, *Ground and Grammar*, 3, citing Bernard Lovell, *In the Centre of Immensities* (London: Hutchinson, 1979), 116.
6 This is not to say, especially for a realist like myself, that the story is untrue—only that we had better not believe it.

Jupiter *must* house intelligent life, as otherwise the splendid spectacle of Jupiter's moons would not be properly appreciated. William Whewell rebutted the suggestion, observing that we cannot know all God's purposes.[7] He was both orthodox in this, and in line with the Enlightenment rejection — the methodological rejection — of an appeal to final causes to predict or fully explain what happens. At least Owen did not conclude that *we* ought to travel to Jupiter so that the spectacle could be enjoyed: implicit in his suggestion was the further thought that we could not be the *only* intelligences. That same thought is probably still powerful: there *must* — so most of us believe — be *other* living creatures elsewhere in so vast a world. What would be the *point* of the cosmos if there were only us? To which, of course, those who prefer another response to the cosmological case may simply say that there is no point at all — except the one we give it. From this latter hope we may move on to a rampant human triumphalism: suppose we are the first and only creatures to understand the cosmos and hope to change it. May we expect, or fantasize, that our descendants will?[8]

The more ancient thought would rather be that we are not, after all, the best and greatest things (Aristotle, *Nicomachean Ethics* 6.1141a35–1141b3), nor is the world devised entirely for our enjoyment. Perhaps the world is indeed fulfilled by being *known*, and exists because it is meant to be known, but do we know the world? And do most of us even care? In times past, we could mostly pay lip service indeed to the conviction that such knowledge mattered, not only to us but to our neighbors. In Alexander Winchell's words (in 1883):

> There are other suns and other planetary systems, and other worlds which possess the conditions of habitability. When we look on the hosts of stars, and consider that if only one habitable planet wanders about each sun, we understand that the number of habitable worlds is countless. In this view, space seems to be densely populated. We have neighbors; they live beyond impassable barriers, but they gaze on the same galaxy, and we know they are endowed

---

7 William Whewell, *Of the Plurality of Worlds*, ed. Michael Ruse (Chicago: University of Chicago Press, 2001 [1853]), 183–84.

8 Dyson, "Time without End."

The Roots of Religion

with certain faculties which establish a community between them and us. However conformed bodily, whatever their modes and means of organic activity, we know that they reason as we reason, and interpret the universe on the same principles of logic and mathematics as ourselves. The orbits which their planetary homes describe are ellipses; they have studied the same celestial geometry as ourselves; they have written their treatises on celestial mechanics; they have felt the impact of the luminous weave of ether; they have speculated on the nature of matter and energy; they have interpreted the order of the cosmical mechanism as the expression of thought and purpose; they have placed themselves in communion with the Supreme Thinker who is so near to all of us that his voice is audible alike to the ear of reason in all the worlds.[9]

Even atheistical naturalists nowadays still usually expect the same, and may hope that those Others know rather more than we do but without radically subverting what we think we know ourselves—though they may doubt that those other creatures will be theists, or share our merely "moral" values. My own suspicion is that if the Others have never been theists they will also not, as it were, be *rationalists* either: they will have no reason to suppose—no logical reason and no natural impulse—that the little effusion of their brains or quasi-brains that they call "thought" could be a model for the universe. Nor need they feel any obligation to find out the truth of things, beyond whatever seems immediately useful. Intelligence, as an evolutionary adaptation, is never likely—on naturalistic terms—to be more than a guide to getting food, and mates, and avoiding being food for long enough to reproduce. Each sort of creature has its own *Umwelt*, constructed from a range of markers that may be invisible to any other kind.[10] These, for any social species, will include social markers, and much

---

9 Alexander Winchell, *World Life or Comparative Geology* (Chicago: S. C. Griggs & Co., 1883), 507–8, cited by Karl S. Guthke, *The Last Frontier: Imagining Other Worlds from the Copernican Revolution to Modern Science Fiction*, trans. Helen Atkins (Ithaca: Cornell University Press, 1990), 344.

10 See Jacob Johann von Uexküll, *Theoretical Biology*, trans. D. L. Mackinnon (London: Kegan Paul, 1926); "A Stroll through the Worlds of Animals and Men," in C. H. Schiller, ed., *Instinctive Behavior* (New York: International University Press, 1957), 5–80.

Can We Believe in People?

of our activity will be directed, in the first place, to keeping a place in our social group — but this is to say that our intelligence, where it is more than "practical," is concerned with gossip and make-believe.[11] What the Real World beyond all little worlds may be we have, as I suggested earlier, no good reason to expect to know — unless we have good reason to believe that we also carry something of the divine in us, that Real Reason is at least an *image* of the one creative intelligence that makes and sustains the world. It is because we still believe or half-believe that human beings are "special" by comparison with more limited living things, and that there is some overriding reason for our existence, that we can so easily imagine that there will be other sort-of-human beings elsewhere: human in the sense defined by Winchell, or something even better.

So what is the likelier, or more credible, or more pragmatically useful thought? If the cosmos is fulfilled in being known, may we expect that this knowledge will be ours? Or are there already knowledgeable witnesses abroad, perhaps very unlike ourselves? Is such knowledge, conversely, what we were made for? Or is that too grandiloquent a thought, and we would be better thinking rather of the here and now, what Stapledon called our little atom of community, irrespective of the wider, colder world?[12] The drive to know and understand the whole, even if that involves a departure from the comforts of our present bodily condition, seems to be a version of the priestly or contemplative endeavor. "Only those who, having disrobed themselves of all created things and of the innermost veil and wrapping of mere opinion, with mind unhampered and naked will come to God."[13] Is this even a safe hope? H. P. Lovecraft had a different slant on things. On the one hand, he found our common concentration on the trivialities of human and animal life absurd, and preferred to fix his gaze on the wider world his science and his imagination showed. On the other hand, he had abandoned any happy illusions that we were equipped to see that world. A quotation from an early, and otherwise inferior tale, "From Beyond" [1920]:

---

11 Robin Dunbar Grooming, *Gossip and the Evolution of Language* (London: Faber, 1996).
12 Olaf Stapledon, *Star Maker* (London: Gollancz, 1999 [1937]), 3, 254.
13 Philo of Alexandria, *Collected Works*, trans. F. H. Colson, G. H. Whitaker, et al., Loeb Classical Library (Cambridge, MA: Harvard University Press, 1929–62), 2:470–73 [*De Gigantibus* 12.53–4].

The Roots of Religion

What do we know... of the world and the universe about us? Our means of receiving impressions are absurdly few, and our notions of surrounding objects infinitely narrow. We see things only as we are constructed to see them, and can gain no idea of their absolute nature. With five feeble senses we pretend to comprehend the boundlessly complex cosmos, yet other beings with a wider, stronger, or different range of senses might not only see very differently the things we see, but might see and study whole worlds of matter, energy, and life which lie close at hand yet can never be detected with the senses we have.[14]

Do we *want* to know that cosmos, even if we could? Stapledon himself had doubts. "If there is a meaning," so Stapledon's Last Men say in their final hours, "it is no human meaning,"[15] and so might as well be no real meaning. When, in another fiction, his peace-loving and peace-making Tibetan mystics finally discover — as they suppose — the truth of things, it is as if they woke to a frozen landscape trampled by indifferent giants.[16] Whether those giants are deaf because they are witless or because they are callous hardly matters; even their ill will — if they are malevolent — is immune to prayer, and so as natural and fixed a fact as any.

In either case, so Stapledon and Lovecraft both agreed, it is part of our duty "as men" to acknowledge that there is more to the worlds than us, and somehow to find, despite the worlds' indifference, a way of living humanely. Our friends, our family, our native soil, our histories don't matter to the wider world or its more powerful residents: they may still matter to us, and those who allow themselves to be infected by indifference, indiscipline, cultish stupidity, are still to be resisted when we can — or even if, in the end, we can't. Lovecraft's partial solution was an appeal to mere tradition.[17]

---

14 H. P. Lovecraft, *The Dreams in the Witch House and Other Weird Stories*, ed. S. T. Joshi (London: Penguin, 2005), 23–29.
   15 Stapledon, *Last and First Men*, 605.
   16 Olaf Stapledon, *Darkness and Light* (London: Methuen, 1942).
   17 See John Kekes, "What Is Conservatism?," *Philosophy* 72.281 (1997): 351–74, for a clear and well-balanced discussion of such appeals.

Can We Believe in People?

Amidst this variability [that is, the relative and changing nature of "the good"] there is only one anchor of fixity which we can seize upon as the working pseudo-standard of "values" which we need in order to feel settled and contented—and that anchor is tradition, the potent emotional legacy bequeathed to us by the massed experience of our ancestors, individual or national, biological or cultural. Tradition means nothing cosmically, but it means everything locally and pragmatically because we have nothing else to shield us from a devastating sense of "lostness" in endless time and space.[18]

Or as John Buchan supposed a savage might speak to a missionary for the wider world:

> Wherefore my brittle gods I make
> Of friendly clay and kindly stone,—
> Wrought with my hands, to serve or break,
> From crown to toe my work, my own.
> My eyes can see, my nose can smell,
> My fingers touch their painted face,
> They weave their little homely spell
> To warm me from the cold of Space.
>
> My gods are wrought of common stuff
> For human joys and mortal tears;
> Weakly, perchance, yet staunch enough
> To build a barrier 'gainst my fears,
> Where, lowly but secure, I wait
> And hear without the strange winds blow.—
> I cannot worship what I hate,
> Or serve a god I dare not know.[19]

---

18 H. P. Lovecraft, *Selected Letters 1911–37*, ed. August Derleth, Donald Wandrei and James Turner (Sauk City, WI: Arkham House, 1965–76), 2:356–57, quoted by S. T. Joshi, *A Subtler Magick: The Writings and Philosophy of H. P. Lovecraft* (Rockville, MD: Borgo Press, 1996), 37.

19 John Buchan, *The Moon Endureth* (Edinburgh: Thomas Nelson, 1923 [1912]), 160–62.

The Roots of Religion

Those who insist on following where Truth leads — the one thing greater than our Reason, so Augustine says[20] — are endorsing a dictum well known to Platonists: "where both are friends [the Truth and one's beloved teacher], true piety is to prefer the Truth."[21] This is always likely to be uncomfortable, and often surprising: "truth must of necessity be stranger than fiction, for fiction is the creation of the human mind, and therefore is congenial to it."[22]

THE GODS OF COMMON STUFF

But perhaps we should return again to Chesterton's, and Joseph Ashkenazi's, thought. The claim to understand and to appreciate the wider world too easily becomes another excuse for thinking ourselves, our human selves, superior, even while we emphasize how vast and strange that wider world may be. It is also a claim that alienates us from the very world we seek to understand. "If we understand humans to be the only creatures in God's image, then we isolate those qualities that set human beings apart ... repressing those aspects of our own being that unite us with all life."[23] Chesterton himself frequently criticized what he considered an "over-intellectualizing" attitude, one that looked away from immediate, felt experience. He identified the error in both vivisectionists and vegetarians:

> It is not a human thing, it is not a humane thing, when you see a poor woman staring hungrily at a bloater [a smoked herring], to think, not of the obvious feelings of the woman, but of the unimaginable feelings of the deceased bloater. Similarly, it is not human, it is not humane, when you look at a dog to think about what theoretic discoveries you might possibly make if you were allowed to bore a hole in his head. Both the humanitarians' fancy about

---

Buchan appended the poem to a distinctly Lovecraftian story, "Space," about what lurks around us in some normally invisible direction.

20 Augustine, *The Teacher, The Free Choice of the Will, Grace and Free Will*, trans. R. P. Russell (Washington, DC: Catholic University of America Press, 1968), 144 [*De Libero Arbitrio* 2.13.35].

21 Aristotle, *Nicomachean Ethics* 1.1096a16, after Plato, *Republic* 10.595c.

22 G. K. Chesterton, *The Club of Queer Trades* (London: Darwen Finlayson Ltd., 1960 [1905]), 82.

23 Seidenberg, *Kabbalah*, 32.

the feelings concealed inside the bloater, and the vivisectionists' fancy about the knowledge concealed inside the dog, are unhealthy fancies, because they upset a human sanity that is certain for the sake of something that is of necessity uncertain. The vivisectionist, for the sake of doing something that may or may not be useful, does something that certainly is horrible. The anti-Christmas humanitarian, in seeking to have a sympathy with a turkey which no man can have with a turkey, loses the sympathy he has already with the happiness of millions of the poor.[24]

Chesterton might have thought a little differently about the turkey, or even the herring, if he had occasion to consider the realities of modern farming and fishing, on the one hand, and our better understanding of our cousins' lives on the other. He certainly had no sympathy with those who denied that "animals" had any feelings or perceptions, or reckoned them insignificant. Indeed, it seems likely that he would have agreed with Jennings's appeal to the "natural recognition" of mind and feeling in others, even if he was startled by Jennings's judgment on amoebas:

> The writer is thoroughly convinced, after long study of the behavior of this organism, that if Amoeba were a large animal, so as to come in the everyday experience of human beings, its behavior would at once call forth the attribution to it of states of pleasure and pain, of hunger, desire, and the like, on precisely the same basis as we attribute these things to the dog. This natural recognition is exactly what [Hugo] Münsterberg [1863–1916] has emphasised as the test of a subject. In conducting objective investigations we train ourselves to suppress this impression, but thorough investigation tends to restore it stronger than at first.[25]

---

24 G. K. Chesterton, *All Things Considered* (London: Methuen, 1908), 216. Chesterton also remarks that "a turkey is more occult and awful than all the angels and archangels" (ibid., 220). This is an exaggeration, but if it were true we should surely have some respect for turkeys.

25 H. S. Jennings, *Behavior of the Lower Organisms* (New York: Columbia University Press, 1906), 336.

The Roots of Religion

Chesterton still wished to insist that human beings must be thoroughly different from non-human, even while disclaiming any deep knowledge of the non-human — which seems to involve a pragmatic contradiction: if turkeys are as incomprehensible as he supposed, how is it that he knew so much about them?

But his principal point still has some force: all policies that aim at a supposedly greater good, visible only to the enlightened, are liable to ignore present realities and the effects those policies will have on those least well equipped to bear them. How much do global understanding and long-term strategizing matter? Should not that silent language of affection described by John Paul II have rather more to offer? Should we not allow some force to the criticisms of a "distant deity"?

Consider John Wren-Lewis's exasperated response, back in 1961, to Sir Julian Huxley's paean in praise of evolution and the human spirit:

> Many people call Sir Julian an atheist: he probably calls himself one. His article in last week's *Observer*, however, makes it clear that he is nothing of the kind, and many Christians like myself will wish profoundly that he would be an honest-to-God atheist! In fact, as his regular readers will have known for many years, he is a profoundly religious writer, whose God is evolution. He says that evolution should be the controlling idea in all our thinking, both scientific and ethical. He describes the universe as an "all-embracing evolutionary process," and the whole tone of his language shows that he gives mankind a religious significance because evolution has at this point "strangely and wonderfully" acquired the power of conscious self-direction. *This*, Sir, is *exactly* the sort of thing William Blake was referring to when he said that if men had not the religion of Jesus, they would have the religion of Satan. When the prophets of the Bible raved about idolatry, they meant just this sort of mystical subordination of man to the great system of nature. Against this, those who have the religion of Jesus want to assert that people do *not* acquire significance by performing any sort of function, however lofty, in any larger system, however universal. They can have absolute significance *as individuals*, by

Can We Believe in People?

the simple process of giving it to each other in ordinary personal relationships. The Christian believes this because he holds that the Absolute God, whose name is love, is present in personal relationships, but he might welcome a *real* atheist who held the same personalist values, in the name of what [H. J.] Blackham [1923–2009] calls "the self-sufficiency of perishable things," as an ally against all attempts to resurrect the Great God Pan. As I see it, the achievement of Darwin was that he drove the last shreds of mystical value out of nature by exposing its apparently creative processes as purely relative and random. Let us on no account go back on this, whether at the behest of scientists like Sir Julian or supposedly Christian writers like Teilhard de Chardin.[26]

"Personalist" values—the emphasis on *personal* relationships—have their own dangers when combined with the unargued claim that *only* human beings are thus "personal." Wren-Lewis (1923–2006), it is to be feared, assumed too easily that "animals" were only "natural," and that our redemption lay in escaping nature and our likeness to the beasts. But this was not to be by devotion to an impersonal, abstract, intellectual reality, but by actually loving our neighbors, and helping to bring a new "human" world to birth:

> We may *say* that man is an insignificant animal crawling on the surface of a speck of cosmic dust, who should eschew all large-sounding pretensions, but we act in practice as if we believed that given enough hard work the natural order can be tamed and the world "made a better place" in our efforts to realize the human values that are summed up in the word "love," and this is precisely what the Christian vision would amount to if expressed in modern terms—the vision that man can have dominion over nature because love is more real than nature.[27]

"Dominion," once again, is still a dangerous term.

26 *Observer Letter Page*, September 10, 1961.
27 John Wren-Lewis, "What I Believe," in G. Unwin, ed., *What I Believe* (London: Allen & Unwin, 1966), 221–36.

The Roots of Religion

But how can we avoid the thought that we are indeed a marginal matter? We may be able to convince ourselves that we can discover the wider world, and learn to live with that understanding, and without any fervent hope that life will ever be different (as Russell claimed to do). That there is a deep epistemic contradiction here may be disputed, but only if we are already firmly convinced that "intellect" is lord. What if we were instead to put our trust in the more immediate recognition of the Other's value, if the truth were made known in love? And yet the thought of the wider world may continue to sap our resolve, to diminish our personal attachments (which are only, in the end, a biological norm) as well as our rational pretensions. One answer may be to reconsider what our intellectual belief in the wider world amounts to.

Amongst the commonest cosmological observations is the thought that the world stretches out immensely, unimaginably, far in space and time. If the whole story of this earth's existence were represented as a single year, humans would be appearing only in the last few seconds of the year. If the whole expanse of the cosmos were represented in little, we would be an infinitesimal point, a minor planet around a minor star in a minor galaxy that is itself only a dot within the expanse of Laniakea (a network of galactic superclusters). As William Whewell posed the question (without endorsing a merely negative answer), "can the Earth be thus the centre of the moral and religious universe, when it has been shewn to have no claim to be the centre of the physical universe?"[28] Though the details are different, this is actually old news. In the *Dream of Scipio*, one of the core texts of medieval thought, we are told that Scipio, in his visionary ascent through the planetary spheres, saw

> stars which we never see from here below, and all the stars were vast far beyond what we have ever imagined. The least of them was that which, farthest from heaven, nearest to the earth, shone with a borrowed light. But the starry globes very far surpassed the earth in magnitude. The earth itself indeed looked to me so small as to make me ashamed of our empire, which was a mere point on its surface.[29]

---

28 Whewell, *Plurality*, 19.
29 Macrobius, *Commentary on the Dream of Scipio*, trans. William Harris Stahl (New York: Columbia University Press, 1952), 72.

Can We Believe in People?

The same thought is present in Boethius's *Consolation of Philosophy*:

> It is well known, and you have seen it demonstrated by astronomers, that beside the extent of the heavens, the circumference of the earth has the size of a point; that is to say, compared with the magnitude of the celestial sphere, it may be thought as having no extent at all.[30]

Notoriously, that this Earth was "central" meant only that it was at the bottom. But what do place and distance and duration amount to? We may measure distance by duration, by how long it takes us to travel from one spot to another. We may measure duration by distance, by how far the hour or minute hands move on a clock face while we wait. Our *experience* depends on our biology, on personal temperament, or contemplative practice. If there was no one to experience the passage of time from the "Big Bang" till the first beginnings of life then the time involved had no *experienced* duration. Indeed, if there were no creatures with more than a moment's memory until "quite late" in terrestrial history, there was still no real experienced duration. As Chesterton pointed out,

> It is curious that [H. G. Wells's] first fairy-tale was a complete answer to his last book of history. *The Time Machine* [1895] destroyed in advance all comfortable conclusions founded on the mere relativity of time. In that sublime nightmare the hero saw trees shoot up like green rockets, and vegetation spread visibly like a green conflagration, or the sun shoot across the sky from east to west with the swiftness of a meteor.[31]

If there were sentient and time-binding entities from early on in the cosmos' history, then how *long* that history was for them will have depended on their biology, their personal temperament and contemplative practice. All moments, for God as we have roughly meant that term, are infinitely

---

30 Boethius, *Consolation of Philosophy*, trans. V. E. Watts (Harmondsworth: Penguin, 1969), 73 [Bk. 2, ch. 7].

31 Chesterton, *Everlasting Man*, 13.

divisible and easily endured. None is longer than another, any more than anything is larger or more significant, for God, than any other. An infinite God need spend no more time and energy on a supercluster than a quark, an aeon than a nanosecond. Laniakea is no larger than Little Gidding: literally so — there are as many "points" in one as in the other. Leibniz was probably wrong to suppose that there was no "bottommost" scale of material things, and that infinite worlds like ours were to be found in every seemingly small section, at whatever level of magnification.[32] Different scales, it seems, also have different rules, so that one might, in principle, locate what *level* a particular world-pool occupies. But that does not alter the chief moral: that *our* scale is as real as any other, and not diminished in significance because there are either larger or smaller scales.[33]

In brief, the acres of dusty eternity that we have imagined into being are just that: *imagined* worlds. We need not suppose ourselves to be "marginal" or "minor" players. Even if — as I am inclined myself to believe — there really is such a cosmos, it is no larger than it needs to be, nor longer-lived. Our lives and portions are not diminished by it. Wren-Lewis responded to Bertrand Russell's lament, his warning that "Omnipotent Matter" would inevitably obliterate whatever mattered to us, by observing that science was founded rather on a belief in "Potent Man."

> Real science knows nothing of Omnipotent Matter, for it is a continual process of changing both our concepts and our experience of matter. The only constant factor in real science — the science of the experimental method — is Potent Man, man who constantly strives to use matter to express the creativity of his own inner life.

---

[32] "Whence it appears that in the smallest particle of matter there is a world of creatures, living beings, animals, entelechies, souls. Each portion of matter may be conceived as like a garden full of plants and like a pond full of fishes. But each branch of every plant, each member of every animal, each drop of its liquid parts is also some rich garden or pond. And though the earth and the air which are between the plants of the garden, or the water which is between the fish of the pond, be neither plant nor fish; yet they also contain plants and fishes, but mostly so minute as to be imperceptible to us." G. W. Leibniz, *Monadology and Other Philosophical Writings*, trans. Robert Latta (Clarendon Press: Oxford 1898 [1714]), 256 [*Monadology*, 65–67].

[33] See Mariam Thalos, *Without Hierarchy: The Scale Freedom of the Universe* (New York: Oxford University Press, 2013) for a compelling argument against the usual assumption that the smallest scale must rule all others.

> Omnipotent Matter is as much a paranoid fantasy as the traditional concept of Omnipotent God, and serves the same neurotic purpose of providing grounds for not taking the inner life of human beings really seriously in its own right. Where traditional religion insists upon the subordination of man's inner life to the supposed Divine Plan behind the scenes, materialism overrides the inner life by dismissing it in the name of a "tough-minded" assertion of man's utter insignificance in face of the inflexible laws of an indifferent universe.[34]

Other Christian thinkers have made similar remarks. So, for example, Benedict XVI:

> It is not the laws of matter and of evolution that have the final say, but reason, will, love — a Person. And if we know this Person and he knows us, then truly the inexorable power of material elements no longer has the last word; we are not slaves of the universe and of its laws, we are free.[35]

We may find that Person wherever we find *any* person. And "person" does not simply mean a creature capable of forethought and responsibility, but simply one to which, to whom, we do and should respond in "personal" ways. Everything is an image of that One, a daughter — as Plotinus put it — of the Father.[36]

> Could expanding God's image to the more-than-human world and removing humanity from its pedestal have the unintended effect of trivializing human life? If we do so consciously, I think not. When we come to expand *tzelem*'s reach, its original meaning is also intensified. Imagine, or remember, the awe you feel standing

---

34 John Wren-Lewis, *What Shall We Tell the Children?* (London: Constable, 1971), 70, commenting on Bertrand Russell, "The Free Man's Worship," 56.

35 Benedict XVI, *Spe Salvi: On Christian Hope* (November 30, 2007), §5, cited by Stratford Caldecott, *All Things Made New: The Mysteries of the World in Christ* (San Rafael, CA: Angelico Press, 2013), 21.

36 Plotinus, *Ennead* II.9 [33].15.33–16.10.

at the edge of the Grand Canyon, or descending into a forest, or witnessing an extraordinary storm or sunset. What would it be like to look at another person and feel that kind of awe? Imagine regarding a bus driver or a stranger who sits down beside you, or even an enemy, with those eyes. Imagine or remember what it is like to see a lover or a child with those eyes.[37]

Pagan philosophers generally supposed that the trivialities of common life were mere distractions, and that we needed above all to isolate ourselves from them, and from whatever we shared with "beasts" both wild and tame. Even when they insisted that only *human* beings could possibly be "like God," they did not mean that it was by "reasoning," "remembering," "choosing" that we achieved that likeness: God, after all, has no need of reasoning, nor memory, nor choice. But we can now turn the story round: it is in these trivialities, when properly perceived, that we can find the way.

> In every sphere, in every relational act, through everything that becomes present to us, we gaze toward the train of the eternal You; in each we perceive a breath of it, in every you we address the eternal You, in every sphere according to its manner. All spheres are included in it, while it is included in none. Through all of them shines the one presence.[38]

OMENS AND THE HIDDEN ORDER

Anthropologists and biologists enquiring into the nature and the origin of "religion" have emphasized its role in building up communities, united through ceremonies, familiar stories, invocations, torturous initiations. The question of what such religious folk "believe" is often beside the point: "belief," as holding to particular propositions that purport to describe this world or any other, may be no more than the repetition of stories that inspire much more than they explain. Especially in pre-literate societies the stories may themselves be embodied, as it were, in the surrounding landscape or in significant buildings: to walk through the landscape or the

37 Seidenberg, *Kabbalah*, 313.
38 Buber, *I and Thou*, 150.

temple, or even to look up at the night sky, is to be reminded of imagined gods and heroes, and the part they—or their remembrance—play in common life. To take away the land, or to take the nation from the land, is to take away their past as well.[39] This is not to say simply that known battlesites or the birthplaces of national heroes may be pointed out to fond enquirers, as if the historical memory is contained elsewhere and merely applied to the landscape. The land itself, as it is intensely imagined and perceived, is a great mnemonic: the art of memory is no recent invention, however often it is rediscovered.[40] A nation's whole history may be stored, in the form of images, in the imagined landscape, and the narrator need then only walk around her land to find the story, or recount the story to have a vivid perception of the land. Cathedrals and parish churches were expressly designed to house such stories, to provide gigantic models for the houses of memory that all believers must construct in their souls. There are other such landmarks, even ones that have been deliberately constructed to house the images which speak to the well-informed of our nation's past (for good or ill). The beauties of such parks and houses are more than contemporary: that is to say, they are "beautiful," aesthetically moving, in ways that could not be duplicated overnight. First, it takes time to create a living landscape and architecture: as in ecology, a "climax community" cannot be quickly restored—so that farmers who first chop down a long-established hedgerow and then speak of "replanting it," as if such hedgerows were no more than a row of nursery-bred wallflowers, are deceiving themselves. Secondly, their beauties are the greater because we know where they began, and what they have lived through: it is not a mistake to think that originals are more valuable than even good reproductions, that we would be being fooled if we were fobbed off with a building or painting that had no genuine material connection with the thing it represents.[41] Forgeries are like fake relics.

Sometimes the gods and heroes visible in landscape and architecture can also be invoked to shape the words and actions of particular persons: priests

---

39 K. Lynch, *The Image of the City* (Cambridge, MA: MIT Press, 1960), 125–26.
40 See Gary Snyder, *The Good, the Wild and the Sacred* (London: Five Seasons Press, 1984).
41 R. Elliot, "Faking Nature," *Inquiry* 25 (1983): 81–93; Eric Katz, *Nature as Subject: Human Obligation and Natural Community* (Lanham, MD: Rowman and Littlefield, 1997), 93–108.

or shamans or accomplished actors. For nine months in the year, Hari Das, for example, is a manual laborer and prison guard. In the remaining three months, he is the medium of a Hindu god: "you become the deity. You lose all fear. Even your voice changes. The god comes alive and takes over. You are just the vehicle, the medium. In the trance it is God who speaks, and all the acts are the acts of the god—feeling, thinking, speaking."[42] The interpretation easier for Western common sense is that this is a form of theatre, hardly different from the techniques used by actors to evoke (rather than invoke) a character. There may be moments when a great actor does manage almost to incarnate a spirit, almost to "become" the part she plays. But the participants in shamanic rituals do not consider themselves great actors, nor do they think that the gods are their own hidden selves, as though Hari Das's evocation of the god Vishnu were evoking only Hari Das's Vishnu. On the other hand, neither do they necessarily have any opinion about the *metaphysics* of the event. They accept the obvious reality of the experience, and the efficacy of the techniques that support it, without troubling to devise a cosmological system to fit.

Gods and spirits, that is, may be found in the surrounding landscape, in temples and cathedrals, in the stars, and in sacred theatre. Sometimes the discovery may be easier simply because a tree, a rock, a particular confluence of cloud and water momentarily *looks* just like a man, a lion, an eagle. This is not to say that people are making mistakes, as if the willingness to see such patterns, selected because it paid our ancestors to notice lions and eagles and human enemies, has primed us to see them when they aren't there. The sculptor or woodworker who *sees* the shape she wants to find in a stone or a bare log of wood is not deceived. And her talent, to play the evolutionary game, has other explanations than oversensitivity.

Nor is it always foolish to hear the voices of birds, or see their flight, as omens: they spell out for us what we might already guess. The crows cry "Cras, Cras" for Latin-speakers ("Tomorrow, Tomorrow"), whether in hope or longing or despair, just as human infants, babbling "Da Da," are heard by their devoted Roman grandfather as saying "Give!"[43] The audience need

---

42 William Dalrymple, *Nine Lives: In Search of the Sacred in Modern India* (London: Bloomsbury, 2009), 31.

43 Marcus Cornelius Fronto, 164 AD, in Noelle K. Zeiner-Carmichael, ed., *Roman Letters: An*

not have been deceived: it is enough that the words are heard, whether or not the birds or infants meant them.

And yet there is some good reason to let the world speak for itself, and to clear away what we first see and hear in it. When Athanasius, in the passage I cited before, proclaimed that Christ had exorcised the demons that infested woods and springs, he did not intend to leave them without their own being and value, as though they were to be only "stuff" for human purposes henceforward. Rather we were to see them as they are.

> We must see things objectively, as we do a tree; and understand that they exist whether we like them or not. We must not try and turn them into something different by the mere exercise of our minds, as if we were witches.[44]

In so doing we may find, probably we will find, a deeper and more abiding pattern. Our species' first acquaintance with lawlike regularity, we may suspect, was in the motions of the heavens. The sun, moon and stars marked out the moments of the night and day, the seasons and even the Platonic Year (though this last observation needed many generations to identify). We also came to understand that those bright lights were only echoes of the bodily realities that made them: their motions could be calculated more exactly, and more understandably, by pairing them with the cogs of astrolabes like the Antikythera mechanism.[45] Until the astronomers had some material model of the stars and planets (or at least the planetary spheres) they could not have understood just why those "decorations in the sky" were moving as they did (Plato, *Republic* 7.529). The Antikythera mechanism and its — probably Babylonian — predecessors provided another model, one that led on to the Ptolemaic picture of the heavens.

Anthology (Chichester: John Wiley, 2014), 167. He was pleased to find the child liked grapes — and small birds.

44 *Illustrated London News*, November 22, 1913, in G. K. Chesterton, *Collected Works*, vol. 29: *Illustrated London News* 1911–13, ed. Lawrence J. Clipper (San Francisco: Ignatius Press, 1988), 589.

45 See Jo Marchant, *Decoding the Heavens: Solving the Mystery of the World's First Computer* (London: Windmill Books, 2009) for a readable account of the discovery and workings of the device.

The Roots of Religion

In other words, epicycles were not a philosophical innovation but a mechanical one. Once Greek astronomers realized how well epicyclic gearing in devices such as the Antikythera mechanism replicated the cyclic variations of celestial bodies, they could have incorporated the concept into their own geometrical models of the cosmos.[46]

The heavenly order we had seemed to see was gradually revealed as only the result of merely terrestrial motions: the earth does not stand still beneath the heavens after all, but revolves, and orbits, and wobbles on its axis to create the grand impression of the heavens' order. But this is not to say that the heavens *aren't* ordered: we only have to learn a different language to describe the thing, to talk of "solar systems," "galaxies," "superclusters" and the expanding cosmos. As Heraclitus said, "the hidden order is stronger than the apparent."[47] Those images as well turn out to be less than real: the cosmos, we might conclude, is a complex mathematical object realized both in "physical" things and in the multiplicity of appearances.[48]

Religion, in the broadest sense, is the set of ceremonies, stories, speculations and enactments that we have devised in various modes to keep us in tune with both the human and the wider world. In some hands, and at some times, it embodies suggestions, very variously interpreted, about the original cause and purpose of the cosmos, as well as of the social worlds we have imagined into being. Sometimes it supports modes of oppression, giving both oppressor and oppressed some rationalized account of what is going on. Sometimes it foments rebellion against the powers that be, or at least against the powers that claim unbridled authority over the here-and-now.

---

46 Jo Marchant, "Ancient astronomy: Mechanical inspiration," *Nature* 468 (2010): 496–98; 498.
47 DK 22B54, in Waterfield, *First Philosophers*, 40.
48 Tegmark, *Our Mathematical Universe*; see also Plotinus, *Ennead* V.1 [10].6. Many scientific critics of Tegmark's playful hypotheses, especially about the real existence of every possible cosmos and alternate history (which I do not myself endorse), seem to believe that what cannot now be shown by experimental data to be superior to alternative hypotheses cannot be either true or worth exploring. Neither claim seems sensible, however much I may myself dislike the notion of the Multiverse (on which see Alexander Vilenkin, "The principle of mediocrity," *Astronomy and Geophysics* 52.5 [2011]: 33–36 [doi.org/10.1111/j.1468-4004.2011.52533.x], together with some suggestions for how the story might be confirmed). Failing to prove p does not often amount to proving not-p.

Can We Believe in People?

Our war is "against principalities, against powers, against the rulers of the darkness of this world, against spiritual wickedness in high places."[49] Without some sense that there is something that lies *beyond* the present powers it is difficult to sustain morale: whether that "beyond" is the heavenly realm itself, or some future aeon, or only the long memory of living things, is not to be settled here.

What is worth noticing is that many or even most of those who wish to empty the world of spirits, omens and other "unnatural" forms will usually themselves accept, without compunction, such social lies as national boundaries, the value of bits of paper, and above all the absolute rights of "scientific man" to use the world as he pleases.

> The ancient traditions of devotion and reflection, of worship and enquiry, have seen themselves as *schools*. Christianity and Vedantic Hinduism, Judaism and Buddhism and Islam are schools . . . whose pedagogy has the twofold purpose—however differently conceived and executed in the different traditions—of weaning us from our idolatry and purifying our desire.[50]

Merely ignoring the ancient symbols while continuing to adore or fear the continuing realities is hardly an advance. Nor is it likely that we ever could, or should, entirely empty our minds and hearts of these apparently foolish distinctions. Apparently they signify or represent something that matters to us from the start.

> Those who think, for instance, that the thing called superstition is something heavily artificial, are very numerous; that is those who think that it has only been the power of priests or of some very deliberate system that has built up boundaries, that has called one course of action lawful and another unlawful, that has called one

---

49 Eph 6:12; see also 2 Cor 4:3–4.
50 Nicholas Lash, *The Beginning and the End of "Religion"* (Cambridge: Cambridge University Press, 1996), 21. See also Moses Maimonides, *The Guide of the Perplexed*, trans. Chaim Rabin, ed. Julius Guttman (Indianapolis: Hackett, 1995 [1190]), 178 [Bk. 3, ch. 29]: "the first purpose of the whole law is to remove idolatry and to wipe out its traces and all that belongs to it, even in memory."

piece of ground sacred and another profane. Nothing it would seem, except a large and powerful conspiracy could account for men so strangely distinguishing between one field and another, between one city and another, between one nation and another. To all those who think in this way there is only one answer to be given. It is to approach each of them and whisper in his ear: "Did you or did you not as a child try to step on every alternate paving-stone?"[51]

Children dress up, and bind themselves by rules, apparently unaware that they are securing their own oppression. Just so we may, even in adulthood, devise all manner of ceremonials and engaging stories, while still being conscious that reality is beyond our grasp, but not beyond our reach.

Just as the sun and the moon and the heavens and the earth and the sea are common to all, but are called by different names by different peoples, so for that one rationality which keeps all these things in order and the one Providence which watches over them and the ancillary powers that are set over all, there have arisen among different peoples, in accordance with their customs, different honors and appellations. Thus men make use of consecrated symbols, some employing symbols that are obscure, but others those that are clearer, in guiding the intelligence toward things divine, though not without a certain hazard. For some go completely astray and become engulfed in superstition; and others, while they fly from superstition as from a quagmire, on the other hand unwittingly fall, as it were, over a precipice into atheism.[52]

---

51 G. K. Chesterton, "The Philosophy of Islands," in *The Venture Annual*, ed. Laurence Housman and W. Somerset Maugham (London: John Baillie's, 1903), 2–9; reprinted in Chesterton, *The Spice of Life*, ed. D. Collins (Beaconsfield: Finlayson, 1964).
52 Plutarch, *Moralia*, 5:157 [*Isis and Osiris* 67.377f6–378a9].

7

Alien Life on Earth and Elsewhere

IMAGINING OTHER LIVES

We have been imagining other lives than ours for as long as our records reach, whether those lives are almost-human (elves, dwarves, giants, mermen and the like) or mysteriously talking beasts. We have also been inclined to mold our own nature and expectations in deliberate contrast to what we take to be "other," even when the "otherness" is a difference only in emphasis. For Westerners in the last centuries, "savages," "heathens," "blacks," "Arabs" and "Orientals" have served as convenient contrasts. Ancient Greeks, perhaps more bluntly, reckoned the Northern barbarians slavish (as moved solely by impulses of desire, fear and anger) and the Eastern barbarians slavish in another mode (as contemptibly submissive to imperial rule). Other nations, equally convinced of their own central importance in the world, have noted other disparities. Nowadays, we Westerners often abjure as "other" characteristics also found in our immediate forebears, which we have only recently identified and rejected. Believing ourselves "like gods" we need to locate other creatures who aren't, if only to know what likeness it is we mean. But there is another option: maybe there are creatures *more* like gods than we are, whether we should hope to imitate them, to worship them, or merely fear them. In the last few hundred years we have imagined them elsewhere, either in the heavens or in the distant past.

We cannot, at the moment, tell whether there are, or aren't, extraterrestrial species of a more or less "human" sort. We cannot even tell whether there were, or weren't, similarly alien species of an intelligent kind in the terrestrial past.

> Nature has employed at least two very different ways of making a brain—indeed, there are almost as many ways as there are phyla in the animal kingdom. Mind, to varying degrees, has arisen or is

embodied in all of these, despite the profound biological gulf that separates them from one other, and us from them.[1]

And how could we tell what those past brains may have done? Any future archaeologically inclined species, arising many millions of years after our extinction, would maybe find some traces of the so-called Anthropocene,[2] perhaps in whatever form plastic debris in the oceans will have taken after those many years—but there would be no certain evidence of our sometime existence, nor of our character. The geological layer is likely to be very narrow. Neither do we now have any certain evidence of any past industrial or similarly interventionist civilization, nor of the absence of any such.[3] The issue is made more difficult because we can no longer feel the confidence with which Winchell asserted that "however conformed bodily, whatever their modes and means of organic activity, we know that [those other creatures] reason as we reason, and interpret the universe on the same principles of logic and mathematics as ourselves."[4] Nor do we know what they would build, or how. It may be doubted that we could even be sure about their anatomy.

> Suppose that in some convulsion of the planets there fell upon this earth from Mars, a creature of a shape totally unfamiliar, a creature about whose actual structure we were of necessity so dark that we could not tell which was creature and which was clothes. We could see that it had, say, six red tufts on its head, but we should not know whether they were a highly respectable head-covering or simply a head. We should see that the tail ended in three yellow stars, but it would be difficult for us to know whether this was part of a ritual or simply a tail.[5]

---

[1] Oliver Sacks, *The River of Consciousness* (New York: Alfred A. Knopf, 2017), 76–77.
[2] See Jeremy Davies, *The Birth of the Anthropocene* (Oakland, CA: University of California Press, 2016).
[3] Gavin A. Schmidt and Adam Frank, "The Silurian hypothesis: Would it be possible to detect an industrial civilization in the geological record?," *International Journal of Astrobiology* 18.2 (2019): 142–50 [doi:10.1017/S1473550418000095].
[4] Winchell, *World Life*, 508.
[5] Chesterton, "Philosophy of Islands."

Alien Life on Earth and Elsewhere

We might not even be sure of the distinction between head and tail, nor even whether they needed "brains" to be intelligent agents in some unfamiliar sense.

Lovelock proposed that we could tell, even from a distance, whether there was or wasn't "life" on another planet, by discovering whether the planet was or wasn't at chemical equilibrium.[6] Whether there was or wasn't "intelligent" life seems less easy to determine, even if we insist that "intelligence" is shown in practical activity of a sort that needs social cooperation, patience and imaginative forethought. Not even all human beings take much thought for tomorrow, or seek to alter the conditions in which they live. Conversely, many non-human species whom we doubt are really "intelligent" build complex houses, regulate their temperature and lay up stores for winter. Encountering a planetary city, or what looked exactly like a city, would still not *prove* that its inhabitants and builders were more like us than like ants.

Why does this matter to us? Why do we still hope, or even expect, that there are other creatures far away (or even long ago) whom we might consider "intelligent" in something like a human sense? What is that sense, and what account of things would make it likely, or even possible, that there are such creatures even if we cannot hope to *meet* them? Why do we trouble to imagine them, in whatever mode, when we are already acquainted with very many non-human lives and minds? We can neither prove nor disprove the suggestion that there were many non-human "intelligent" species in the past which practiced agriculture and industry on the human scale (perhaps to their own destruction). But we can easily show that there are very many non-human intelligent species *now*, which have adopted other modes of consciousness and action. We cannot even claim, at least without self-deception, that the human species is the *dominant* form of life here-now, nor yet the kind most likely to last the aeons. The world, we might more reasonably judge, is ruled by the bacterial cloud, or by the mass of eusocial insects — to both of which I shall return.

Travel to other planets in the neighborhood will probably be possible sometime in this century. Travel to other stars is likely to take much longer, whether by robotic proxy, multi-generational starships or magical shortcuts

---

6 Lovelock, *Gaia*, 5–9.

through hyperspace. The one partly convincing argument against even the possibility of such travel is simply that we should long ago have been visited by the inhabitants of other systems far away.[7] On the other hand, we might not know that we have been, or that we won't be fairly soon. The fantasies may nonetheless be helpful in discerning what it is we think or hope for. Mere "rocks," even of planetary size, would be promptly regarded as no more than convenient sources of whatever ores had been laid down in past lifeless ages. Living worlds would be more exciting—but almost all our fantasies suggest that we would be rather disappointed, or even a little afraid, if we could not identify some species that we might agree was "sapient." Bacterial infections, poisonous plants or ravenous predators could defeat our colonial ambitions easily, and there be no way of coming to any agreement with these dangers. The thought lies at the back of "social contract" theories of morality and the State: we can come to peaceful terms only with creatures who could make and have reason to keep a bargain. Outside such real or tacit or merely imagined contracts, it is said, there is no chance of justice—which is why both Stoics and Epicureans have denied that human beings have any duties to non-humans, nor the latter any rights against us, nor yet duties towards us. A just peace is only possible, it is thought, between "rational" beings who can understand the options, and bind themselves to peace (perhaps with the help of Hobbes's Leviathan).

At the same time we may think that it is only such "rational" species that constitute a lasting danger: others will mostly be confined to their own planetary realms. The long sad history of our own species, of course, would at once suggest that such sapient creatures were either "primitives" to be patronized, enslaved or killed, or else dangerous rivals to be conciliated or defeated. The prospect of locating vastly superior creatures who would then treat our species as we have so often treated others has often been enough to deter too loud attempts to attract the attention of any aliens "out there." A more hopeful outcome might be the discovery that our needs and wishes were so disparate as to occasion no conflict—but even this more optimistic idea might falter in the thought that there is time to come. Even if we are not rivals *now*, our descendants might find new uses for material and

7 Stephen Webb, *If the Universe Is Teeming with Aliens... Where Is Everybody? Fifty Solutions to Fermi's Paradox and the Problem of Extraterrestrial Life* (New York: Copernicus Books, 2002).

worlds that are at the moment valueless. Even the thought that we might engage in *trade*, without recourse to violence, seems naïve in the face of human history. Contracts were made to be broken — and will be unless the Hobbesian Sovereign is longer lived, more powerful and far craftier than any of its cheating subjects, or unless we somehow all internalize a better moral.

Chesterton was persuaded that it is really wrong — among other things — to steal, and that this truth is more certain and more universal than any merely contingent description of "the facts":

> Reason and justice grip the remotest and the loneliest star. Look at those stars. Don't they look as if they were single diamonds and sapphires? Well, you can imagine any mad botany or geology you please. Think of forests of adamant with leaves of brilliants. Think the moon is a blue moon, a single elephantine sapphire. But don't fancy that all that frantic astronomy would make the smallest difference to the reason and justice of conduct. On plains of opal, under cliffs cut out of pearl, you would still find a notice-board, "Thou shalt not steal."[8]

What counts as "stealing" may of course be debatable. And there may be many more prohibitions, even injunctions, that are both more significant and far more fixed. But can the imagination of strange "sapient" forms of life throw any doubt on them all? Like other mammals, and many other vertebrates, we are, for example, assiduous in our care for our cubs: as I remarked before, it is very odd that modern moral theories make such care merely marginal, as if we only minded about babies for their supposed "potential." But it is relatively easy to imagine (or identify) animal species that are "r-selecting" rather than "K-selecting":[9] they produce so many offspring that there is no need to provide much care, or any care, for them. Even human societies sometimes invest less in their offspring, knowing that infants will often die irrespective

---

8 G. K. Chesterton, "The Blue Cross" (1911), in *The Father Brown Stories* (London: Cassell, 1929), 27.

9 See Eric R. Pianka "On r- and K-Selection," *The American Naturalist* 104.940 (1970): 592–97, after R. MacArthur and E. O. Wilson, *The Theory of Island Biogeography* (Princeton, NJ: Princeton University Press, 1967).

Can We Believe in People?

of the care their parents take. The young may achieve full significance, or a voice, only after adolescent initiation. The labor of production, and parental bonds, make it unlikely that we would ever entirely abandon the impulse to parental care—unless, perhaps, we replace our "natural" reproductive habits with more technological, extra-uterine techniques. Might not other species have very different attitudes to the young, as imagined (for example) by C. J. Cherryh,[10] whose *regul* give their respect only to mature, immobile adults, and whose young are lucky to survive adult anger or disappointment? In her *Foreigner* sequence, her *atevi* don't owe any special duty to chance acquaintance, sometime colleagues, lovers, or even family members, even if they have enjoyed their company. "Assassinate someone of the same *man'chi*, the same hierarchical loyalty? That was shocking. Assassinate a relative? That was possibly a rational solution."[11] The *kif* of her *Chanur* saga are yet more uncompromisingly alien, though strangely like what some political theorists assume we humans are: they are egoists, who eat their own kind and do not feel guilt.[12] The joke (perhaps) in Cherryh's story is that they can be brought to see the advantages of clear bargains, and to keep them more reliably than other more "sentimental" kinds. Are all these real possibilities, or must we rather suppose that *any* sapient species will eventually uncover the fundamental laws of justice and propriety? Darwin suggested that "if men were reared under precisely the same condition as hive-bees, there can hardly be any doubt that our unmarried females would, like worker bees, think it a sacred duty to kill their brothers, and mothers would strike to kill their fertile daughters, and no one would think of interfering."[13] Henry Sidgwick's mildly witty response (cited by Darwin in later editions) that "a superior bee would aspire to a milder solution of the population problem"[14]

---

10 C. J. Cherryh, *The Faded Sun Trilogy: Kesrith* (1978); *Shon'jir* (1978); *Kutath* (1979) (London: Penguin, 2000).

11 C. J. Cherryh, *Invader* (London: Random House, 1996), 84.

12 C. J. Cherryh, *The Chanur Saga: The Pride of Chanur* (1981); *Chanur's Venture* (1984); *The Kif Strike Back* (1985) (New York: Daw Books, 2000); *Chanur's Endgame* (*Chanur's Homecoming* [1986]; *Chanur's Legacy* [1992]) (New York: Daw Books, 2007).

13 Darwin, *Descent of Man*, 1:86.

14 Henry Sidgwick, "Review of Frances Cobbe's *Darwinism in morals*," *The Academy* III, no. 50 (15 June 1872): 230–31; see Darwin *Descent of Man*, 1:99. Darwin commented in turn that "the habits of many or most savages" show that "man solves the problem by female infanticide, polyandry and promiscuous intercourse; therefore it may well be doubted whether it would be

testifies to a common faith that a humane ethic *must* prevail among the rationally intelligent. But are we sure?

There are, of course, more optimistic fantasies, including Olaf Stapledon's account of the rise of symbiotic and self-aware intelligence, culminating in a Cosmic Marriage of creature and creator, despite the manifold missteps and planetary catastrophes on the way to that conclusion. Maybe there could be — maybe there already is — at least a Galactic Commonwealth that could supervise the local, planetary tribes till they are wise and careful enough to be allowed out into the expanse. Maybe our maturity as genuinely *humane* creatures will come when we understand how different, and how very much the same, all living creatures are, of whatever star and whatever strange descent. Looking back from a very distant future our descendants will feel affectionate pity for their planetary forebears, and wonder how we could have lived like this. Maybe we are already living in that distant future, briefly enjoying a virtual reality adventure to uncover our beginnings[15] — or the beginnings of some minor species mostly unknown to the Manifold.

All such fancies, both the pessimistic and the hopeful, have their place.[16] All offer us the chance to specify what it is we mind about, what it is we reckon significantly "human," "rational," "sapient," "intelligent," and so on. All tend to reveal a little of our parochial character, our absurd assumption that the really alien will somehow be familiar. Even those who step beyond the simply humanoid very often imagine *feline* species as our rivals or — perhaps — companions, as though domestic cats are the furthest we can conceive as rivals or companions. We might as easily and sensibly, it could be said, expect that any creatures we encounter will, obviously, speak English, as that they will be comprehensible at all. If our first Galactic

---

by a milder method." See Hallvard Lillehammer, "Methods of ethics and the descent of man: Darwin and Sidgwick on ethics and evolution," *Biology and Philosophy* 25 (2010): 361–78 [doi.org/10.1007/s10539-010-9204-8]. Lillehammer, it should be said, proposes that although "it is reasonable to think that an improved understanding of the natural origins of our ethical beliefs would put into question some deeply treasured yet grossly prejudiced aspects of different systems of human morality... it is hard to seriously foresee this process as resulting in an unlimited license to torture one's neighbours for fun" (375).

15 Nick Bostrom, "Are you living in a computer simulation?," *Philosophical Quarterly* 53 (2003): 243–55.

16 See Jack Cohen and Ian Stewart, *What Does a Martian Look Like?: The Science of Extraterrestrial Life* (New Jersey: John Wiley, 2002).

contact were with Anglophones we should either conclude that the envoys had been watching us for ages and had learnt a useful language, or that Galactic civilization had long ago been infiltrated, by accident, by English refugees, or (least plausibly) our distant Saxon ancestors had learnt a truly Galactic tongue from some stranded alien. We would not, we may hope, conclude that English was the universal speech, the natural outcome of all linguistic history. If we encounter elsewhere any creatures with whom we can communicate and bargain we might have similar qualms: why may they not indeed be as "occult and awful" as turkeys, squids or slime molds?

One answer might be that we are "in the image and likeness of God" — and that God the Creator has scattered equivalent images everywhere. If we can explain the veracity of our rational intelligence by acknowledging that God has made us to understand the world, may we not expect that there will be other intelligences elsewhere, at least as well equipped as we, whatever their merely biological beginnings? Finding human or almost-human life Out There might at least give us cause to suspect a common ancestral origin, or an evolutionary history guided by the humane archetype. Maybe the Logos, the Word of God, is born in many worlds, whether in a particular incarnation or simply as the light that "lightens every man" (Jn 1:9), or rather every *hnau*. And perhaps that provides another and better answer to the question, why we want and hope that we shall find "intelligence" Out There. We want there to be someone who can speak for a whole world, who can be the representative of living things to us and to the powers. Just as humanity may incorporate and stand for the whole range of terrestrial life, so may there be other "images" elsewhere. Conversely, if that is what we secretly hope to find elsewhere, we need to begin again to comprehend our cousins here, and speak for them, to each other and the powers. This notion still tends to elevate our human status, as if it were our job to *lead*.

> The ultimate destiny of the universe is in the fullness of God, which has already been attained by the risen Christ, the measure of the maturity of all things. Here we can add yet another argument for rejecting every tyrannical and irresponsible domination of human beings over other creatures. The ultimate purpose of other creatures

is not to be found in us. Rather, all creatures are moving forward with us and through us towards a common point of arrival, which is God, in that transcendent fullness where the risen Christ embraces and illumines all things. Human beings, endowed with intelligence and love, and drawn by the fullness of Christ, are called to lead all creatures back to their Creator.[17]

Better perhaps to recall the Lorax: "I am the Lorax. I speak for the trees. I speak for the trees, for the trees have no tongues."[18] And what if the Lorax were to turn into a Once-ler?

THE BACTERIAL CLOUD

When the story of the Earth is compared to a single year, the first faint signs of prokaryotic life appear in, as it were, late February, 3.8 billion years ago. Eukaryotes — creatures whose cells contain distinct nuclei — do not appear till "mid-July," and the principal animal phyla with which we are now acquainted not till mid-November.[19] The story is a familiar one, often cited, as I remarked on an earlier page, to show our insignificance (which it does not). The more significant point is that life on Earth was prokaryotic for half the planet's existence. The symbiotic partnership that created eukaryotes was apparently not an easy or obvious step. We cannot conclude very much from this: perhaps the step is taken "accidentally" earlier or later in other developing biospheres. But if terrestrial history is taken to be typical, by the easy — but unproven — "principle of mediocrity,"[20] then most living things Out There are probably also microbes.

Must this mean that "intelligence" is also long delayed? The question must seem absurd: how can *microbes* reason their way to any conclusion about the world, or even about *their* worlds? And yet we cannot quite exclude the thought:

---

17 Francis, *Laudato Si'*, §83.
18 Dr. Seuss (aka Theodor Seuss Geisel), *The Lorax* (New York: Random House, 1971), 23.
19 See, for example, https://biomimicry.net/earths-calendar-year/ (accessed December 21, 2019).
20 "The principle of mediocrity [is] that we should assume ourselves to be typical in any class that we belong to, unless there is some evidence to the contrary" (Vilenkin, "Principle of Mediocrity").

The idea that microbes might know their world, not merely bump into it, is controversial but unoriginal. At the beginning of the 20th century, Jennings (1905) claimed the behavior of the "lower animals," notably paramecia but including bacteria, could tell us much about the behavior of the "higher animals," including humans.[21]

After outlining the considerable evidence that microbes both can and do respond distinctively to features of their world, and that they can communicate their findings, Lyon concludes with a statement of belief:

> I believe there is something going on at the microscopic level that doesn't just "look" cognitive, it is cognitive, or, more accurately, it is typically considered cognitive when studied in animals more like us.

The world that microbes inhabit can be mapped within those microbes' anatomy and DNA. They can also do more than merely communicate: the transfer of genetic information enables them to adapt to circumstances. Though we may describe different sorts of microbe as if they were members of distinctive species, there are no long-lasting, distinct kinds of microbe, as there are of larger eukaryotic organisms like us. This is part of what ensures that any attempt to go to war with microbes, even with such bacteria as are now associated with our disease or death, is certain to end in our defeat.

The suggestion can be misunderstood. We are not to suppose that microbes are "little people," with some clear sense of their own particularity, confronting the world as we do and having to balance the impulse to preserve and promote "our selves" and the impulse rather to promote our kind (whatever we take that to be). That is a product of precisely the dubious notion that I am examining: that human beings are somehow the primary template for all life and all intelligence, and that every other living thing is less than us, by how much they differ from us. Maybe that is true, but even to understand the claim, let alone to find reason to believe it, we must consider alternatives. Microbes are constantly splitting and merging in the bacterial sea, infecting

---

21 P. Lyon, "The cognitive cell: bacterial behavior reconsidered," *Frontiers in Microbiology* 6.264 (2015) [doi.org/10.3389/fmicb.2015.00264], after H. S. Jennings, *Behavior of the Lower Organisms* (New York: Columbia University Press, 1905).

or communicating elements of their own selfhood, and with no impulse to put their "own" wellbeing over that of "others." They may also be capable of "quantum superposition," being in more than one, apparently exclusive, state at the same time, and communicating by "quantum entanglement": the issue is not settled, though serious suggestions have been made to explain the odd efficiency, for example, of photosynthesis. Their logic and mathematical theory, if such items exist in the cloud, are likely to be rather unlike ours. The closest, perhaps, that we can get to imagining what these lives are like would be to take the Buddhist story seriously: there are no *selves* at all, but only notions, sensations, perceptions, process, *dukkha*. It is true both that nothing lasts and that anything may turn up again, replicated or resurrected infinitely many times in a boundless, endless world. What we — or microbes — can do with this insight or illusion is for others, somehow, to intuit or to plan.

Whatever life is like for the bacterial cloud, it is evident that the rest of us cannot survive without it. All later eukaryotic life is built around and upon the earlier, and microbial life is present both in our individual bodies and in the wider world. "The number of bacterial cells residing in a human body is ten times the number of human cells which ensures that the human kingdom is practically immersed in the bacterial world."[22] Each cell of our bodies depends on mitochondria for its energy. Our digestive system depends on gut bacteria. Bacterial infections may bring useful variations to our DNA. Trace elements are concentrated or compounds synthesized in the wider world on which our life depends. A few science fiction writers have played with the notion of a bacterial civilization capable of manipulating the responses of eukaryotes like us,[23] but their fantasies are not so distant from the truth, even if merely *terrestrial* microbes are perhaps (how should we tell?) not yet so far farsighted.

In brief: if the bacterial cloud is not, after all, the viceroy of the Lord, whether to represent that Lord to all His creatures or to represent His

---

22 Sarangam Majumdar and Sukla Pal, "Bacterial intelligence: imitation games, time-sharing, and long-range quantum coherence," *Journal of Cell Communication and Signaling* 11.3 (2017): 281–84 [link.springer.com/article/10.1007%2Fs12079-017-0394-6].

23 For example, Greg Bear, *Blood Music* (London: Gollancz, 1985); Orson Scott Card, *Xenocide* (London: Orbit, 2013 [1991]).

creatures to each other and Himself, then something else needs saying about the Human. We should consider once again what our relationship with *angels* may be. On the one hand, angels — by hypothesis — are immeasurably our superiors: immortal, hyperintelligent and unconstrained by any bodily passion. On the other, by tradition, they are to consent to bow before "us."

> We created you and then formed you and then We said to the Angels, "Prostrate before Adam" and they prostrated except for Iblis [which is the Arabic term for Satan]. He was not among those who prostrated. God said, "What prevented you from prostrating when I commanded you?" He (Iblis) replied, "I am better than him. You created me from fire and You created him from clay." God said, "Descend from heaven. It is not for you to be arrogant in it. So get out! You are one of the abased."[24]

Does it seem odd to compare bacteria to angels? That is perhaps our residual dualism at work. The fact that bacteria are made of "chemical stuff," mostly formed in stars and scattered through the cosmos in galactic dust, is not at odds with an "angelic" status: something more than transient animal organisms, and replicating the structure of the worlds they have a hand in making.

THE EUSOCIAL OPTION
The other familiar notion explored by xenobiologists, both scholarly and science-fictional, is that most successful multicellular organisms are likely to be "eusocial," whether they are biologically programmed to form nests and hives or are the mechanical heirs of earlier successful life. In either case, the creatures that make up eusocial societies are molded for their roles, and interchangeable within those roles. The more mechanical versions may be repaired and constantly reinvented for the larger purpose. Such possibilities have been explored at least since Wells's *First Men in the Moon*,[25] and generally suppose that "human beings," by contrast, are individual agents only casually linked with others of their kind, and easily able to opt out of any assigned stations. The fantasy may also be projected onto human tribes,

---

24 Koran 7.11–13.
25 H. G. Wells, *The First Men in the Moon* (London: George Newnes, 1901).

Alien Life on Earth and Elsewhere

most often in "the East," who are supposed to be careless of individual human lives, and to accept their programmed roles without complaint. Such human collectivities may make their members' lives more hopeful by the thought that there are after all individual souls who may get other lives hereafter: they are not *essentially* Brahmins, nobles, or Dalits, nor even essentially male or female, nor human or non-human, however harshly they are judged for stepping outside their present roles in life.

This xenobiological fantasy is more consistent., and has this merit at least, that eusocial forms have indeed evolved many times in terrestrial history: many contemporary species of ants, termites, bees, and even naked mole rats make it clear that this is a successful form of life that can appear in many distinct lines. Some sociobiologists, exploring human possibilities, have urged that human beings could not maintain such a form: the genetic interest of humans must always (they thought) preclude the possibility that only a dominant female reproduce the clan, and force all or most of her offspring to be merely aunts and uncles. This may be so—but even mammals have either adopted the style entirely, or at least come close to it: as a solution to the problem of the surplus male it may have merits that the more usual answers (war or strict monogamy) do not. But let it be supposed that indeed the *human* form is not entirely suited to eusociality: what does that show about the future? Science fiction writers may have generally supposed that the human style, promoting individual variety united only through conscious contracts, will have more success than the insectile or robotic forms they imagine—but perhaps they are mistaken. Individual humans are not really as inventive or original as they suppose, and eusocial insects (and robots) can afford to vary their ways and invent new varieties to fit new worlds.

The eusocial fantasy echoes some past political theory: city-states (*poleis*), so Plato thought, could display, writ large, the very same vices and virtues, the very same form and structures, as human individuals (*Republic* 2.368e). Aristotle indeed suggested that "a city (*polis*) is naturally prior to the household and to each of us, just as any organism is prior to its parts" (*Politics* 1.1252a19). We do not, generally, form cities by simple association: rather we are all born into households and into cities, and come to responsible adult life by being brought up properly. Some recent African philosophers and activists have suggested that this is a thought peculiar to Bantu philosophy: "a person is a person through other persons," in one summary of the concept of "*Ubuntu*":

> This maxim has descriptive senses to the effect that one's identity as a human being causally and even metaphysically depends on a community. It also has prescriptive senses to the effect that one ought to be a mensch, in other words, morally should support the community in certain ways.[26]

It may be true that Bantu philosophy—and common moral sense—is more respectful of tradition and community than some modern Western philosophies—but that perhaps says more about modern Western philosophies than about our own European tradition.

Just as a human individual's being lies in her *choice* of what to do and be, so also a city's identity lies in its constitution, its way of life embodied in institutions and day-to-day decisions (Aristotle, *Politics* 3.1276b10). Of course, its citizens, its component parts, can sometimes survive in exile, or may even join with others to form new cities. The same is true of more obviously singular creatures: sponges squeezed through silk can reconstitute themselves, and slime molds can exist both as a crowd of distinct bits, and as single, sluglike organisms on the way to a better life elsewhere. Any animal, as Aristotle says, is like a well-governed *polis* (*De Motu* 703a29), at least until it falls apart. The political message may often be used oppressively, to suggest to the downtrodden poor that they should serve the central organs of a state (its leaders), but so can almost any political theory. That too is not a notion found only in "the West."

> The Western concept of the body politic, a conceptual metaphor that can be traced back to Plato and clearly articulated by John of Salisbury (c. 1120–1180) in the twelfth century, also has a similar

---

26 Thaddeus Metz, "Toward an African Moral Theory," *Journal of Political Philosophy* 15.2 (2007): 321–41, 323; see also Fainos Mangena, "Hunhu/Ubuntu in the Traditional Thought of Southern Africa," *Internet Encyclopedia of Philosophy* (2016) [http://www.iep.utm.edu/hunhu/, accessed 14th June 2019].

Alien Life on Earth and Elsewhere

expression in Chinese political thinking. According to John of Salisbury, the king is "the head in the republic," the senate its heart, "judges and governors of provinces" perform "duties of the ears, eyes and mouth," officials and soldiers are the hands, while those who assist the king are "comparable to the flanks."[27] Li Gang (1083–1140), a Chinese statesman of the Song dynasty, also described the state or "all under heaven" as "just one human body. The royal house inside is the heart, offices outside reaching in four directions are the four limbs, and laws, rules, and penal codes are the veins and arteries."[28] This of course reminds us of Dong Zhongshu's description of the human body as similarly constituted as that of heaven or the universe in an essentially social and political theory.[29]

But it may still be difficult for most ordinary human beings fully to agree that they are merely cells, limbs, or organs, of the "body politic." We are far readier to believe that ants or bees or termites are cells or organs of their hives or nests.[30] But in the past such "super-organisms" were admired: bees, for example, have something of the divine about them, unlike wasps (Aristotle, *De Generatione Animalium* 3.761a5). Their societies, just in that they are so close to being fully united organisms, were to be admired, and maybe copied. Stapledon's own future "history" is full of such macro-organisms, world souls that experience life through many distinct members, though (inevitably) they continue to sound like Stapledon. Even American science fiction, through the 1950s, seemed to prefer such model societies, in which business and education are managed from on high, perhaps with the aid, or

---

27 John of Salisbury, *Policraticus: Of the Frivolities of Courtiers and the Footprints of Philosophers*, 5:2, in Cary J. Nederman and Kate Langdon Forhan, eds., *Medieval Political Theory—A Reader: The Quest for the Body Politic, 1100–1400* (London: Routledge, 1993), 38. See also Plato, *Republic* 5.464b.

28 Li Gang, "On Curing the State," *Liangxi ji (Li Gang's Collected Writings)*, juan 157, in *Siku quanshu (Complete Collection of the Four Treasuries)* (Shanghai: Shanghai guji, 1987 reprint), vol. 1126, 683b–684a.

29 Zhang Longxi, "Heaven and Man: From a Cross-Cultural Perspective," in *Comparative Political Theory and Cross-Cultural Philosophy: Essays in Honor of Hwa Yol Jung*, ed. Jin Y. Park (Plymouth: Lexington, 2009), 139–50, 146.

30 See Eugène Marais, *The Soul of the White Ant*, trans. Winifred de Kok (London: Methuen, 1950 [1937]).

on the orders, of an advanced computer. In the most extreme versions of that trope the computer is even responsible for creating transient individuals for particular tasks, or to complete the picture. On the other hand, fantasists also presented such eusocial forms as aliens, at odds with maverick human intelligences unconstrained by any duty to obey the group, or maintain tradition.

Might eusocial collectives be rather more like God? The Christian Church, after all, is self-defined as "the Body of Christ," and her members are instructed to think of each other as serving particular roles within the wider whole. "For as in one body we have many members, and the members do not all have the same function, so we, though many, are one body in Christ, and individually members one of another" (Rom 12:4–5). Churches, to be sure, are rather a different sort of collective than tribes or even cities: membership is by baptism and adoption, not by birth (Jn 1:12–13). And it is vital to their being that each member is so by her own "personal" choice (however much that choice may, in reality, be influenced). "There is no compulsion in religion."[31]

> While [King Ethelbert of Kent] was pleased at [his subjects'] faith and conversion, it is said that he would not compel anyone to accept Christianity; for he had learned from his instructors and guides to salvation that the service of Christ must be accepted freely and not under compulsion. Nevertheless, he showed greater favour to believers, because they were fellow-citizens of the kingdom of heaven.[32]

The contest played out in late 20th-century science fiction, and human politics, between "collectivists" and "individualists" was more often, in fact, only a contest between differing collectives. Even the "escape from Earth" imagined in James Blish's saga of the star-travelling cities merely carried the collectives further: the otherwise deathless citizens he imagined were to be summarily executed if someone else could perform their function better.[33] What lasts,

---

31 Koran: al-Baqarah 2:256.
32 Bede, *Ecclesiastical History of the English People, with Bede's Letter to Egbert and Cuthbert's Letter on the Death of Bede*, trans. Leo Sherley-Price (London: Penguin, 1990 [731]), 77.
33 James Blish, *Cities in Flight: They Shall Have Stars* (1956); *A Life for the Stars* (1962); *Earthman Come Home* (1955); *The Triumph of Time* (1959) (London: Gollancz, 2000), 211, 219.

it seems, is the collective — and individual persons only as elements in those long-lasting wholes. The Party is immortal (as Orwell's O'Brien said[34]): what steps outside that whole is cast aside, is hardly anything, not even a beast, let alone — as Aristotle allowed — a god (*Politics* 1.1253a29; see also *Nicomachean Ethics* 9.1169b17–20). On the other hand, even the Party only exists in its individual members, with their own proclivities and preferences.

If ants, bees, churches and Stapledonian "group minds" form "super-organisms," it is also evident that our own selves are colonies. We multicellular organisms only manage to survive with the aid of our microbiomes on the one hand, and the entire surrounding environment (both human and natural) on the other. To resurrect one human body is to resurrect a world.[35] If super-organisms are taken to be the template, then we might also apply the preference for a non-hierarchical, genuinely *cooperative* form of life to our human existence. Rather than the trope that our selfhood resides in "reason" or "the brain" we might better consider that it is our whole bodies, and their allies, that sustain our selves.

> We are apes — political, shortsighted, self-serving, affectionate and tender, clever and emotional. But we are also like paper wasps, driven by the urge to make things; industrious ants, moving earth and tending gardens for the future; responsible honeybees, filled with civic duty — and the densely intertwining fungi that pulse beneath the soil. Like all these superorganisms, we share our resources and nurture our ecosystems, and strive to create something better than what came before.[36]

---

34 George Orwell, *Nineteen Eighty-Four*, ed. Thomas Pynchon (London: Penguin, 1989 [1949]), 261.

35 In passing: it is sometimes suggested that Paul (1 Cor 15:44) supposed that we were to be raised as "spiritual (*pneumatika*) bodies," being of the same homogenous substance as the stars, and having no material parts or symbionts. This was later judged a heresy by Christian theologians, and is probably not what Paul intended. See Rom 8:19–21: "The creation waits in eager expectation for the children of God to be revealed. For the creation was subjected to frustration, not by its own choice, but by the will of the one who subjected it, in hope that the creation itself will be liberated from its bondage to decay and brought into the freedom and glory of the children of God."

36 Tamsin Woolley-Barker, *Teeming, How Superorganisms Work to Build Infinite Wealth in a Finite World* (Ashland, OR: White Cloud Press, 2017), 64.

Can We Believe in People?

CLIMBING UP TO HEAVEN

The bacterial and eusocial options have turned up so often or survived so long in our terrestrial history that we could not reasonably be surprised to find some similar lives Out There. There may of course be many other sorts of creature, including many wholly unlike any known terrestrial organism. There are many unique solutions to life's problems which we could not have expected, and may have difficulty ever understanding. Panpsychists, rejecting both eliminative materialism (that subjectivity, weirdly, is an illusion) and the inexplicable "emergence," magically, of consciousness from wholly non-conscious elements, may wonder whether even rocks are sometimes sentient. A rock, of course, is only an arbitrary fragment of some geological stratum, formed entirely by external forces. And yet there may be some moment when a rock becomes a genuine unity. A Greek verse, coined by Nilus the Scholastic, gives a voice to a sculpture: "I laugh because I marvel how, put together out of all sorts of stones, I suddenly become a satyr."[37] Quite how we might imagine *being* such a living rock, or how we could ever verify our thought, is doubtful. How might living rocks be acquainted with what surrounds them, or what other rocks might feel? Perhaps they might be changed by the passage of cosmic radiation, as well as by the warmth and light of the sun? What needs would living rocks have, or how might they or would they resist erosion or fragmentation? It may seem that, having no need to know, nor any way of knowing, what is happening nearby they also have no need of sentience at all—and yet there are also plainly living animal organisms that can float uncaring in the sea, enjoying light. The nudibranch *Elysia viridis* absorbs photosynthetic algae early in its active life, and thereafter does not need to eat, but only to float in the upper ocean. That we don't know how a living rock would live is no proof that it couldn't.

Moving on from the merely mineral, we may also reconsider the status of the "vegetable" kingdom, which we always assume, along with Aristotle, is insentient, immobile, barely alive at all (except that there is a difference between a living plant and a dead one). Recent research shows that trees *communicate* with each other, through a fungal network laced around their

---

37 Nilus the Scholastic (5th century), *Planudean Appendix* (*Greek Anthology*, bk. 16), epigram 247, quoted by Gervase Mathew, *Byzantine Aesthetics* (London: John Murray, 1964), 76.

roots: they can warn their neighbors of coming predators, and to prepare toxins to repel them.[38] They may not — currently — move from where they are planted, except that they can send out shoots and gradually move their focus across the ground. What gambits their descendants may devise (or what gambits extraterrestrial "plants" manage) we cannot accurately guess. Maybe their seeds, one day, will fly rather than merely be carried by the wind. Maybe they will leave their roots behind for others to use in their travels. Or maybe they will be content to communicate from a distance — which is the fable most common in science fiction circles. We cannot at least be as confident as Plotinus, that plants are the rashest of the rebels or refugees from the company of heaven, sticking their hands in the earth and oblivious to the wider world![39] We might instead consider them a primary image or likeness of the cosmos, which is itself, in a way, a tree, comprising more than merely roots, fruits and leaves, but also the bacterial, fungal, animal life that feeds and lives within it. Prue Shaw notes that Dante, in "an arresting visual image [in *Paradise* 27.118–120], describes time as a tree with its roots in the *primum mobile*":[40] the image is derived, by whatever route, from Plotinus. We are, Plotinus reckoned, "maggots (*eulai*)" in that tree (*Ennead* IV.3 [27].4, 26–30). The whole cosmos is, as it were, flowering from a single root, and "those that are closer to the root [which is to say, the stars] remain for ever (*emenen aei*), and the others are always coming into being (*egineto aei*), the fruits and the leaves."[41]

Which brings us to the stars. Our predecessors were almost all persuaded that the stars were living, and intelligent: even that they are gods. They were, apparently, both everlasting and orderly, as well as individually glorious: "neither the evening nor the morning star are as fair," perhaps, as Justice (*Ennead* I.6 [1].4, 10f.), but their beauty is enough to show that beauty is more than any symmetry of parts (since they appear to us as mere points). Our own perception and concept of the stars is bound to be somewhat different: that they are points of light, and orderly, and everlasting, are

---

38 Peter Wohlleben, *The Hidden Life of Trees: What They Feel, How They Communicate*, trans. Jane Billinghurst (Vancouver: Greystone Books, 2016).
39 *Ennead* V.2 [11].2, after Plato *Timaeus* 91c and Aristotle, *De Partibus Animalium* 4.686a25ff.
40 Prue Shaw, *Reading Dante: From Here to Eternity* (New York: W. W. Norton, 2015), 160.
41 *Ennead* III.3 [48].7, 10–24; see also III.8 [30].10.

only figments of our location on a turning earth. Stars have lifespans, even if they aren't living, and their orderliness does not prevent their crashing into each other, or poaching each other's substance. They last longer than we do, and provide both light and warmth to any living planets in their sway, while also being capable of destroying worlds — and forming them. They also provide the very material on which our own lives rest: carbon and other heavy elements are formed in stars, and spread throughout the neighborhood by the stars' explosion.

Do the problems I raised for sentience in rocks apply also to stars? Possibly not: stars, after all, are emitting radiation in all appropriate wavelengths, and that radiation reveals, even to us, their composition and their character. Does that radiation impinge on other stars to modify and alert them (as trees alert each other)? Must the conversation be long delayed while electromagnetic radiation potters along at light speed over many light-years? Or might we expect that they have solved the problem of quantum entanglement, to remain in touch with entities born of the same root?

Can we imagine being stars? And what might the imagination show us of ourselves? One easier answer might be that there are solar beings in the stars, as there are organisms in many another seemingly hostile place. Aristotle expected that there were creatures, even intelligent creatures, living in the lunar fire (*De Generatione Animalium* 3.761b22–24). Stapledon, in one of his lesser known fables, imagined these as flames, born in the sun's troposphere and condemned to live out a cold and intermittent existence on solid earth since the planets were formed. The late world war, and its manifold fires, have brought them out of hibernation in the dust of the air, and they sense the possibility of forming a symbiotic alliance with us: we to provide the environment within which they can live, they to provide the mental stability and community awareness we supposedly lack. If we cannot agree, the flames' other option is to instigate nuclear spasm: "then at last, with the whole planet turned into a single atomic bomb, and all the incandescent continents hurtling into space, we should have for a short while conditions almost as good as those of our golden age in the sun."[42]

---

42 Olaf Stapledon, *The Flames* (London: Secker & Warburg, 1947), 61.

Alien Life on Earth and Elsewhere

Allegorically, of course, the flames are simply those technological powers whose use may lead to utopia or to disaster. Or else they are a shifting image of the individual-in-community, less inclined than we to imagine that they are independent individuals, rather than elements within the global, or the stellar community, and by the same token all too ready to ignore the needs and passions of each such element, and fall into the little death of the hive-mind. The story even allows him what he does not attempt elsewhere, the thought that present individuals are fallen creatures, forever reaching towards a perfection they have lost: "each new experience came to us with a haunting sense of familiarity and a suspicion that the new version was but a crude and partial substitute for the old."

But the flames (and their assorted cognates in other science fiction) are a little too anthropomorphic to be very interesting. So even are the living stars of Stapledon's other work. There is more to be learnt, perhaps, from an older synthesis: the stars are visible gods, and perhaps we too may join them in their felicity. On Plotinus's account they have no need of memory, since everything important is always accessible to them. Nor need they have the problems with a fractured self that we humans have: their choices are always already made, and they have no rebellious segments. Climbing up to heaven, so pagan philosophers thought, was to divest ourselves of the properties we had acquired in our descent through all the planetary spheres. According to Macrobius, we pick up "reason and understanding" (*logistikon* and *theoretikon*) in the sphere of Saturn, "in Jupiter's sphere, the power to act, called *praktikon*; in Mars' sphere, a bold spirit or *thymikon*; in the sun's sphere, sense-perception and imagination, *aisthetikon* and *phantastikon*; in Venus's sphere, the impulse of passion, *epithymetikon*; in Mercury's sphere, the ability to speak and interpret, *hermeneutikon;* and in the lunar sphere, the function of moulding and increasing bodies, *phytikon*."[43] Lunar influence isn't merely *physical* (as it might seem): below the Moon is the realm of the transient, the mutable, and its power allows us instability, for good as well as ill.

---

43 Macrobius, *Commentary*, 136 (I.12); see my "Climbing up to Heaven: The Hermetic Option," in *Purgatory: Philosophical Dimensions*, ed. Kristof K. P. Vanhoutte and Benjamin W. McCraw (London: Palgrave-Macmillan, 2017), 151–74.

Can We Believe in People?

None of these powers or virtues are manifest as they should be here below:

> What comes from the stars will not reach the recipients in the same state in which it left them. If it is fire, for instance, the fire down here is dim, and if it is a loving disposition (*philiake diathesis*) it becomes weak in the recipient and produces a rather unpleasant kind of loving (*ou mala kalen ten philesin*); and manly spirit, when the receiver does not take it in due measure, so as to become brave, produces violent temper or spiritlessness; and that which belongs to honor in love and is concerned with beauty produces desire of what only seems to be beautiful, and the efflux of intellect produces knavery (*panourgia*); for knavery wants to be intellect, only it is unable to attain what it aims at. So all these things become evil in us, though they are not so up in heaven. (*Ennead* II.3 [52].11)

Whether we must shed them entirely, or accept their purified versions, may be emphasized differently by different pagan writers. What they are like in their proper forms, in the stars that we were or may be, is hardly for us to imagine except in the simplest terms. According to Hildegard of Bingen, before Adam fell "what is now gall in him sparkled like crystal, and bore the taste of good works, and what is now melancholy in man shone in him like the dawn and contained in itself the wisdom and perfection of good works."[44] And Pseudo-Dionysius:

> Their fury of anger represents an intellectual power of resistance of which anger is the last and faintest echo; their desire symbolizes the Divine Love; and in short we might find in all the irrational tendencies and many parts of irrational creatures, figures of the immaterial conceptions and single powers of the Celestial Beings.[45]

So why are not these the proper likenesses, and corresponding images, of the Divine? Mainstream Christians have insisted instead that it is idolatry

---

[44] R. Klibansky, E. Panofsky and F. Saxl, *Saturn and Melancholy* (Edinburgh: Nelson, 1964), 80.

[45] Ps-Dionysius, *The Celestial Hierarchy* (Whitefish, MT: Kessinger Publishing, 2004), 34.

Alien Life on Earth and Elsewhere

to worship the stars of heaven, and wrong to suppose even that we should ever be "like them." So Gregory Palamas, writing in the thirteenth century:

> These people have arrived at a certain conception of God, but not at a conception truly worthy of Him and appropriate to His blessed nature. For their "disordered heart was darkened" by the machinations of the wicked demons who were instructing them. For if a worthy conception of God could be attained through the use of intellection, how could these people have taken the demons for gods, and how could they have believed the demons when they taught man polytheism? In this way, wrapped up in this mindless and foolish wisdom and unenlightened education, they have calumniated both God and nature. They have deprived God of His sovereignty (at least as far as they are concerned); they have ascribed the Divine Name to demons; and they were so far from finding the knowledge of beings — the object of their desire and zeal — as to claim that inanimate things [that is, the stars] have a soul and participate in a soul superior to our own. They also allege that things without reason are reasonable, since capable of receiving a human soul; that demons are superior to us and are even our creators (such is their impiety); they have classed among things uncreated and unoriginate and coeternal with God, not only matter, and what they call the World Soul, but also those intelligible beings not clothed in the opacity of the body, and even our souls themselves.[46]

Some of the condemnation turned on familiar misunderstandings, but the principal point is probably worth considering. Angels, gods and *daimones*, even if they are real and more powerful or cleverer than us, are still not to be worshipped. As a later Platonist insisted:

> These gods are visions of the eternal attributes, or divine names, which, when erected into gods, become destructive of humanity....

---

46 Palamas, *150 Chapters*, 26 [I.1.18].

Can We Believe in People?

> When separated from man or humanity, who is Jesus the Saviour, the vine of eternity, they are thieves and rebels, they are destroyers.[47]

The aphorism that we, as human beings, may err by becoming or imitating "beasts" (*Ennead* III.2 [47].8, 9–13) in this life or another, should be balanced by a similar warning against too readily thinking ourselves "gods": "as intemperance and sensuality make us Beasts; so Pride and Malice make us Devils."[48] Pagan Platonists, though they too reckoned that gods and *daimones* were only our fellow creatures, and not to be given any absolute authority, preferred to remember that they were our natural superiors, and at least deserved *respect* (*Ennead* II.9 [33].9, 53–60) — though it was also important that they be contained within Zeus or Kronos rather than rebelling against Him. Whereas Christians in particular were persuaded that this world here was fallen, and that there might and should "one day" be a better world, God's Kingdom, pagan Platonists thought this too disrespectful: how could there be a better *material* world than this?

> Despising the universe and the gods in it and the other noble things is certainly not becoming good. Every wicked man, in former times too, was capable of despising the gods, and even if he was not altogether wicked before, when he despised them he became so by this very fact, even if he was not wicked in everything else.[49]

As I suggested earlier, it is the Christian Gospel (and perhaps also the Abrahamic thought) that the divine is to be found in simple, vulnerable things, like us, rather than in the splendor of the heavens, and that we are to look toward a future, earthly, kingdom, rather than escape aloft. There may be living stars. They may even merit our admiration and respect. But perhaps it is still better to think that a defenseless and wounded animal is the better image.

---

47 Blake, *Complete Writings*, 571.
48 Benjamin Whichcote, *Moral and Religious Aphorisms* [1703], in George Patrides, ed., *The Cambridge Platonists* (Cambridge: Cambridge University Press, 1980 [1969]), 327.
49 *Ennead* II.9 [33].16, 1–5; see also II.9 [33].4, 25–32.

8

Do We Have a Future?

OMEGA POINTS

Chesterton and Teilhard de Chardin both conceded that, considered simply as a biological species, humankind was but a twig upon the tree of life. Both nonetheless insisted that humankind was something special, not simply because they were both — like myself and (presumably) my present readers — members of that species. Teilhard de Chardin, indeed, followed Aristotle in insisting that "man is the most characteristic, most polar and most living form of life."[1] It is a doctrine also found in China:

> "Man is above and beyond all ten thousand things," Dong Zhongshu [179–104 BC] declares in no ambiguous terms, "and is thus the noblest of all under heaven." "When we look at the human body," he says, "how much higher above everything else it is, and how much closer to heaven!" He goes on to argue that because other creatures take less of the essence of heaven and earth, when compared with human beings, they all are shaped in such a way as to bend down or prostrate when they move, while "man alone stands erect and is truly worthy."[2]

Longxi rightly disparages the common claim that "Asian values" are needed to overcome mistaken "Western" notions of human dominance: Dong Zhongshu's notion of the "unity of man and heaven" entailed a strictly hierarchical, anthropocentric order. Longxi's further remarks

---

1 Pierre Teilhard de Chardin, *Man's Place in Nature*, trans. R. Hague (London: Harper & Row, 1966), 17; see Aristotle, *De Partibus Animalium* 656a7; Clark, *Aristotle's Man*, 28–30.

2 Zhang Longxi, "Heaven and Man," 147, citing Dong Zhongshu's *Exuberant Dews of the Spring and Autumn*; see Wing-tsit Chan, ed., *Sourcebook in Chinese Philosophy* (Princeton, NJ: Princeton University Press, 1963), 281–82; Clark, *Aristotle's Man*, 46.

on the importance of a comparative and global philosophy are worth noting here:

> The appreciation of man as the noblest and superior creature on earth is indeed shared by both the humanistic tradition in the West and by the Confucian tradition in China. Dong Zhongshu definitely put man on top of all other creatures under heaven. In fact, Confucian teachings are clearly human-centered. As we read in the Analects, when Confucius came back home one day and found the stable in his house burned down in a fire, he immediately asked: "Is anybody hurt?" But he did not ask about the horses. For him, the supreme virtue of *ren* or benevolence meant nothing but to "love human beings." To put human beings above other creatures, however, does not necessarily mean to destroy the balance between man and nature, and it is misleading to insist that either you have to conquer and destroy nature or you must give up all human interests and desires to preserve nature. Such an "either-or" opposition is false and unhelpful, serving only to intensify the cultural differences and confrontations between the East and the West. What we need in our world today is an open-minded acceptance of different perspectives and views that bring to us the best of all cultures. In fact, in the world's great cultures and traditions, we can find ideas, insights, and visions that are fundamentally commensurate and mutually enriching, and it is the task for a scholar and an intellectual to recognize the values of humanity's common ideas, insights, and visions and promote the mutual understanding, rather than the confrontation, of Asia and Europe, the East and the West. It is not so much Asian values as human values that we must learn to appreciate, and in this effort, cross-cultural understanding offers the hope of true knowledge, the hope of humanity's more peaceful and promising future.[3]

---

3 Longxi, "Heaven and Man," 116–17, cites Liu Baonan (1791–1855) as his authority for the story and its interpretation: *Lunyu zhengyi* (*The Correct Meaning of the Analects*), x.17, xii.22, in *Zhuzi jicheng* (*Collection of Distinguished Philosophical Works*), vol. 1, 228, 278.

Do We Have a Future?

Teilhard de Chardin's own contribution to the debate lay in his suggestion that evolution was a progressive force whose growing tip was now to be found in our species, and destined to culminate in the complete "hominization" of the cosmos as the "Noosphere" emerges to take control of things. Someday the cosmos will have been remade and repurposed. Someday the perfected form of humankind, visible already in a Jewish Hasid, will sit on the throne of heaven. Someday the whole cosmos will be brought into a unity, a joyfully experienced whole (perhaps with the same hope as Isaiah 11:6-10). Stapledon had some similar dreams — except that he did not expect that it would be biological humans who were thus elevated, nor that the Cosmic Spirit would find itself any closer to the Infinite and Incomprehensible Creator.[4]

That "evolution" is always a "progressive" force is not a claim that serious Darwinists could make, and Darwin himself explicitly disowned it. But the claim is part of the common, "optimistic" understanding of Darwinian theory which decrees that what is "later" must also be "more successful" and therefore also "better" — and so also are some associated claims, reminiscent of Wells's attitude to "black or yellow or mean-white squatters."[5]

> The task confronting biology, physiology and medicine is not only to master scientifically the maladies and phenomena of counterevolution (sterility and physical weakening) which undermine the growth of the noosphere — but to produce by various means (selection, control of the sexes, action of hormones, hygiene, etc.) a superior human type.... What attitude should the advancing sector of humanity adopt towards static and decidedly unprogressive ethnic groups?[6]

Or consider Haldane's wishful fantasy of future evolution, when such self-regarding sentiments as pride, "a personal preference concerning mating" and pity ("an unpleasant feeling aroused by the suffering of other

---

4 Stapledon, *Star Maker*, 233-34.
5 Wells, *Anticipations*, 263.
6 Teilhard de Chardin (1937), cited by R. Speaight, *Teilhard de Chardin: A Biography* (London: Collins, 1967), 233-34.

individuals") have been bred out of the species.[7] Stapledon, to similar effect, incorporated in some of his forwardlooking fantasies doctrines of a superior humanity disdainful of our present smallminded morals, which were soon to be dreadfully embodied in the here and now. The utopian researchers of his future "histories" regularly experiment on children, eliminate "the unfit," commit genocide, and see themselves as heralds of a greater dawn, licensed to do just what they please to those they judge inferior. At each stage they might discover, but rarely do, that they themselves are inferior to yet "higher" forms. Readers sometimes fail to notice this. One of the author and critic Brian Aldiss's most extraordinary critical judgments, for example, is his description of *Odd John* as a "pleasant superman tale," with a "light and cheerful mood."[8] John is a multiple murderer, who treats human beings as vermin, experimental animals or pets, and is critical of totalitarian barbarism only because he thinks himself and his companions superior to those despots. They all end in mass suicide rather than collaborate with ordinary people, whom they despise as an "inferior species." The Flames described in another work entertain the project of initiating nuclear spasm, "through loyalty to the spirit in us," if they should decide that the human species was doomed to self-destruction sooner or later,[9] rather as the Fifth Men of his future history destroy the inhabitants of Venus, on the plea that they are less developed and failing creatures: this slaughter, incidentally, produces in its agents on the one hand an "unreasoning disgust with humanity" and on the other a "grave elation" expressing itself in the thought that "the murder of Venerian life was terrible but right."[10] Odd John assures his biographer bluntly "if we could wipe out your whole species, we would,"[11] though in the end he and his fellows refrain. These may be extreme opinions — but all utopian planners are in danger of disrespecting *present* realities for the sake of an imagined future whose properties they cannot possibly guarantee. Only One who already knows all possible outcomes, and has all needful power to avoid the unintended consequences of action or inaction, can

---

7   J. B. S. Haldane, *Possible Worlds* (London: Chatto & Windus, 1930), 303.

8   Brian Aldiss, *Billion Year Spree* (London: Weidenfeld & Nicolson, 1974), 235, speaking of Olaf Stapledon, *Odd John* (London: Gollancz, 1935).

9   Stapledon, *Flames*, 60.

10 Stapledon, *Last and First Men*, 232.

11 Stapledon, *Odd John*, 216.

afford to be a consequentialist! Which is not to say that He is: after all, He is Himself responsible for bringing the effects, whatever they are, about! "It is certain that the practice of any vice or the commision of any crime is attended with an immediate punishment in this life. The infinitely wise providence of God hath joyned moral and natural evil together"[12] — but these things are wrong because God forbids them, and not because they lead to disaster. On the contrary, they usually lead to disaster because God has forbidden them, and chooses that way to make His displeasure clear. On this account, we cannot argue that if there be some occasion when the vicious act does not lead to disaster it isn't "really" wrong on that occasion: it remains wrong even if God delays or softens the punishment.

But perhaps we can afford even such grandiose and murderous thoughts some sympathy, and see how they might be developed with greater care. Stapledon himself repented his suggestions. "Were the masters of Buchenwald my ministers?" asks Stapledon's imagined God with heavy irony.[13] Surely not: any advantage won by deceit or violence is "outweighed by a greater hurt in the future, namely damage to the tradition of kindliness and reasonableness"[14] — though this consequentialist argument is not likely to convince the romantic revolutionary. Teilhard de Chardin might also have modified his conclusions, if he had been engaged more carefully and courteously by his ecclesiastical superiors and theological peers during his lifetime.

He was not the only evolutionary theorist to try to trace patterns in the development of earthly life, and to suggest that there was a clear, though gradual and sometimes interrupted, increase in "complexity": the complexity of individual organisms, and of the relations between them. It may have taken aeons for prokaryotes (archaebacteria and eubacteria) to create eukaryotes, and multicellular creatures (plant, fungi, animals). It may have taken further ages for individual eukaryotic and multicellular creatures to band together to care both for each other and their young. Human history likewise moves by stages from merely familial groupings to tribes and nations and cities.

---

12 George Berkeley, *Sermon on Charity: Sermons, Essays and Letters*, in *Works*, vol. 7, ed. A. A. Luce and T. E. Jessop (Edinburgh: Thomas Nelson, 1967), 36.

13 Olaf Stapledon, *The Opening of the Eyes*, ed. Agnes Stapledon (London: Methuen, 1954), 8.

14 Olaf Stapledon, *Philosophy and Living* (Harmondsworth: Penguin, 1939), 101.

Nowadays we must somehow find a way of assimilating, accommodating, learning from all manner of hitherto separate tribes, nations, and cultures. At the same time we have learnt to *record* our stories and discoveries in terms that anyone, of whatever tribal or linguistic origin, can, with an effort, discover and criticize. None of last century's evolutionary theorists and futurists quite envisaged the Internet, and the corresponding availability, in principle, of all recorded knowledge and fable to anyone. But they did expect that knowledge would always be increasing, and always available to "scientists." Few thought that there was any case *against* the coming Union. Those who imagined or hoped for a World Government most often reckoned that "scientists" — and perhaps especially "psychologists" — would be able to understand and guide all human beings into a fruitful peace (with or without their knowledge or consent). Stapledon, to be fair to him, was one of the few who noticed that there were many possible ideals, and that rebels against the Union might have a point. Eugenicists of the kind all-too-familiar in the thirties imagined that they could breed a "better" sort of humanity, but all the experiments that Stapledon imagines end in calamity, partly because the eugenicists themselves had no clear or sound ideas of what "better" means, and partly, as Plato knew, because the world disrupts our careful plans. Shall we breed for manual dexterity, or musical sensitivity, or ecological wholeness, or Great Brains ("huge bumps of curiosity equipped with cunning hands," operating "a very accurate behavioristic psychology," but with no inner understanding of their subjects, either civil or experimental),[15] or ecstatic flight (all of which ideals — and others — are explored in *Last and First Men*)?

And yet the hope or fantasy remains. May we not imagine that we could achieve a humane union, even incorporating other forms of life? Metz summarized the philosophy of "Ubuntu" as follows:

> An action is right just insofar as it promotes shared identity among people grounded on good-will; an act is wrong to the extent that it fails to do so and tends to encourage the opposites of division and ill-will.[16]

15 Stapledon, *Last and First Men*, 212.
16 Metz, "African Moral Theory," 338.

Do We Have a Future?

Nothing says that "people" here need only mean those of our own current species. May we not imagine that—over many millions of years—there could even be a society, or a someone, who could enjoy the cosmos as a whole, experiencing it from all its many places, and with every power it needed to sustain and improve that whole? Perhaps that will not happen until long after the stars are dead, and all remaining life is sustained by presently unknown processes, perhaps including Hawking radiation from black holes. How such a society or someone could communicate with itself over immeasurably many years and light years is hardly for us to say, or even to imagine. What it would find to do is also moot: supposing it would have reason, for example, to dream us into existence assumes too much about its wholly unknown psychology! So what is the point of the story? What would be its point even if we restrict the union to this Earth or this small solar system, leaving Laniakea to be? The hope, perhaps, is Peirce's: if truth is what would be decided at the end of all our enquiries, by enquirers wholly capable of understanding reasons, then we must hope that there will indeed be such an eventual decision. Maybe the thought experiment of "Wigner's Friend" has also some effect. Schrödinger proposed a thought experiment:

> One can even set up quite ridiculous cases. A cat is penned up in a steel chamber, along with the following diabolical device (which must be secured against direct interference by the cat): in a Geiger counter there is a tiny bit of radioactive substance, so small, that perhaps in the course of one hour one of the atoms decays, but also, with equal probability, perhaps none; if it happens, the counter tube discharges and through a relay releases a hammer which shatters a small flask of hydrocyanic acid.[17]

Until the container is opened, the thought goes, the cat is just as much "superpositioned" (both dead and alive, in multiply many postures) as the decay itself. It is usually forgotten that Schrödinger intended this as a

---

17 John D. Trimmer, "The Present Situation in Quantum Mechanics: A Translation of Schrödinger's 'Cat Paradox' paper [1935]," *Proceedings of the American Philosophical Society* 124.5 (1980): 323–338.

reductio ad absurdum of the whole idea that such events had no definite nature till they were observed — a story that some had thought could be confined to the atomic realm. Eugene Wigner, by considering instead how someone else might report on whether a photon has been observed by an experimenter, allows for a further development of Schrödinger's story: suppose the cat, the container and the experimentalist are all confined in a closed room. Until someone from outside opens the door to see, the whole system is similarly superpositioned: the experimentalist has both opened the container to find a dead cat, and opened it to find a living (once again, in all manner of different postures and locations).[18] This is one step towards a profligate Multiverse, in which all physically possible outcomes are equally real. Or else some final observer fixes the final outcome.

It seems to follow that either the Multiverse is, horribly, a fact, or else the "real" history of the cosmos will not have been decided until the very end, until the Final Unsurpassed Observer opens the final box. As the story so far goes this will not be any *decision* by the Observer: only what he/she/it/they happen to discover. But maybe we should hope for more. The Final Observer, let us say, *determines* what the history of the cosmos is. And are we here and now therefore already in that thread which the Final Observer vindicates, or are we rather one of the stories that will turn out never to have been at all? Might we give the Observer any reason to prefer *our* thread?[19] Or should we rather hope that he/she/it/they won't? "History is a nightmare from which I am trying to awake," so Joyce caused his Stephen Daedalus to say in response to a jolly anti-Semite.[20] Perhaps we should hope that the Final Observer has enough power, knowledge and empathy to discover the best available history, whether that decision is to ratify the history we "know" or to relegate us all to the realm of "might have been."

> There is no way to remove the observer — us — from our perceptions of the world.... In classical physics, the past is assumed to exist as a definite series of events, but according to quantum physics,

---

18   Eugene P. Wigner, "Remarks on the mind-body question," in I. J. Good, ed., *The Scientist Speculates* (London: Heinemann, 1961), 284–302.
19   The thought is explored by Stephen Baxter in *Timelike Infinity* (London: Collins, 1992).
20   James Joyce, *Ulysses* (Oxford: Oxford University Press, 1993 [1922]), 34.

Do We Have a Future?

the past, like the future, is indefinite and exists only as a spectrum of possibilities.[21]

Robert Lanza takes the point further:

> If we, the observer, collapse these possibilities (that is, the past and future) then where does that leave evolutionary theory, as described in our schoolbooks? Until the present is determined, how can there be a past? The past begins with the observer, us, not the other way around as we've been taught.[22]

As far as I know no evolutionary theorists have taken up the challenge posed by this suggestion, that our evolutionary past has been *selected*, or will have been selected, out of many possible lines that "were" in some sense equally real until the decision will someday have been taken.

THE DOOMSDAY ARGUMENT

It has at least been plausibly argued that we are most likely to be in or very near the largest generation of humankind: to suppose otherwise would be to violate the principle of mediocrity. If you were to find yourself, blindfolded, in a room containing an unknown number of people, and were told that there were indefinitely many rooms, each containing ten times the number of the previous room (from ten to who knows how many millions), you should bet that you are in the largest actual room. If you then found, once the blindfold was removed, that you were in a room containing only — let us say — five thousand, you would have less reason to believe that there were many or any rooms containing more.[23] An only slightly less daunting

---

21 Hawking and Mlodinow, *Grand Design*, 105.

22 Robert Lanza, "Why Are You Here? A New Theory May Hold the Missing Piece," *Huff-Post Contributor Platform* (11/12/2010; updated November 17, 2011); see also Robert Lanza and Bob Berman, *Biocentrism: How Life and Consciousness Are the Keys to Understanding the True Nature of the Universe* (Dallas: BenBella, 2009).

23 John Leslie, *The End of the World: Science and Ethics of Human Extinction* (London: Routledge, 1996), after Brandon Carter and W. H. McCrea, "The anthropic principle and its implications for biological evolution," *Philosophical Transactions of the Royal Society of London* 310.1512 (1983): 347–63 [doi:10.1098/rsta.1983.0096].

calculation[24] — the so-called Copernican Calculation — suggests that there is a 95% probability that humankind has something between 1/39th and 39 times its past yet to go: that is, that we are somewhere within the central 95% of its total span. Assuming that our species emerged circa 100,000 years ago, that leaves us anything between 2,500 and 3,900,000 years: but *civilization* "has been around for only 5,500 years, giving 95% confidence that its future longevity will be longer than 140 years but less than 214,000 years."[25] There is a 50/50 chance that we are in the middle third of civilized humanity, and there is somewhere between 1,667 and 15,000 years to go. So even if the species lasts considerably longer than we have any other good reason to expect, the probability is high that *civilization* — by which I mean an ordered society with written records and urban conglomerates — will have a much earlier end, and more probably, we may reasonably fear, within the next few hundred years. This is not, of course, a definite prediction. Since there *are* people in the smaller rooms, we may be amongst them. And there is a 5% chance that we lie outside the central 95% (and the end may as easily come tomorrow as in half a million years). It may turn out that we here-now are *astonishingly* early hominins, and that practically every human person who ever lives will live in artificial habitats orbiting black holes, long after the last star has died (assuming that these far-future descendants would be willing to think themselves human), or in the Great Redoubt of Hodgson's Night Land. It is easy to think that something like this is plausible, until we realize how odd it would make our own present perspective on the world. The point of the arguments is to make it clear that such futures cannot be expected with any confidence. Certainly, if they are valid, then all previous generations should also have been convinced by them — and all those previous generations, it now seems, would have been wrong. We have already lasted longer than the ancient Egyptians would have had reason to expect, and may in turn outlast the Pyramids. But we shouldn't count on it. "Can you tell me, in a world that is flagrant with the failure of civilisations, what there is particularly immortal about yours?"[26]

---

24 Richard J. Gott, *Time Travel in Einstein's Universe* (London: Weidenfeld & Nicolson, 2001), 206ff.
25 Ibid., 224.
26 G. K. Chesterton, *The Napoleon of Notting Hill* (Harmondsworth: Penguin, 1946 [1904]), 25.

Do We Have a Future?

So what might our future be? Two improbable stories both rely on our being improbably early hominins. In one, the species spreads up into the heavens, inhabiting human technospheres around and between the stars.[27] Someday there will be as many human species as there are vertebrate. In another, we remain here on the Earth, populating its least crevice until the sun expands into its red giant phase: maybe our descendants will then emigrate, if not to Neptune (as Stapledon imagined), then to some Outer Moon. In that future, there will probably only be a single species, markedly homogeneous, unless we choose to breed or engineer sub-species for particular rôles and habitats. Either way, most human beings will prove to have lived long after us — and that is what is improbable. The first story can be checked for plausibility another way: if it were at all likely that our species would one day rule the heavens, we must assume that it is even likelier that some other kind already does. Astronomical and historical phenomena should routinely be explained as engineering work by the Great Galactics. If that is not an acceptable account, then neither is the prediction of our own success. "The answer to Fermi's question [why the Great Galactics are not already here] ... is that a significant proportion of all intelligent observers must still be sitting on their home planet, just like you: otherwise, you would be special."[28] The second story (that humankind will fully colonize and cultivate the Earth, but go no further) presumes a power and knowledge in some ways greater than would be needed to spread beyond the Earth. At least we could *experiment* with building extraterrestrial habitats: conducting an experiment inside and on our only home would hasten our extinction more probably than defer it. So the more probable scenario must be that human population will soon begin to decrease, whether catastrophically or by degrees. Civilization will begin to be eroded, falling back from its global peak into more isolated enclaves, until at last our descendants — like other human populations such as the Tupi-Guarani[29] — abandon the decaying and laborious cities to recreate themselves as human animals reliant on

---

27 Stephen R. L. Clark, "From Biosphere to Technosphere," *Ends and Means* 5 (2001): 3–21.
28 Gott, *Time Travel*, 237.
29 See Pierre Clastres, *Society against the State: Essays in Political Anthropology*, trans. Robert Hurley (Brooklyn: Zone Books, 1987 [1974]).

oral histories within the larger jungle. That jungle may be the merely biological one — or it may even be a technosphere of sorts, populated by machinery grown autonomous.

So the more probable future of our species, contrary to happy expectations of continued progress or expansion, is one in which our descendants will look back with puzzlement, awe or horror at a vastly inflated urban order, whose relics will be largely uninterpretable by those who follow after: the story has been often told, by Crowley and Hoban amongst others. Indeed, it was told, by implication, long ago, by Aristotle.[30] The argument does not predict that the outcome is immediate: *probably* you and I, and even our grandchildren, will still be living high, for some decades to come. The argument does not predict that the outcome I have described is certain: *possibly*, our great-grandchildren will have taken the first steps to "Forever," and be spreading out across the universe, hoping to remodel everything before the End. And if they do succeed, we might even imagine that they will also create experimental enclaves where they can play at being early hominins! Maybe we are indeed living in the largest array of humankind, but are simply deluded about our actual situation. Perhaps this is a virtual universe, a collective hallucination, from which we shall wake into the unimaginable company of all intelligence, the literally infinite array of being. But though I think that story *possible*, it would be very odd to say that it was certain. An only slightly less surprising story — that the colonization period has already happened, but that all colonies (including the one that we call home) regress — might allow there to be many unknown civilizations Out There as long as almost none of them turn into the Great Galactics. And though that story too is *possible*, it does not predict that *we* are likely to be the colonizers. Over all, we had better, sudden revelation aside, conclude, as before, that civilization is not here to stay, and that the species itself will not survive forever, nor even for as long as extinct species of the remoter past. If you continue to doubt that possibility, recall the flocks of passenger pigeons that once filled the skies, no more than a century or so ago. Remember bison. Remember, for that matter, that Rome and Babylon are fallen.

30 *On Philosophy*, fr. 8 Rose, in Ross, *Works of Aristotle*, 12:77 [fr.10]; cf. John Crowley, *Engine Summer* (London: Gollancz, 2013 [1979]); Russell Hoban, *Riddley Walker* (London: Jonathan Cape, 1980).

Do We Have a Future?

> Cities and Thrones and Powers
> Stand, in Time's eye,
> Almost as long as flowers,
> Which daily die:
> But, as new buds put forth
> To glad new men,
> Out of the spent and unconsidered Earth
> The Cities rise again.
> This season's Daffodil,
> She never hears,
> What change, what chance, what chill,
> Cut down last year's;
> But with bold countenance,
> And knowledge small,
> Esteems her seven days' continuance
> To be perpetual.
> To Time that is o'er kind
> To all that be,
> Ordains us e'en as blind,
> As bold as she:
> That in our very death,
> And burial sure,
> Shadow to shadow, well persuaded, saith,
> "See how our works endure!"[31]

If Babylon is fallen—and if we too shall yet see Babylon fall—how can we reorient our lives, in prospect, for that other life? Is there, by the way, a paradox here? By the account I am giving, almost all the years of humankind's existence will probably be occupied by humans who live in small groups and enclaves, without any expectation that they rule the world. So if that is so, are we not special after all? No paradox: most

---

31 Rudyard Kipling, *Rudyard Kipling's Verse: Definitive Edition* (London: Hodder & Stoughton, 1940), 479. This is not to endorse the false analogy that treats species and cultures as mortal individuals, as though they must *inevitably* grow old and die. It is only to agree that species and cultures *do* end.

individual human beings will prove to have lived in civilization's heyday, but the aeons of non-civilized existence will, most probably, prove longer.

And how will Babylon fall? To that, we need have no single answer. Nineteenth-century fantasy envisaged plague. Twentieth — especially towards its end — expected war or famine. We may now think about the confluence of disasters issuing from climate change on the one hand and radical injustice on the other: flood, drought, the death of oceans, mass migration and the use by alienated individuals of powers that have been cultivated by civilized states for their own purposes. Maybe we shall so transform ourselves through nanotechnology, genetic engineering and computer interfaces as to bring about an end of singular intelligence (and so avoid the Carter Catastrophe by reducing the number of intelligences and exalting their power). Or we may prefer to contemplate a future in which our artefacts become the masters: perhaps by the bloody means employed in *Terminator* or by more gradual enchantments (nanotechnology, genetic engineering and computer interfaces). Meteor strikes, solar flares and supernovae, unpredictable variations and transformations of the underlying structure of space-time, and yet more unpredictable invasions by the Great Galactics, all feature in our nightmares or our wistful dreams. But the end need not be sudden. Only the weight of habit holds us to the daily round, the common task, which hide from us the gradual changes that will be evident to all a little later. *Then* our descendants or supplanters will look back and wonder how we could have been so blind (but they will be blind too).

If you and I here-now are really citizens of the Infinite City, disguised as early hominins, then the focus of our real lives is not the *expected* future: living for that extrapolated world is living for an illusion. If, on the other hand, we really are alive here-now, we have much less reason than we sleepily suppose to think that our future is a gradual improvement and expansion of our present civilized condition. Either way, we had better not focus wholly on an expected future: let us instead look sideways, "out of time." The present moment is our only opening. Consider an older allegory: the chances of being born *human*, a Buddhist text informs us, is as if a blind turtle swimming in the Great Ocean were inadvertently to poke its head out through a single life-belt floating at random in that

Ocean.[32] A more modern allegory could rest on Gott's suggestion that our only way of improving the survival chances of our species and our civilization is to seize the opportunity to spread out from the Earth, an opportunity that is vanishingly unlikely to recur.[33] Our very existence as creatures capable of changing the focus of our attention is so wildly improbable — on most naturalistic assumptions — that we would be very foolish to imagine that we shall have another chance. But I am less assured than Gott that the Great Migration would make us much less vulnerable: it is possible it might, in a way, be safer than to leave all humankind upon one fragile Earth. But by the same token such an expansion of our borders would increase the chances of encountering something lethal, and the diaspora itself would generate new kinds and internecine wars. The Copernican Calculation and Carter Catastrophe will always apply, and every age of humankind will have some reason to think that it will be the last. I am temperamentally inclined to vote with Gott, and to take the chance — but Diaspora is not the real answer.

> The human diaspora, the human scattering, is the *problem*... The rate of growth that sustains the technological capacity that makes civilization possible is now exceeding the rate of cultural adaptation, and distance is exceeding our communications. The end will become more and more like the beginning, scattered tribes of humans across an endless plain, in pointless conflict — or isolate stagnation.[34]

So our ancestors were right: we should not suppose that *here* we have a continuing city (cf. Heb 13:14), but rather look sideways, "out of time and to eternity," from the eternal now. As long as we think of here and now as being this very place and moment, we must admit that it is always being lost, and that our extrapolated futures will not come to pass in quite the way we think of them. Notoriously, to make God laugh we need only tell Him

---

32 Bhikku Bodhi, *The Connected Discourses of the Buddha: A Translation of the Samyutta Nikaya* (Somerville, MA: Wisdom Publications, 2000), 1871–72 [Saccasamyutta 47–48].

33 Gott, *Time Travel*, 232.

34 C. J. Cherryh, *Cyteen* (London: NEL, 1989), 472.

our plans. Sacrificing the present for the sake of the future is suicidal. Nor can a merely material, temporal future ever be enough to satisfy us. "If the many become the same as the few when possess'd, More! More! is the cry of a mistaken soul; less than All cannot satisfy Man."[35]

So the moral of my story about the future of our species must be just this: don't live for any imagined future; time is always short. Seize the occasion to look outward, whether literally or analogically. The peril in that advice is that it may seem to support the short-termism or presentism of too many of our present leaders, cued to respond to immediate crisis without any care to consider where their response will lead. To look aside to eternity is to seek that pattern of living which is appropriate to *any* age and climate, not simply to discount the future in the name of a present passion. The peril that we face — which may be the proximate cause of our expectable decline — is our concern with short-term *outcomes* at the expense of *values*. Short-term expediency in forgetfulness of the eternal and without any imaginative grasp of a likely future almost guarantees that the temporal end is near.

IN THE BEGINNING, GOD

Religion often offers inspiration rather than explanation, a project rather than a metaphysic. This is not to say that there are no metaphysical implications of standard religious theses, and especially of theistic forms. We could not easily convince ourselves that "all shall be well, and all shall be well, and all manner of thing shall be well," as Julian of Norwich assured us,[36] in a cosmos that is not governed, in the end, by some enduring moral purpose. But the hope is founded on a present experience, or a prayer, rather than a metaphysical, still less a "scientific," inquiry.

> Quick now, here, now, always—
> A condition of complete simplicity
> (Costing not less than everything)
> And all shall be well and
> All manner of thing shall be well

---

35 Blake, *Complete Writings*, 97.
36 Julian, *Revelations of Divine Love*, trans. Barry Windeatt (Oxford: Oxford University Press, 2015), 74 [ch. 27].

Do We Have a Future?

> When the tongues of flame are in-folded
> Into the crowned knot of fire
> And the fire and the rose are one.[37]

As Plantinga has acidly remarked in a review of Daniel Dennett's work *Darwin's Dangerous Idea*,

> [Christians] don't *postulate* the existence of God, as if this were a scientific hypothesis of some kind. They don't typically propose the existence of God (let alone other characteristic Christian doctrines, such as Trinity, Incarnation, Atonement) as a kind of *hypothesis*, designed to explain organized complexity or other phenomena. They don't believe in God because God's existence and activity is a good hypothesis, a good explanation of organized complexity in the world. When God spoke to Moses from the burning bush, Moses didn't say, "Hey, look at that weird bush! It's on fire but isn't burning up! And listen to those sounds coming out of it! What's the best explanatory hypothesis I can think of? Perhaps there is an all-knowing, all-powerful wholly good being who created the world, and he is addressing me from that bush. Yes, that must be it, that's a good explanation of the phenomena."[38]

Of course, as he also adds, the doctrine may turn out to explain many other things, once it has been conceived and properly considered, but its beginning is in "faith," which is to say, in an immediate response of trust and admiration to a perceived revelation or ambition. The beginning of Mosaic theism is the demand "to let My people go," and the subsequent display of a program of mutual respect and civil order. The people were given that choice between Life and Death that, so the story has it, our first ancestors thoroughly muffed. The revelation or insistence that "death shall have no dominion" (Rom 6:9), and that justice will in the end be done, is a promise or a project, not an hypothesis.

---

37 T. S. Eliot, "Little Gidding," *Four Quartets* (London: Faber, 1944), 43.
38 Alvin Plantinga, "Darwin, Mind and Meaning," *Books and Culture*, May/June 1996.

> The opening statement [of Genesis] that in the beginning God created the world ... was not meant as a speculation about the origin of the natural order in past history at all, but rather as a poem about the world which *could* be created by God-in-man if man lived up to his full human stature; nature appears in the story as the No-thing out of which the world is to be made, the chance realm which is fundamentally "without form and void," although it throws up, purely *by* chance, patterns which can be starting-points for creating a world.[39]

"Nature," in the Hebrew Scriptures, is not the unalterable context of all our actions, nor the pattern by which we need to rule our lives. Aristotle, like most other Greek philosophers, was concerned with what happens "always or for the most part" as the proper subject of "scientific" inquiry (*Metaphysics* 6.1027a), and a fairly reliable guide to what we need to do (though not a final one: a topic I touch on in a little while). The Israelites knew better: it is the anomalous happening, the unpredictable opportunity, that opens the way for us. Abram's father Terah leaves Ur of the Chaldees and its astrological governance behind; so also Abram leaves Haran and is transformed to Abraham. Gideon requires his God to provide assurance of victory by ensuring both that a fleece is wet in the morning after being left out all-night and that next day it is dry (Jdg 6:36–40). Elijah summons fire to burn up the wet offering (and so defeat the priests of Baal, 1 Kgs 18:20–40).[40] Wren-Lewis identified this shift of attention with the growth of modern science, which also depends on noticing anomalies, and of modern technology, which is not content with how things worked before. "Potent Man ... constantly strives to use matter to express the creativity of his own inner life."[41]

---

39 Wren-Lewis, "What I Believe," 236.

40 Was the pyre drenched in *water*, or in some more combustible, purificatory, liquid, naphtha (see 2 Macc 1:19–36)? If the latter, this was not a cheat, but a demonstration that things aren't what they seem, but may be what we need!

41 Wren-Lewis, *What Shall We Tell*, 70. It is unfortunate that Wren-Lewis thought, without thinking clearly, solely about "Man" rather than Humanity, or even, more broadly, Life: like Blake, perhaps, he was inclined, at least at that stage of his life, to equate "Nature," "the Female" and "Oppression": "Thou, Mother of my mortal part," said Blake, "With cruelty didst mould my heart, / And with false self-deceiving tears / Didst bind my nostrils, eyes, and ears; / Didst close my tongue in senseless clay, / And me to mortal life betray: / The death of Jesus set me

Do We Have a Future?

But though there is some force in Wren-Lewis's exegesis, he seems not to have fully noticed that Genesis says God *created* that formless void. His own story more closely resembles the original "Bronze Age Myth," according to which the Primeval Mound, Atum, the very first thing, simply appeared from Emptiness, and then proliferated, via paired forces, into the world of "persons" and dysfunctional families who gradually made a *human* world from Chaos.[42] Similarly in Babylon, Apsu plots against the younger gods and is destroyed by Ea, who in turn gives way to Marduk who fights with his grandmother Tiamat and her new monstrous offspring. According to the Hittite text, Kumarbi castrates Anu, swallows the phallus and so bears Weather and the Euphrates.[43] In each case complexity and personality gradually emerge from Chaos, younger gods seize their power from the older, and peace is somehow established. Or rather, Law is established: "Peace" is projected back into the rule of Kronos, or of Osiris before his murder. Ethiopians (Homer, *Iliad* 1.421–422) and Hyperboreans may somehow retain their innocence, but we here-now can only rely on Law, on the order that we, somehow, establish. And Law won't last:

> The father will not agree with his children, nor the children with their father, nor guest with his host, nor comrade with comrade; nor will brother be dear to brother as aforetime. Men will dishonor their parents as they grow quickly old, and will carp at them, chiding them with bitter words, hard-hearted they, not knowing the fear of the gods. They will not repay their aged parents the cost of their nurture, for might shall be their right: and one man will sack another's city. There will be no favor for the man who keeps his oath or for the just or for the good; but rather men will praise the evil-doer and his violent dealing. Strength will be right and reverence will cease to be; and the wicked will hurt the worthy man, speaking false words against him, and will swear an oath upon

---

free: / Then what have I to do with thee?" (Blake, *Complete Works*, 22: "To Tirzah" [1801]).

42 See Jan Assmann, *Moses the Egyptian* (Cambridge, MA: Harvard University Press, 1997); Erik Hornung, *Conceptions of God in Ancient Egypt*, trans. John Baines (Ithaca, NY: Cornell University Press, 1982).

43 Walter Burkert, *Babylon, Memphis, Persepolis: Eastern Contexts of Greek Culture* (Cambridge, MA: Harvard University Press, 2004), 92.

them. Envy, foul-mouthed, delighting in evil, with scowling face, will go along with wretched men one and all. And then *Aidos* and *Nemesis* [that is, Shame and Indignation], with their sweet forms wrapped in white robes, will go from the wide-pathed earth and forsake mankind to join the company of the deathless gods: and bitter sorrows will be left for mortal men, and there will be no help against evil. (Hesiod, *Works and Days* 175–201)

What human beings have created, human beings can also dismantle: Chesterton made the remark in optimistic vein, with reference to the overthrow of ancient tyranny, symbolized in the Bastille.

> The destruction of the Bastille was not a reform; it was something more important than a reform. It was an iconoclasm; it was the breaking of a stone image. The people saw the building like a giant looking at them with a score of eyes, and they struck at it as at a carved fact. For of all the shapes in which that immense illusion called materialism can terrify the soul, perhaps the most oppressive are big buildings. Man feels like a fly, an accident, in the thing he has himself made. It requires a violent effort of the spirit to remember that man made this confounding thing and man could unmake it. Therefore the mere act of the ragged people in the street taking and destroying a huge public building has a spiritual, a ritual meaning far beyond its immediate political results. It is a religious service. If, for instance, the Socialists were numerous or courageous enough to capture and smash up the Bank of England, you might argue for ever about the inutility of the act, and how it really did not touch the root of the economic problem in the correct manner. But mankind would never forget it. It would change the world.[44]

Sadly, we can also dismantle whatever *good* we create (and of course the world can do the job for us as well).

---

44 G. K. Chesterton, *Tremendous Trifles* (London: Methuen, 1904), 18.

Do We Have a Future?

So Potent Man may after all be nothing but a dream: as Pindar put it: "man is a shadow's dream (*skias onar*)." He added, more consolingly, that "when (a) god sheds a brightness then shining light is on earth, and life is as sweet as honey" (*Pythian* 8.95–97). Wren-Lewis himself came to realize that the life he had himself devised was transient, and correspondingly that our hopes of a grand remaking of the cosmos were jejune. His marriage, his Anglican identity and his career in science collapsed because he could not believe that they were founded in anything more reliable than the wishful thinking he had blamed for other people's belief in a hidden, humane order. The glory went away. He was saved from penury, as he says, "by the fact that [his] writings apparently contained sufficient insights of inspirational or scholarly value to cause people in various parts of the world to want [his] occasional services as a teacher."

By 1983 Wren-Lewis was unhappily convinced that there was no chance of finding any transcendental or even *apparently* transcendental element in human experience. It was then, on a bus in Thailand during a joint investigation, with his second wife Ann Faraday, of shamanic practices amongst the Senoi, that he was poisoned almost to death, and had a near death experience which transformed his life:

> I came round with a radically "altered state of consciousness" wherein the mundane shell of so-called ordinary human life was completely gone. Subjectively the state was utterly different from anything I'd experienced with psychedelics (or for that matter in experiments with trance or meditation), but more significantly, *it has remained with me ever since*, an effect not found with any drug yet known. In fact this consciousness feels so utterly natural that terms like "drugged" or "tranced" seem more appropriate for my earlier life, and I now know firsthand, from more than ten years' continuing daily (and nightly) experience, why at the mystical core of most religious traditions there is found the notion of "awakening" from an age-long collective human nightmare. I also know from firsthand experience why those who've actually experienced mystical wakening so often resort to paradox or negation when trying to say anything about it, and frequently resort to terms like

"ineffable." Almost all human speech derives from that old collective nightmare of separate individuals struggling in an alien space-time world for survival, satisfaction and meaning, whereas I now experience myself and everyone else — indeed every thing else — as more like the continuous dance-like activity of a universal, truly infinite Consciousness/Aliveness whose very nature is satisfaction and "meaning" in an eternal Presentness, from which Separation (space) and activity (time) are continuously created. This must surely be what terms like God-consciousness originally meant, yet from the ordinary human perspective such theological expressions inevitably suggest a separate human "me" being conscious of God. My experience, however, is God — Infinite Aliveness — cognizing me (and everyone and everything else) into existence instant by instant, and this consciousness finds everything "very good." And this must surely also be what Hinduism and Buddhism mean by Nirvana extinguishing the illusion of separate selfhood, though from the ordinary human standpoint such expressions have a punitive sound. My sense, by contrast, is of selfhood as the continuing product of infinite lovingness, which to my never-ceasing astonishment takes the sting of suffering out of even the most humanly "unpleasant" situations, including the prospect of personal extinction. And so it is that mystical awakening, which came to me by a complete act of grace (through something remarkably like a literal process of death and resurrection), has enabled me late in life to find meaning I never suspected in a great many of humanity's religious attempts to express transcendence. Yet because it is a meaning so utterly at odds with all conventional understanding of such expressions, I can now see very clearly why, at each phase of my earlier life, heart-opening always came more through breaking away from religious forms than from conforming to them. I now look back with gratitude on all those earlier struggles with religion as my personal twentieth century version of what mystical traditions have called the Way of Negation.[45]

---

45 John Wren-Lewis, "The Dazzling Dark: A Near-Death Experience Opens the Door to a Permanent Transformation" [www.nonduality.com/dazdark.htm and www.angelfire.com/electronic/awakening101/dazzledark.html (accessed June 15, 2019)]; see also Wren-Lewis,

Do We Have a Future?

In other and still more detailed attempts to talk around the unsayable — reminiscent indeed of Plotinus's humorous efforts to do the same — Wren-Lewis described his experience, using a phrase of Henry Vaughan, as of a "dazzling darkness":[46]

> It was as if I'd emerged freshly made (complete with all the memories that constitute my personal identity) from a vast blackness that was somehow radiant, a kind of infinitely concentrated aliveness or pure consciousness that had no separation within it, and therefore no space or time.[47]

This experience, he said, did not convince him of any post-mortem personal existence, but rather of the irrelevance of that idea: it was as if his personal consciousness had been, was continually being, recreated from an infinite and eternal joy.

> It feels quintessentially natural that personal consciousness should be aware of its own Ground, while my first fifty-nine years of so-called "normal" consciousness, in ignorance of that Ground, now seem like a kind of waking dream. It was as if I'd been entranced from birth into a collective nightmare of separate individuals struggling in an alien universe for survival, satisfaction and significance.

The details of Wren-Lewis's revelation are not my present concern.[48] The thought that he acknowledges, and that reverses his earlier attacks on a "transcendent" and "hidden" order, is that we here-now are dreaming — as Marcus Aurelius said, our lives are but a "dream and a delirium" (*Meditations*

"A Mystical Awakening," in Monica Furlong, ed., *Our Childhood's Pattern: Memories of Growing Up Christian* (London: Mowbrays, 1995), 107–23: 121–23.

46 Henry Vaughan, *Silex Scintillans* (Charleston: Bibliobazaar, 2008 [1650]), 300.

47 Wren-Lewis, "Dazzling Dark"; see also Wren-Lewis "The darkness of God: A personal report on consciousness transformation through an encounter with death," *Journal of Humanistic Psychology* 28 (1988): 105–22.

48 Stephen R. L. Clark, "The Case of John Wren-Lewis," in Victoria Harrison and Harriet Harris, eds., *Atheisms* (forthcoming): a talk originally addressed to the biennial conference of the *British Society for Philosophy of Religion* in 2013.

2.17.1), and that there is a chance of waking (though not one that Aurelius could comprehend). So what might the "real world" be? We can imagine, playfully, that we are living in a Virtual Reality devised by the alien powers of the End Time, or even by more easily recognized engineers a few centuries in advance of the age in which we dream we're living. The truth of the story probably makes little difference to our lives: even if it is so, we cannot anticipate our waking, and must abide by the rules of the game our makers or directors set. But what if the story is a myth, a metaphor, expressing a deeper reality, namely that this world here, "the cloud-capped towers, the gorgeous palaces, the solemn temples, the great globe itself" (Shakespeare, *The Tempest*, Act 4, scene 1) can be wrapped up as a garment, to be put aside (Heb 1:12)? What will then stand revealed? Can we really suppose that the real and eternal world is populated only by abstract intelligences, divorced from any biological companionship? Or should we rather suppose that the connections and affections we experience even in the dream are hints or echoes of the larger world?

> The capacity to see the divine dimension of other creatures is readily imbricated or interwoven with *biophilia*, the sense of solidarity most people have with other creatures, and their love for the richness and diversity of the more-than-human world. The term "*biophilia*" was coined by E. O. Wilson, the great evolutionary biologist, to indicate, in part, that loving other creatures is not something that lifts human beings out of Nature, but is rather an instinct that comes from Nature, and from our nature. He writes, "humanity is exalted not because we are so far above other living creatures, but because knowing [the other creatures] well elevates the very concept of life." By understanding our desire for the more-than-human world, and binding ourselves to other creatures in this way, we are enriching the meaning of our own humanity. According to Wilson, who is in this point remarkably parallel to Rav [Avraham Yitshak] Kook (1865–1935), our humanity is enriched because we are enriching the meaning of Life itself. This provides a wonderful, holistic picture of humankind's uniqueness, one that complements the holistic anthropology of the rabbis and that helps

us make sense of our purpose in relation to the whole of Creation. In this vein, *biophilia* may be understood as a uniquely human power that connects us to both the Creator and to Creation, and is part of God's image within us.[49]

Though once again the claim to be *unique* in this seems to have no clear warrant. And the implications for our moral and political lives seem unexplored, or not acted on.

There is also an ethical dimension to the insight that we should focus on the exceptional, the anomalous, the strange. It is tempting to equate "what happens always or for the most part" with what generally *ought* to happen, and to treat anyone or anything that deviates from that pattern as "freakish," "abnormal," "unnatural," and the like. If human beings (and most other vertebrates) are either male or female, then anyone who is "betwixt and between," either in biological sex or in gender stereotype, is to be "re-educated" as forcefully as the left-handed once were. If God created humanity as male and female, separated from some primordial unity so as to achieve a different sort of community, then such a conjunction is normative, and all other sorts of coupling are to be deplored or punished. But the world, and humankind, is not so rigidly confined. There are always "inbetweeners" in any workable taxonomy, and always fresh ways of achieving

---

49 Seidenberg, *Kabbalah*, 171, citing E. O. Wilson, *Biophilia* (Cambridge, MA: Harvard University Press, 1984), 22. See also Francis *Laudato Si'*, §92: "Moreover, when our hearts are authentically open to universal communion, this sense of fraternity excludes nothing and no one. It follows that our indifference or cruelty towards fellow creatures of this world sooner or later affects the treatment we mete out to other human beings. We have only one heart, and the same wretchedness which leads us to mistreat an animal will not be long in showing itself in our relationships with other people. Every act of cruelty towards any creature is 'contrary to human dignity' (*Catechism* 2418). We can hardly consider ourselves to be fully loving if we disregard any aspect of reality: 'Peace, justice and the preservation of creation are three absolutely interconnected themes, which cannot be separated and treated individually without once again falling into reductionism' (Conference of Dominican Bishops, Pastoral Letter *Sobre la relación del hombre con la naturaleza*, 21 January 1987). Everything is related, and we human beings are united as brothers and sisters on a wonderful pilgrimage, woven together by the love God has for each of his creatures and which also unites us in fond affection with brother sun, sister moon, brother river and mother earth." It does not seem to me that either Francis or the Catholic Church in general has properly internalized the implications of this rhetoric — any more than the writers of the American Declaration of Independence fully grasped or acted on the logic of their axioms.

a companionable life. It will indeed often be exactly such inbetweeners who are most creatively and piously engaged. But this is a topic too large for the present volume, especially in the light of the recent rise of homophobic and racist movements.

One further gloss: in speaking at times of the forms or norms or ideals which we, and all created beings, are called to realize, I may seem to be suggesting that there is already a completed pattern, an eternal and unchanging Word. The best world, even if it is one that cannot be fully realized in time, is complete and stable. That would indeed seem to be the implication of a consistent pagan Platonism: whatever of beauty is encountered here is only a shadow of eternal beauty, a fragment from the always completed whole. The nature of our experience is to take things one by one, piecemeal, as though we were circling an unchanging mountain, seeing it from one angle or one distance or another, with whatever different eyes. All moments of our experience are equally real, equally partial, aspects of the eternal. But maybe there is another way of considering the world. Maybe really *new* beauties are created, always: we are not engaged only in *discovering* beauty, but actively cooperating, however clumsily, with God or the gods to make "many and beautiful things," as Socrates and Euthyphro agreed (Plato, *Euthyphro* 13b–14b). Those beautiful things are *new*. The whole strange process of evolutionary change is an open-ended exploration of the possibilities, not simply a process set to converge on a pre-established harmony. Time itself is perhaps more real, more innovative, than philosophers and physicists have usually supposed. What will happen next is not now determined.

"Eternity is in love with the productions of time."[50]

---

50 Blake, "Marriage of Heaven and Hell," 7.10, in *Complete Works*, 151.

CONCLUSION

So how shall we conceive humanity, in the context of a world immensely larger, older, stranger than our ancestors imagined? Its size and age, as I have indicated, are not "objective" factors: if we see with anything like a God's-eye view, then the whole cosmos may be no more than a hazelnut, "round as a ball," in a human hand, which "will last and always will, because God loves it."[1] That it is a lot stranger than we thought should have been no surprise: "'my thoughts are not your thoughts, neither are your ways my ways', declares the Lord. 'As the heavens are higher than the earth, so are my ways higher than your ways and my thoughts than your thoughts'" (Is 55:8–9). "Truth must of necessity be stranger than fiction."[2]

Most of us sophists and intellectuals, while complimenting ourselves on noticing this truth, still reckon that our intellectual gifts, our pattern-sensing habits, our logical investigations, are what we can rely upon to find "the Mind of God," or "think God's thoughts" for ourselves. We barely notice the additional maxim, that *children* are the ones who "own" the Kingdom (Mk 10:14): not because children are always innocent (they aren't) or playful, happy and adventurous (they aren't), nor even because they are moved by love more than by rational calculation (some sometimes are), but solely because they are children, and must rely on others. Just occasionally, perhaps, their faces show that awed delight in beauty that, perhaps, is what we all should feel. Occasionally, perhaps, all adults feel that same irrational, unconditional affection that is the source of beauty.

> Let us suppose we are confronted with a desperate thing—say Pimlico. If we think what is really best for Pimlico we shall find the thread of thought leads to the throne of the mystic and the arbitrary. It is not enough for a man to disapprove of Pimlico; in that case he will merely cut his throat or move to Chelsea. Nor, certainly, is it enough for a man to approve of Pimlico; for then it will remain

---

1 Julian, *Revelations*, 45 [ch. 5].
2 Chesterton, *Club of Queer Trades*, 82.

Can We Believe in People?

> Pimlico, which would be awful. The only way out of it seems to be for somebody to love Pimlico; to love it with a transcendental tie and without any earthly reason. If there arose a man who loved Pimlico, then Pimlico would rise into ivory towers and golden pinnacles; Pimlico would attire herself as a woman does when she is loved. For decoration is not given to hide horrible things; but to decorate things already adorable. A mother does not give her child a blue bow because he is so ugly without it. A lover does not give a girl a necklace to hide her neck. If men loved Pimlico as mothers love children, arbitrarily, because it is *theirs*, Pimlico in a year or two might be fairer than Florence. Some readers will say that this is mere fantasy. I answer that this is the actual history of mankind. This, as a fact, is how cities did grow great. Go back to the darkest roots of civilization and you will find them knotted round some sacred stone or encircling some sacred well. People first paid honour to a spot and afterwards gained glory for it. Men did not love Rome because she was great. She was great because they had loved her.[3]

Though perhaps they came to love her later for all the wrong reasons, after all.

Everything that is, so Plotinus said, depends on something to make it one rather than many disparate and dissolving parts. Its welfare, as well as its being, depends on how well it is focused.

> It is like a choral dance: in the order of its singing the choir keeps round its *koruphaios* but may sometimes turn away so that he is out of their sight, but when it turns back to him it sings beautifully and is truly with him; so we are always around him—and if we were not, we should be totally dissolved and no longer exist—but not always turned towards him; but when we do look to him, then we are at our goal and at rest and do not sing out of tune as we truly dance our god-inspired dance around him.[4]

---

3 Chesterton, *Orthodoxy*, 47.
4 Plotinus, *Ennead* VI.9 [9].8, 38ff.

Conclusion

In the ancient chorus that "*koruphaios*" is the lead dancer, or perhaps the musician seated in the center of the dance: in Plato's account, that is the god, Apollo, "who sits in the center, on the navel of the earth, and is the interpreter of religion to all mankind" (*Republic* 4.427c).[5] Abrahamists may similarly be directed towards the Unknowable God, recognizing that their very best conception of that God must always fall short of His reality. All three main branches of the Abrahamic tradition also recognize the importance of that God's self-expression, both in the Word by which the world was (is) made, and the Spirit that gazes back at its Origin. For Jews that Word is the Torah, or the Wisdom it embodies:

> In human practice, when a mortal king builds a palace, he builds it not with his own skills, but with those of an architect. Moreover, the architect does not build it out of his head, but employs plans and diagrams to know how to arrange the chambers and the wicket doors. Thus God consulted the Torah and created the world, while the Torah declares, "In the beginning God created" (Gen 1:1), "beginning" referring to the Torah, as in the verse, "The Lord made me as the beginning of His way" (Prov. 8:22).[6]

Generally that Wisdom is reckoned the first thing that God *made*, before the foundation of the world, and is everlasting rather than eternal — but perhaps the logic of the story must be that it is rather *uncreated*: how, save by Wisdom herself, could He have made Wisdom? Plotinus too insisted that "it is already clear that the thought of [for example] a horse existed if [God] wanted to make a horse; so that it is not possible for him to think

---

5 See further in my forthcoming commentary on *Ennead VI.9* (Las Vegas: Parmenides Press, 2020).

6 *Bereisheet Rabbah* [c. 500 AD] 1:10, cited by Yakov Z. Meyer, "Parashat Teruma: The Primordial Torah," *Haaretz*, January 30, 2014: "In the way of the world, a king of flesh and blood who builds a castle does not do so from his own knowledge, but rather from the knowledge of an architect, and the architect does not build it from his own knowledge, but rather he has scrolls and books in order to know how to make rooms and doorways. So too Hashem gazed into the Torah and created the world. Similarly the Torah says, 'Through the reishis Hashem created [the heavens and the earth],' and reishis means Torah, as in 'Hashem made me [the Torah] the beginning (reishis) of His way' (Mishlei [*Proverbs*] 8:22)" [www.sefaria.org/Bereishit_Rabbah.1.1?lang=bi, accessed November 10, 2018].

it in order to make it, but the horse which did not come into being must exist before that which was to be afterwards" (*Ennead* VI.7 [38].8, 6–9). The blueprint, or the Will and Reason expressed in the blueprint, always precedes the building. "How can the Logos, being the Counsel and Will of the Father, come into being Himself by an act of will and purpose?"[7] Muslims (or at least Sunni Muslims) seem to have drawn the same conclusion: the Koran, as the Wisdom of God and the plan for creation, is itself *uncreated*.[8] Christians also affirm that the Word is "begotten and not made": not an arbitrary or contingent thing, but someone (with many caveats about the appropriateness of that language), not merely some thing, and "of one substance with the Father." The surprising notion that defines the Christian branch is that this Word "became flesh and dwelt among us," not simply as a fixed, authoritative text but as a "person," a human animal, subject to the same laws as ourselves. He is the true "image and likeness" of God, with whom we can, perhaps, be united, "through the breaking of bread." He is also the representative, and template, of all created being.

Is that story now incredible? Or is it only, as it always was, surprising? Those who believe that only that is true which can be proved true by impeccable extrapolation from known truths may still decline to believe it — but that rule has notorious problems, as it disallows almost all sane doctrines (and cannot itself be proved). The better program is to try out hypotheses, and see where they may lead: to live, in short, by faith, while still acknowledging our ignorance of what is and has been, as well as what is yet to come.

---

[7] G. L. Prestige, *God in Patristic Thought* (London: SPCK, 1952), 151, after St. Athanasius.

[8] See a brief discussion by Shari L. Lowin and Nevin Reda, "Scripture and exegesis: Torah and Qur'an in historical retrospective": *Routledge Handbook of Muslim-Jewish Relations*, ed. Josef W. Meri (London: Routledge, 2016), 57–76; 61. It is significant that effectively the same dispute about the origin of the Word occurs in both Muslim and in Christian history: on the one hand, whether the Koran is merely *created* or exists eternally as an *uncreated* expression of what God requires of us, and on the other, whether the Son is truly of God's substance or only the first (perhaps) of all created things. In both spheres, the notion that it was "created" was preferred by rulers, as it suggested both that the Word as it had been previously declared might turn out to be obsolete, and — by analogy — that their own arbitrary commands were valid. See Hugh Kennedy, *The Caliphate* (London: Penguin, 2016), 114–16. This does not seem, as far as I can tell, to be raised as an issue in Jewish thought.

EPILOGUE

To Mercy, Pity, Peace, and Love
All pray in their distress;
And to these virtues of delight
Return their thankfulness.

For Mercy, Pity, Peace, and Love
Is God, our father dear,
And Mercy, Pity, Peace, and Love
Is Man, his child and care.

For Mercy has a human heart,
Pity a human face,
And Love, the human form divine,
And Peace, the human dress.

Then every man, of every clime,
That prays in his distress,
Prays to the human form divine,
Love, Mercy, Pity, Peace.

And all must love the human form,
In heathen, Turk, or Jew;
Where Mercy, Love, and Pity dwell
There God is dwelling too.[1]

---

1 Blake, "The Divine Image," *Complete Works*, 117.

WORKS CITED

Aldiss, Brian. *Billion Year Spree*. London: Weidenfeld & Nicolson, 1974.
Almond, Philip. "Adam, Pre-Adamites, and Extra-Terrestrial Beings in Early Modern Europe." *Journal of Religious History* 30.2 (2006): 163–74.
Altizer, Thomas J. J. and William Hamilton. *Radical Theology and the Death of God*. Indianapolis: Bobbs-Merrill, 1966.
Anscombe, G. E. M. *Metaphysics and the Philosophy of Mind*. Oxford: Blackwell, 1981.
———. "Paganism, Superstition and Philosophy" [1985]. In *Faith in a Hard Ground: Essays on Religion, Philosophy and Ethics*, edited by Mary Geach and Luke Gormally, 49–60. Exeter: Imprint Academic, 2008.
Armstrong, A. H. *Plotinus: The Enneads*. Loeb Classical Library. Cambridge, MA: Harvard University Press, 1966–88.
Assmann, Jan. *Moses the Egyptian*. Cambridge, MA: Harvard University Press, 1997.
Athanasius. *On the Incarnation* [318]. London: Geoffrey Bles, 1944.
Augustine. *City of God*. Translated by R. W. Dyson. Cambridge: Cambridge University Press, 1998.
———. *The Teacher, The Free Choice of the Will, Grace and Free Will*. Translated R. P. Russell. Washington, DC: Catholic University of America Press, 1968.
Babbage, Charles. *The Ninth Bridgwater Treatise: A Fragment* [1838]. London: Frank Cass, 1967.
Bacovcin, Helen, trans. *The Way of a Pilgrim*. New York: Doubleday, 2003.
Baker, John L. *Race*. Oxford: Oxford University Press, 1974.
Balme, D. M. "Aristotle's Biology was not Essentialist." *Archiv für Geschichte der Philosophie* 62 (1980): 1–12.
Baxter, Stephen. *Timelike Infinity*. London: Collins, 1992.
Bede the Venerable. *Ecclesiastical History of the English People, with Bede's Letter to Egbert and Cuthbert's Letter on the Death of Bede* [731]. Translated by Leo Sherley-Price. London: Penguin, 1990.
Bekoff, Marc. "Wild Justice and Fair Play: Cooperation, Forgiveness, and Morality in Animals." *Biology and Philosophy* 19 (2004): 489–520.
Benedict XVI. Encyclical Letter *Spe Salvi: On Christian Hope*. November 30, 2007.
———. Message to Archbishop Rino Fisichella on the Occasion of the International Congress "From Galileo's Telescope to Evolutionary Cosmology. Science, Philosophy and Theology in Dialogue" (2009).
Bergfeld, A., R. Bergmann and P. V. Sengbusch. "Phenotypic and Genetic Variation; Ecotypes." In *Botany Online* 1996–2004. http://www1.biologie.uni-hamburg.de/bonline/e37/37b.htm. Accessed December 20, 2019.

Berkeley, George. *Alciphron, or The Minute Philosopher* [1732]. *Works*, vol. 3. Edited by A. A. Luce and T. E. Jessop. Edinburgh: Thomas Nelson, 1950.

———. *Sermons, Essays and Letters. Works*, vol. 7. Edited by A. A. Luce and T. E. Jessop. Edinburgh: Thomas Nelson, 1967.

Berkovits, Eliezer. *Man and God: Studies in Biblical Theology*. Detroit: Wayne State University Press, 1969.

Beston, Henry. *The Outermost House: A Year of Life on the Great Beach of Cape Cod* [1928]. New York: Henry Holt & Co., 1988.

Bett, Henry. *Johannes Scotus Erigena: A Study in Medieval Philosophy*. Cambridge: Cambridge University Press, 2014.

Black, Edwin. *War against the Weak: Eugenics and America's Campaign to Create a Master Race*. New York: Four Walls Eight Windows, 2003.

Blake, William. *Complete Writings*. Edited by Geoffrey Keynes. London: Oxford University Press, 1966.

Blish, James. *Cities in Flight: They Shall Have Stars* [1956]; *A Life for the Stars* [1962]; *Earthman Come Home* [1955]; *The Triumph of Time* [1959]. London: Gollancz, 2010.

Bodhi, Bhikku. *The Connected Discourses of the Buddha: A Translation of the Samyutta Nikaya*. Somerville, MA: Wisdom Publications, 2000.

Boethius. *Consolation of Philosophy*. Translated by V. E. Watts. Harmondsworth: Penguin, 1969.

Bostrom, Nick. "Are you living in a computer simulation?" *Philosophical Quarterly* 53 (2003): 243–55.

Bourget, David and David J. Chalmers. "What Do Philosophers Believe?" *Philosophical Studies* 170 (2014): 465–500.

Buber, Martin. *I and Thou* [1923]. Translated by Walter Kaufmann. New York: Simon & Schuster, 1966.

Buchan, John. *The Moon Endureth*. Edinburgh: Thomas Nelson, 1923.

Burke, Edmund. *Reflections on the Revolution in France*. Edited by Conor Cruise O'Brien. Harmondsworth: Penguin, 1968.

Burkert, Walter. *Babylon, Memphis, Persepolis: Eastern Contexts of Greek Culture*. Cambridge, MA: Harvard University Press, 2004.

Caldecott, Stratford. *All Things Made New: The Mysteries of the World in Christ*. San Rafael, CA: Angelico Press, 2013.

Carter, Brandon and W. H. McCrea. "The anthropic principle and its implications for biological evolution." In *Philosophical Transactions of the Royal Society of London* 310.1512 (1983): 347–63; doi:10.1098/rsta.1983.0096. Accessed December 20, 2019.

Chambers, Robert. *Vestiges of the Natural History of Creation* [1845]. Leicester: Leicester University Press, 1969.

Chan, Wing-tsit, ed. *Sourcebook in Chinese Philosophy*. Princeton, NJ: Princeton University Press, 1963.

Works Cited

Cherryh, C. J. *Chanur's Endgame: Chanur's Homecoming* [1986]; *Chanur's Legacy* [1992]. New York: Daw Books, 2007.

———. *The Chanur Saga: The Pride of Chanur* [1981]; *Chanur's Venture* [1984]; *The Kif Strike Back* [1985]. New York: Daw Books, 2000.

———. *Cyteen*. London: NEL, 1989.

———. *The Faded Sun Trilogy: Kesrith* [1978]; *Shon'jir* [1978]; *Kutath* [1979]. London: Penguin, 2000.

———. *Invader*. London: Random House, 1996.

Chesterton, G. K. *All Things Considered*. London: Methuen, 1908.

———. *Charles Dickens*. London: Methuen, 1906.

———. *The Club of Queer Trades* [1905]. London: Darwen Finlayson Ltd., 1960.

———. *Collected Poems*. London: Methuen, 1950.

———. *Collected Works*, vol. 29: *Illustrated London News 1911–13*. Edited by Lawrence J. Clipper. San Francisco: Ignatius Press, 1988.

———. *The Everlasting Man*. London: Hodder & Stoughton, 1925.

———. *Fancies versus Fads*. London: Methuen, 1923.

———. *The Father Brown Stories*. London: Cassell, 1929.

———. *Four Faultless Felons*. London: Cassell, 1930.

———. *Heretics*. New York: John Lane, 1905.

———. *The Napoleon of Notting Hill* [1904]. Harmondsworth: Penguin, 1946.

———. *Orthodoxy* [1908]. Thirsk: Stratus, 2001.

———. "The Philosophy of Islands." In *The Venture Annual* [1903], ed. Laurence Housman and W. Somerset Maugham, 2–9. London: John Baillie's. https://www.chesterton.org/the-philosophy-of-islands/. Accessed December 20, 2019. Reprinted in Chesterton, *The Spice of Life*.

———. *The Poet and the Lunatics* [1929]. London: Darwen Finlayson, 1962.

———. *The Spice of Life*. Edited by D. Collins. Beaconsfield: Finlayson, 1964.

———. *Tremendous Trifles*. London: Methuen, 1904.

———. *The Well and the Shallows*. London: Sheed & Ward, 1935.

———. *What's Wrong with the World*. London: Cassell & Co., 1910.

Clark, Stephen R. L. *Ancient Mediterranean Philosophy*. London: Continuum, 2013.

———. *Aristotle's Man: Speculations upon Aristotelian Anthropology*. Oxford: Clarendon Press, 1975.

———. "The Case of John Wren-Lewis." In *Atheisms*, ed. Victoria Harrison and Harriet Harris (forthcoming).

———. "Climbing up to Heaven: The Hermetic Option." *Purgatory: Philosophical Dimensions*, ed. Kristof K. P. Vanhoutte and Benjamin W. McCraw, 151–74. London: Palgrave-Macmillan, 2017.

———. *Ennead VI.9 On the Good*. Las Vegas: Parmenides Publishing, 2020.

———. "Elves, Hobbits, Trolls and Talking Beasts." In *Creaturely Theology*, ed. Celia Deane-Drummond and David Clough, 151–67. London: SCM Press, 2009.

———. "The Ethics of Taxonomy: A Neo-Aristotelian Synthesis." *Animal Ethics: Past and Present Perspectives*, ed. Evangelos D. Protopapadakis, 38–58. Berlin: Logos Verlag, 2012.
———. "Folly to the Greeks: Good Reasons to Give up Reason." *European Journal for Philosophy of Religion* 4 (2012): 93–113.
———. "From Biosphere to Technosphere." *Ends and Means* 5 (2001): 3–21.
———. *G. K. Chesterton: Thinking Backwards, Looking Forwards*. West Conshohocken, PA: Templeton Foundation Press, 2006.
———. "God, Reason and Extraterrestrials." In *God, Mind and Knowledge*, ed. Andrew Moore, 171–86. London: Ashgate, 2014.
———. "Is Humanity a Natural Kind?" In *What is an Animal?*, ed. T. Ingold, 17–34. London: Unwin Hyman 1988. Republished in Clark, *The Political Animal*, 40–58.
———. "Orwell and the Anti-Realists." *Philosophy* 67 (1992): 141–54.
———. *Plotinus: Myth, Metaphor and Philosophical Practice*. Chicago: University of Chicago Press, 2016.
———. *The Political Animal*. London: Routledge, 1999.
———. "Religion and Law: Response to Michael Moxter." *Ars Disputandi*, supplementary volume 5 (2011): 57–71.
———. "Therapy and Theory Reconstructed." *Philosophy as Therapy*. Royal Institute of Philosophy Supplementary Volume 66, ed. Clare Carlisle and Jonardon Ganeri, 83–102. Cambridge: Cambridge University Press, 2010.
Clastres, Pierre. *Society against the State: Essays in Political Anthropology* [1974]. Translated by Robert Hurley. Brooklyn: Zone Books, 1987.
Clifford, W. K. "The Ethics of Belief" [1877]. In *Lectures and Essays*, ed. L. Stephen and F. Pollock, 339–63. London: Macmillan, 1886.
Cochran, Gregory and Henry Harpending. *The 10,000 Year Explosion*. New York: Basic Books, 2009.
Cohen, Jack and Ian Stewart. *What Does a Martian Look Like?: The Science of Extraterrestrial Life*. New Jersey: John Wiley, 2002.
Coniaris, Anthony M. *Philokalia: The Bible of Orthodox Spirituality*. Minneapolis: Light & Life, 1998.
Conway Morris, Simon. *Life's Solution: Inevitable Humans in a Lonely Universe*. New York: Cambridge University Press, 2003.
Conway Morris, Simon, ed. *The Deep Structure of Biology: Is Convergence Sufficiently Ubiquitous to Give a Directional Signal?* West Conshohocken, PA: Templeton Foundation Press, 2008.
Couzin, I. D. "Collective cognition in animal groups." *Trends in Cognitive Sciences* 13 (2009): 36–43.
Crowley, John. *Engine Summer* [1979]. London: Gollancz, 2013.
Dalrymple, William. *Nine Lives: In Search of the Sacred in Modern India*. London: Bloomsbury, 2009.
Darwin, Charles. *The Descent of Man*. London: John Murray, 1871.

Works Cited

———. *The Life and Letters of Charles Darwin*. Edited by Francis Darwin. London: Murray, 1887.
———. *On the Origin of Species by means of natural selection, or the preservation of favoured races in the struggle for life*. London: John Murray, 1859.
Davies, Jeremy. *The Birth of the Anthropocene*. Oakland, CA: University of California Press, 2016.
Dawkins, Richard. "Gaps in the Mind." In *The Great Ape Project: Equality Beyond Humanity*, ed. P. Singer and P. Cavalieri, 80–87. London: Fourth Estate, 1993.
Deane-Drummond, Celia. "God's Image and Likeness in Humans and Other Animals: Performative Soul-Making and Graced Nature." *Zygon* 47.4 (2012): 934–48.
Depoortere, Frederiek. "The Faith of Job and the Recovery of Christian Atheism." *Expositions* 4 (2010): 105–13.
Desmond, Adrian J. *Archetypes and Ancestors: Palaeontology in Victorian London 1850–1875*. Chicago: University of Chicago Press, 1982.
Dio Chrysostom. *Discourses*. Translated by J. H. Cohoon. Loeb Classical Library. London: Heinemann, 1939.
Dr. Seuss [Theodor Seuss Geisel]. *The Lorax*. New York: Random House, 1971.
Drew, Liam. *I, Mammal: The Story of What Makes Us Mammals*. Bloomsbury: London, 2017.
Dunayer, Joan. *Speciesism*. Derwood, MD: Ryce Publishing, 2004.
Dunbar, Robin. *Grooming, Gossip and the Evolution of Language*. London: Faber, 1996.
Durkheim, Emile. *The Elementary Forms of the Religious Life: A Study in Religious Sociology*. Translated by J. Swain. London: Allen & Unwin, 1915.
Dyson, Freeman. "Time without End: Physics and Biology in an Open Universe." *Reviews of Modern Physics* 51.3 (1979). Reprinted in *Selected Papers of Freeman Dyson*. Providence, RI: American Mathematical Society, 1996: 529–42; also http://www.aleph.se/Trans/Global/Omega/dyson.txt. Accessed December 21, 2019.
Eisenberg, Ronald L. *What the Rabbis Said: 250 Topics from the Talmud*. Santa Barbara: Preiger, 2010.
Eliot, T. S. *Four Quartets*. London: Faber, 1944.
Elliot, R. "Faking Nature." *Inquiry* 25 (1983): 81–93.
Epictetus. *Discourses*. Translated by W. A. Oldfather. Loeb Classical Library. Cambridge, MA: Harvard University Press, 1925.
Finlan, Stephen and Vladimir Kharlamov, eds. *Theosis: Deification in Christian Theology*. Eugene, Oregon: Pickwick Publications, 2006.
Flecker, James Elroy. *Collected Poems*. London: Martin Secker, 1916.
Francis. *Laudato Si': On Care for Our Common Home*. London: Catholic Truth Society, 2015.
Frymer-Kensky, Tikva. "The Image, the Glory and the Holy: Aspects of Being Human in Biblical Thought." In Schweiker, *Humanity before God*, 18–138.
Galton, Francis. "Composite portraits." *Journal of the Anthropological Institute of Great Britain and Ireland* 8 (1878): 132–42.
Gardner, James N. *The Intelligent Universe: AI, ET and the Emerging Mind of the Cosmos*. Franklin, NJ: Career Press, 2007.

Can We Believe in People?

Gee, Henry. *Deep Time: Cladistics, the Revolution in Evolution.* London: Fourth Estate, 2011.

Ghiselin, M. H. *The Economy of Nature and the Evolution of Sex.* San Francisco: University of California Press, 1978.

Gilhus, Ingvild Saelid. *Animals, Gods and Humans: Changing Attitudes to Animals in Greek, Roman and Early Christian Ideas.* London: Routledge, 2006.

Gödel, Kurt. "Some basic theorems on the foundations of mathematics and their philosophical implications" [1951]. In *Collected Works*, ed. S. Feferman, J. Dawson, W. Goldfarb, C. Parsons, R. Solovay, and J. van Heijenoort (Oxford: Oxford University Press, 1995), vol. 3: 304–23.

Gott, J. Richard. *Time Travel in Einstein's Universe.* London: Weidenfeld & Nicolson, 2001.

Gould, Stephen Jay. *Rocks of Ages: Science and Religion in the Fullness of Life.* London: Jonathan Cape, 1999.

Gregory of Nyssa, *On the Making of Man.* Translated by W. Moore and H. A. Wilson. London: Aeterna Press, 2016.

Guthke, Karl S. *The Last Frontier: Imagining Other Worlds from the Copernican Revolution to Modern Science Fiction.* Translated by Helen Atkins. Ithaca: Cornell University Press, 1990.

Haldane, J. B. S. *Possible Worlds.* London: Chatto & Windus, 1930.

Hawking, Stephen and Leonard Mlodinow. *The Grand Design.* London: Bantam Press, 2010.

Hawking, Stephen. *A Brief History of Time.* London: Bantam, 1988.

Henry, Devin. "Aristotle on the Mechanism of Inheritance." *Journal of the History of Biology* 39 (2006): 425–55.

Hoban, Russell. *Riddley Walker.* London: Jonathan Cape, 1980.

Hollis, Christopher. *The Mind of Chesterton.* London: Cassell, 1970.

Hornung, Erik. *Conceptions of God in Ancient Egypt.* Translated by John Baines. Ithaca, NY: Cornell University Press, 1982.

Horowitz, Alexandra. *Being a Dog: Following the Dog into a World of Smell.* New York: Simon & Schuster, 2016.

Hull, David, ed. *Darwin and his Critics.* Chicago: University of Chicago Press, 1983.

Hume, David. *Dialogues concerning Natural Religion.* Edited by J. C.A. Gaskin. Oxford: Oxford University Press, 2008 [1779].

Hunter, George William. *A Civic Biology: Presented in Problems.* New York: American Book Co., 1914.

Iamblichus of Chalcis. *Letters: Writings from the Greco-Roman World.* Translated by John M. Dillon and Wolfgang Pelleichtner. Atlanta: Society of Biblical Literature, 2009.

James, William. *Pragmatism.* London: Longmans, Green & Co., 1907.

——. *The Principles of Psychology.* New York: Macmillan, 1890.

——. *The Will to Believe.* New York: Longmans, Green & Co., 1897.

Jennings, H. S. *Behavior of the Lower Organisms.* New York: Columbia University Press, 1906.

John Paul II. *Evangelium Vitae: On the Value and Inviolability of Human Life.* London: Catholic Truth Society, 1995.

Works Cited

Joshi, S. T. *A Subtler Magick: The Writings and Philosophy of H. P. Lovecraft*. Rockville, MD: Borgo Press, 1996.
Joyce, James. *Ulysses*. Oxford: Oxford University Press, 1993 [1922].
Julian of Norwich. *Revelations of Divine Love*. Translated by Barry Windeatt. Oxford: Oxford University Press, 2015.
Kant, Immanuel. *Kant's Political Writings*. Edited by Hans Reiss. Cambridge: Cambridge University Press, 1970.
Katz, Eric. *Nature as Subject: Human Obligation and Natural Community*. Lanham, MD: Rowman and Littlefield, 1997.
Kekes, John. "What Is Conservatism?" *Philosophy* 72 (1997): 351–74.
Kennedy, Hugh. *The Caliphate*. London: Penguin, 2016.
Kipling, Rudyard. *Rudyard Kipling's Verse: Definitive Edition*. London: Hodder & Stoughton, 1940.
Kirby, William. *On the Power, Wisdom and Goodness of God as Manifested in the Creation of Animals and in their History, Habits and Instincts as Manifested in the Creation of Animals and in Their History Habits and Instincts*. Cambridge: Chadwyck Healey, 1998 [1835].
Klibansky, R., E. Panofsky and F. Saxl. *Saturn and Melancholy*. Edinburgh: Nelson, 1964.
Koons, Robert C. "Science and Theism: Concord not Conflict." In *The Rationality of Theism*, ed. Paul Copan and Paul Moser, 72–89. London: Taylor & Francis, 2003.
Kragh, Helge. "Big Bang: the etymology of a name": *Astronomy and Geophysics* 54.2 (2013): 28–30; https://academic.oup.com/astrogeo/article/54/2/2.28/302975. Accessed December 21, 2019.
Langlois, Judith H., Lori A. Roggman and Lisa Musselman. "What is Average and What is Not Average about Attractive Faces." *Psychological Science* 5.4 (1994): 214–20.
Lanza, Robert and Bob Berman. *Biocentrism: How Life and Consciousness Are the Keys to Understanding the True Nature of the Universe*. Dallas: BenBella, 2009.
Lanza, Robert. "Why Are You Here? A New Theory May Hold the Missing Piece" (November 12, 2010): https://www.huffpost.com/entry/why-are-you-here-new-theo_n_781055. Accessed December 21, 2019.
Larson, Edward J. "Myth 20: that the Scopes Trial ended in defeat for Anti-Evolutionism." In *Galileo and Other Myths about Science and Religion*, ed. Ronald L. Numbers, 176–86. Cambridge, MA: Harvard University Press, 2009.
———. *Summer for the Gods: The Scopes Trial and America's Continuing Debate over Science and Religion*. Cambridge, MA: Harvard University Press, 1998.
Lash, Nicholas. *The Beginning and the End of "Religion."* Cambridge: Cambridge University Press, 1996.
Leibniz, G. W. *Monadology* [1714] *and Other Philosophical Writings*. Translated by Robert Latta. Oxford: Clarendon Press, 1898.
Leopold, Aldo. *A Sand County Almanac and Sketches Here and There*. New York: Oxford University Press, 1968 [1949].

Leslie, John. *The End of the World: Science and Ethics of Human Extinction.* London: Routledge, 1996.
Levenson, Jon D. *Creation and the Persistence of Evil: The Jewish Drama of Divine Omnipotence.* Princeton, NJ: Princeton University Press, 1994.
Lewis, C. S. *The Abolition of Man.* London: Geoffrey Bles, 1946.
——. *Miracles.* London: Fontana, 1960.
——. *Out of the Silent Planet.* London: Pan Books, 1952 [1938].
——. *Poems.* Edited by Walter Hooper. San Diego: Harcourt, 1964.
Li Gang, "On Curing the State," Liangxi ji *(Li Gang's Collected Writings), juan* 157, in *Siku quanshu (Complete Collection of the Four Treasuries),* vol. 1126, 683b–684a. Shanghai: Shanghai guji, 1987 reprint.
Lillehammer, Halvard. "Methods of ethics and the descent of man: Darwin and Sidgwick on ethics and evolution." *Biology and Philosophy* 25 (2019): 361–78; https://doi.org/10.1007/s10539-010-9204-8.
Long, A. A. and D. N. Sedley, eds. *The Hellenistic Philosophers.* Cambridge: Cambridge University Press, 1987.
Longxi, Zhang. "Heaven and Man: From a Cross-Cultural Perspective." In *Comparative Political Theory and Cross-Cultural Philosophy: Essays in Honor of Hwa Yol Jung,* ed. Jin Y. Park, 139–50. Plymouth: Lexington, 2009.
Lovecraft, H. P. *The Dreams in the Witch House and Other Weird Stories.* Edited by S. T. Joshi. London: Penguin, 2005.
——. *Selected Letters 1911–37.* Edited by August Derleth, Donald Wandrei and James Turner. Sauk City, WI: Arkham House, 1965–76.
Lovejoy, A. O. *The Revolt against Dualism: An Inquiry Concerning the Existence of Ideas.* La Salle, IL: Open Court, 1930.
Lovell, Bernard. *In the Centre of Immensities.* London: Hutchinson, 1979.
Lovelock, James. *Gaia: A New Look at Life on Earth.* Oxford: Oxford University Press, 2000 [1979].
Lowin, Shari L. and Nevin Reda. "Scripture and Exegesis; Torah and Qu'ran in historical perspective." In *Routledge Handbook of Muslim-Jewish Relations,* ed. Josef W. Meri, 57–76. London: Routledge, 2016.
Lynch, K. *The Image of the City.* Cambridge, MA: MIT Press, 1960.
Lyon, P. "The cognitive cell: bacterial behavior reconsidered." *Frontiers in Microbiology* 6 (2015): 264; http://doi.org/10.3389/fmicb.2015.00264.
MacArthur, R. and E. O. Wilson. *The Theory of Island Biogeography.* Princeton, NJ: Princeton University Press, 1967.
MacIntyre, Alastair. *Dependent Rational Animals.* Chicago: Open Court, 1999.
Macrobius. *Commentary on the Dream of Scipio.* Translated by William Harris Stahl. New York: Columbia University Press, 1952.
Maimonides, Moses. *The Guide of the Perplexed.* Translated by Chaim Rabin, edited by Julius Guttman. Indianapolis: Hackett, 1995 [1190].

Works Cited

Majumdar, Sarangam and Sukla Pal. "Bacterial intelligence: imitation games, time-sharing, and long-range quantum coherence." *Journal of Cell Communication and Signaling* 11.3 (2017): 281–84; https://doi.org/10.1007/s12079-017-0394-6.

Mangena, Fainos. "Hunhu/Ubuntu in the Traditional Thought of Southern Africa." *Internet Encyclopedia of Philosophy* (2016). http://www.iep.utm.edu/hunhu/.

Marais, Eugène. *The Soul of the White Ant*. Translated by Winifred de Kok. London: Methuen, 1950 [1937].

Marchant, Jo. "Ancient astronomy: Mechanical inspiration." *Nature* 468 (2010): 496–98; doi:10.1038/468496a.

——. *Decoding the Heavens: Solving the Mystery of the World's First Computer*. London: Windmill Books, 2009.

Margulis, Lynn and Dorion Sagan. *Microcosmos: Four Billion Years of Microbial Evolution*. Berkeley: University of California Press, 1997.

Marx, Karl. "Contribution to the Critique of Hegel's *Philosophy of Right*." In *Critique of Hegel's Philosophy of Right*, trans. Annette Joplin and Joseph O'Malley, ed. Joseph O'Malley, 129–42. Cambridge: Cambridge University Press, 1970 [1843–44].

Mathew, Gervase. *Byzantine Aesthetics*. London: John Murray, 1963.

McKibben, Bill. *The End of Nature*. Harmondsworth: Penguin, 1990.

Metz, Thaddeus. "Toward an African Moral Theory." *Journal of Political Philosophy* 15.2 (2007): 321–41.

Meyendorff, J. *A Study of Gregory Palamas*. Translated by George Lawrence. Leighton Buzzard: Faith Press, 1974.

Meyer, Marvin. *The Unknown Sayings of Jesus*. Boston: Shambhala, 1998.

Meyer, Yakov Z. "Parashat Teruma: the primordial Torah." *Haaretz*, January 30, 2014.

Nahin, Paul J. *Dr. Euler's Fabulous Formula: Cures Many Mathematical Ills*. New Jersey: Princeton University Press, 2006.

Nathan, N. M. L. "Naturalism and Self-Defeat: Plantinga's Version." *Religious Studies* 33.2 (1997): 135–42.

Nederman, Cary J. and Kate Langdon Forhan, eds. *Medieval Political Theory—A Reader: The Quest for the Body Politic, 1100–1400*. London: Routledge, 1993.

Orwell, George. *Nineteen Eighty-Four*. Edited by Thomas Pynchon. London: Penguin, 1989 [1949].

Ostwald, Martin. *Nomos and the Beginnings of the Athenian Democracy*. Oxford: Clarendon Press, 1969.

Palamas, Gregory. *The 150 Chapters*. Translated by Robert E. Sinkewicz. Toronto: Pontifical Institute of Mediaeval Studies, 1988.

Patrides, C. A., ed. *The Cambridge Platonists*. Cambridge: Cambridge University Press, 1980 [1969].

Patterson, Nick, D. J. Richter, S. Gnerre, E. S. Lander, D. Reich. "Genetic evidence for complex speciation of humans and chimpanzees." *Nature* 441 (2006): 1103–8 (June 29, 2006); https://doi.org/10.1038/nature04789.

Pausanias. *Description of Greece*. Translated by W. H. S. Jones and H. A. Ormerod. Loeb Classical Library. London: Heinemann, 1926.
Pearsall Smith, Logan. *All Trivia*. New York: Harcourt, Brace, 1945.
Peirce, J. J. *Foundations of Science Fiction*. Westport, Connecticut: Greenwood Press, 1987.
Perry, T. D. *Moral Reasoning and Truth: An Essay in Philosophy and Jurisprudence*. Oxford: Clarendon Press, 1976.
Philo of Alexandria. *Collected Works*. Translated by F. H. Colson, G. H. Whitaker, et al. Loeb Classical Library. Cambridge, MA: Harvard University Press, 1929–62.
Pianka, Eric R. "On r- and K-Selection." *The American Naturalist* 104. 940 (1970): 592–97; https://doi.org/10.1086/282697.
Plantinga, Alvin. "Darwin, Mind and Meaning." *Books and Culture*, May/June 1996.
——. *Warrant and Proper Function*. New York: Oxford University Press, 1993.
Plumwood, Val. "Nature in the Active Voice" In *Handbook of Contemporary Animism*, ed. Graham Harvey, 441–53. Durham: Acumen, 2013.
Plutarch of Chaeronia. *Lives*. Volume 6. Translated by Bernadotte Perrin. Loeb Classical Library. London: Heinemann, 1918.
——. *Moralia*. Volume 5. Translated by Frank Cole Babbitt. Loeb Classical Library. Cambridge, MA: Harvard University Press, 1936.
——. *Moralia*. Volume 12. Translated by Harold Cherniss. Loeb Classical Library. Cambridge, MA: Harvard University Press, 1936.
——. *Moralia*. Volume 13. Translated by Harold Cherniss. Loeb Classical Library. Cambridge, MA: Harvard University Press, 1976.
Prestige, G. L. *God in Patristic Thought*. London: SPCK, 1952.
Pritchard, James, ed. *Ancient Near Eastern Texts Relating to the Old Testament*. Princeton, NJ: Princeton University Press, 1969 [1950].
Pseudo-Dionysius. *The Celestial Hierarchy*. Whitefish, MT: Kessinger Publishing, 2004.
Purves, Libby. *Holy Smoke: Religion and Roots*. London: Hodder & Stoughton, 1998.
Reid, Chris R., Tanya Latty, Audrey Dussutour and Madeleine Beekman. "Slime mold uses an externalized spatial 'memory.'" *Proceedings of the National Academy of Sciences* 109.43 (2012): 17490–94; doi:10.1073/pnas.1215037109.
Reydams-Schils, Gretchen. "'Becoming like god' in Platonism and Stoicism." In *From Stoicism to Platonism: The Development of Philosophy, 100 BCE–100 CE*, ed. T. Engberg-Pedersen, 142–58. Cambridge: Cambridge University Press, 2017.
Richards, Richard A. *The Species Problem: A Philosophical Analysis*. Cambridge: Cambridge University Press, 2010.
Ricoeur, Paul. "Religion, Atheism and Faith" [1966]. Translated by Charles Freilich. In *The Conflict of Interpretations: Essays in Hermeneutics*, ed. Don Ihde, 436–63. Evanston, IL: Northwestern University Press, 2004.
Rorty, R. M. *Philosophy and the Mirror of Nature*. Oxford: Blackwell, 1980.
Rosenberg, A. *Sociobiology and the Pre-emption of Social Science*. Baltimore: Johns Hopkins Press, 1980.

Works Cited

Ross, W. D., ed. *Works of Aristotle*. Volume 12: *Select Fragments*. London: Oxford University Press, 1952.

Rossi, Vincent. "Presence, Participation, Performance: The Remembrance of God in the Early Hesychast Fathers." In *Paths to the Heart: Sufism and the Christian East*, ed. James S. Cutsinger, 64–111. Bloomington, IN: World Wisdom, 2004.

Russell, Bertrand. "The Free Man's Worship" [1903]. In idem, *Mysticism and Logic*, 46–57. London: Allen & Unwin, 1918.

Sachedina, Abdulaziz. "Human Vicegerency: A Blessing or a Curse?" In Schweiker, *Humanity before God*, 31–54.

Sacks, Oliver. *The River of Consciousness*. New York: Alfred A. Knopf, 2017.

Schmidt, Gavin A. and Adam Frank. "The Silurian hypothesis: would it be possible to detect an industrial civilization in the geological record?" *International Journal of Astrobiology* 18.2 (2018): 142–50; doi:10.1017/S1473550418000095.

Schwartz, Richard H. *Judaism and Vegetarianism*. New York: Lantern Books, 2001.

Schweiker, William, Michael A. Johnson, Kevin Jung, eds. *Humanity Before God: Contemporary Faces of Jewish, Christian and Islamic Ethics*. Minneapolis: Fortress Press, 2006.

Seidenberg, David M. *Kabbalah and Ecology: God's Image in the More-Than-Human World*. New York: Cambridge University Press, 2015.

Seidenberg, David M. "Being Here Now: This Creation is the Divine Image." *Tikkun* 132.1 (2017): 62–64.

Shaw, Prue. *Reading Dante: From Here to Eternity*. New York: W. W. Norton, 2015.

Shestov, Lev. *All Things Are Possible*. Translated by Bernard Martin. Athens, GA: Ohio University Press, 1977.

Snyder, Gary. *The Good, the Wild and the Sacred*. London: Five Seasons Press, 1984.

Sober, Elliot. *The Philosophy of Biology*. Boulder, CO: Westview Press, 1993.

Speaight, R. *Teilhard de Chardin: A Biography*. London: Collins, 1967.

Spengler, Oswald. *The Decline of the West*. Abridged by Helmut Werner and Arthur Helps; translated by C. F. Atkinson; introduced by H. Stuart Hughes. New York: Oxford University Press, 1991 [1924, 1926].

Sprat, Thomas. *History of the Royal Society*. New York: Elibron, 2005 [1722; 3rd ed.].

Stapledon, Olaf. *Darkness and Light*. London: Methuen, 1942.

——. *The Flames*. London: Secker & Warburg, 1947.

——. *Last and First Men* [1930] and *Last Men in London* [1932]. London: Penguin, 1972.

——. *Odd John: A Story between Jest and Earnest*. London: Gollancz, 1935.

——. *The Opening of the Eyes*. Edited by Agnes Stapledon. London: Methuen, 1954.

——. *Philosophy and Living*. Harmondsworth: Penguin, 1939.

——. *Saints and Revolutionaries*. London: Heinemann, 1939.

——. *Star Maker*. London: Gollancz, 1999 [1937].

Stewart, Balfour and Peter Guthrie Tait. *The Unseen Universe, or Physical Speculations on Future State*. London: Macmillan, 1879.

Can We Believe in People?

Stoczkowski, Wiktor. *Explaining Human Origins: Myth, Imagination and Conjecture.* Translated by Mary Turton. Cambridge: Cambridge University Press, 2002.

Tanzella-Nitti, Giuseppe. "Jesus Christ, Incarnation and Doctrine of Logos." In *Interdisciplinary Encyclopedia of Religion and Science*, ed. G. Tanzella-Nitti and A. Strumia. Rome: Interdisciplinary Documentation on Religion and Science, 2008. doi: 10.17421/2037-2329-2008-GT-2. Accessed December 21, 2019.

Tegmark, Max. *Our Mathematical Universe: My Quest for the Ultimate Nature of Reality.* London: Allen Lane, 2014.

Teilhard de Chardin, Pierre. *Man's Place in Nature.* Translated by R. Hague. London: Harper & Row, 1966.

Thalos, Mariam. *Without Hierarchy: The Scale Freedom of the Universe.* Oxford: Oxford University Press, 2013.

Torrance, T. E. *The Ground and Grammar of Theology: Consonance Between Theology and Science.* Edinburgh: T&T Clark, 2001 [1980].

Traherne, Thomas. *Centuries of Meditations.* London: Bertram Dobell, 1908.

Trimmer, John D. "The Present Situation in Quantum Mechanics: A Translation of Schrödinger's 'Cat Paradox' Paper." *Proceedings of the American Philosophical Society* 124.5 (1980): 323–38; www.jstor.org/stable/986572.

Urbach, Ephraim E. *The Sages: Their Concepts and Beliefs.* Translated by Israel Abrahams. Cambridge, MA: Harvard University Press, 1979.

Vaughan, Henry. *Silex Scintillans.* Charleston: Bibliobazaar, 2008 [1650].

Vilenkin, Alexander. "The principle of mediocrity." *Astronomy and Geophysics* 52.5 (2011): 33–36; https://doi.org/10.1111/j.1468-4004.2011.52533.x.

Von Rad, Gerhard. *Genesis: A Commentary.* Revised edition. Translated by John H. Marx. London: SCM, 1972.

Von Uexküll, Jacob. "A stroll through the worlds of animals and men." In *Instinctive Behavior*, ed. C. H. Schiller, 5–80. New York: International University Press, 1957.

——. *Theoretical Biology.* Translated by D. L. Mackinnon. London: Kegan Paul, 1926.

Waterfield, Robin, ed. *The First Philosophers: The Presocratics and Sophists.* New York: Oxford University Press, 2000.

Webb, Stephen. *If the Universe Is Teeming with Aliens ... Where Is Everybody? Fifty Solutions to Fermi's Paradox and the Problem of Extraterrestrial Life.* New York: Copernicus Books, 2002.

Weiss, Amaroq E., Timm Kroeger, J. Christopher Haney and Nina Fascione. "Social and Ecological Benefits of Restored Wolf Populations." *Transactions of the 72nd North American Wildlife and Natural Resources Conference* (2007), 297–319.

Wells, H. G. *Anticipations* [1903] *and Other Works.* London: Fisher Unwin, 1924.

——. *First Men in the Moon.* London: George Newnes, 1901.

——. *Mr. Belloc Objects to "The Outline of History."* London: Methuen, 1926.

Whewell, William. *Of the Plurality of Worlds.* Edited by Michael Ruse. Chicago: University of Chicago Press, 2001 [1853].

Works Cited

Wigner, Eugene P. "Remarks on the mind-body question." In *The Scientist Speculates*, ed. I. J. Good, 284–302. London: Heinemann, 1961.

——. "The Unreasonable Effectiveness of Mathematics in the Natural Sciences." *Communications in Pure and Applied Mathematics* 13 (1960): 1–14.

Wilmot, John. *Selected Poems*. Edited by Paul Davis. Oxford: Oxford University Press, 2003.

Wilson, E. O. *Biophilia*. Cambridge, MA: Harvard University Press, 1984.

——. *On Human Nature*. Cambridge, MA: Harvard University Press, 1978.

Winchell, Alexander. *World Life or Comparative Geology*. Chicago: S. C. Griggs & Co., 1883.

Wink, Walter. *Naming the Powers: The Language of Power in the New Testament*. Minneapolis: Fortress Press, 1984.

Wittgenstein, Ludwig von. *Philosophical Investigations*, 4th ed. Edited by P. M. S. Hacker and Joachim Schulte; translated by G. E. M. Anscombe, P. M. S. Hacker and Joachim Schulte. Oxford: Wiley-Blackwell, 2009.

Wohlleben, Peter. *The Hidden Life of Trees: What They Feel, How They Communicate*. Translated by Jane Billinghurst. Vancouver: Greystone Books, 2016.

Woolley-Barker, Tamsin. *Teeming: How Superorganisms Work to Build Infinite Wealth in a Finite World*. Ashland, OR: White Cloud Press, 2017.

Wren-Lewis, John. "The darkness of God: A personal report on consciousness transformation through an encounter with death." *Journal of Humanistic Psychology* 28 (1988): 105–22.

——. "The Dazzling Dark: a Near-Death Experience Opens the Door to a Permanent Transformation." Online at http://www.nonduality.com/dazdark.htm and http://www.angelfire.com/electronic/awakening101/dazzledark.html. Accessed December 21, 2019.

——. "A Mystical Awakening." In *Our Childhood's Pattern: Memories of Growing Up Christian*, ed. Monica Furlong, 107–23. London: Mowbrays, 1995.

——. "What I Believe." In *What I Believe*, ed. G. Unwin, 221–236. London: Allen & Unwin, 1966.

——. *What Shall We Tell the Children?* London: Constable, 1971.

Zeiner-Carmichael, Noelle K., ed. *Roman Letters: An Anthology*. Chichester: John Wiley, 2014.

Žižek, Slavoj. *The Puppet and the Dwarf: The Perverse Core of Christianity*. Cambridge, MA: MIT Press, 2003.

INDEX OF NAMES

Abrahamic tradition, 8, 193
Achilles, 15
Actium, Battle of, 13
Adam, 8–9, 18, 99, 117, 152, 162
Aemilius Paulus, 57
Aldiss, Brian, 168
Al-Ghazali, 10 n21
Altizer, Thomas, 116
Anscombe, G. E. M., 22 n4, 32 n23
Anubis, 13
Aphrodite, 13
Apollo, 67, 193
Aquinas, *see* Thomas Aquinas
Aristotle, xi, xiii–xvi, 5–6, 9, 12, 27, 34, 36–37, 39, 45, 55, 74–77, 83, 110, 120, 125 n21, 153–55, 157–60, 165, 176, 182
Ashkenazi, Joseph, 117, 125
Athanasius of Alexandria, 5, 17, 62–63, 136, 194 n7
Athena, 15, 18
Augustine of Hippo, 54 n26, 92, 125

Babbage, Charles, 79–80
Babies, 25, 111, 145
Babylon, 176–78, 183
Bacchus, 13
Bacon, Francis, 118
Bede, Venerable, 156 n32
Bekoff, Marc, 104 n31
Belloc, Hilaire, 9 n20, 93 n8
Benedict XVI, 30, 31 n20, 132
Bentham, Jeremy, 110
Bergson, Henri, xi–xii
Berkeley, George, 51, 54 n27, 63, 169 n12
Beston, Henry, 107
Big Bang, 32, 34, 130
Birds, 44, 80, 81 n15, 85, 101, 135–36

Blackham, H. J., 128
Blake, William, 60 n40, 127, 164 n47, 180 n35, 182 n41, 183, 190 n50, 195 n1
Blish, James, 156
Boethius, 130
Bostrom, Nick, 29 n16, 147 n15
Buber, Martin, 106, 133 n38
Buchan, John, 124
Buddha, Buddhism, 99 n24, 179 n32
Burke, Edmund, 48 n11

Caldecott, Stratford, 132 n35
Carpenter, Nathanael, 91
Catechism of the Catholic Church, 6–7, 104, 189 n49
Chambers, Robert, 80–81, 86, 93 n6
Cherryh, C. J., 146, 179 n34
Chesterton, G. K., xvi, 3, 5, 9, 22 n2, 23 n7, 29, 30 n17, 46 n8, 61, 72–73, 86–89, 93–99, 103, 105–7, 115–17, 125–27, 130, 136 n44, 139 n51, 142 n5, 145, 165, 174 n26, 184, 191 n2, 192 n3
China, Chinese, 155, 165–66
Christ, 14, 17–18, 40, 116, 136, 148–49, 156
Chrysippus, 42
Chrysostom, John, *see* John Chrysostom
Cicero, 6, 16, 57
Clastres, Pierre, 175 n29
Coleridge, Samuel Taylor, x, 9
Crowley, John, 176

Dalrymple, William, 135 n42
Dante, 159
Darwin, Charles, 21–22, 28, 46–49, 54, 65, 71–74, 78–82, 86–88, 92–96, 102–3, 128, 146–47, 167, 181
Dawkins, Richard, 66, 102
Deane-Drummond, Celia, xv–xvi, 3 n8, 113

Dennett, Daniel, 181
Descartes, René, x
Dio Chrysostom, 57–58, 59 n37, 112
Diogenes Laertius, 39, 109 n46
Dionysius the Areopagite, 112 n49, 162
Disraeli, Benjamin, 93 n6
Domestic, domestication, 11, 42, 44–45, 67 n50, 69, 75–76, 94, 96, 104 n34, 147
Dong Zhongshu, 155, 165–66
Dreams, dreaming, 16, 24–25, 59–62, 167, 178; *see also* simulation
Durkheim, Emile, 59 n38
Dyson, Freeman, 53 n21, 68, 120 n8

Egyptian(s), x–xi, 1, 2 n5, 13, 34 n26, 174, 183 n42
Eliot, T. S., 181 n37
Epictetus, 11, 14, 36 n32
Epicureanism, 47, 56, 99, 144
Eriugena, *see* John Scotus Eriugena
Ethelbert of Kent, 156
Eubacteria, 41, 169
Euclid, 46
Euler, Leonhard, 33
Eusocial, 53, 56, 143, 152–53, 156, 158; *see also* social insects

Fermi, Enrico, 144 n7, 175
Forgive, forgiveness, 104 n31, 114
Francis, Pope, 2 n6, 104 n32, 108 n44, 149 n17, 189 n49
Fronto, Marcus Cornelius, 135 n43

Galileo, 24 n8, 27, 31 n20
Galton, Francis, 92, 93 n5
Geisel, Theodore Seuss, 149 n18
Genesis (book of), 2 n4, 5, 8, 91, 112 n49, 182–83
Gödel, Kurt, 33
Gott, Richard J., 174 n24, 175 n28, 179
Greek(s), Hellenes, xv, 24 n9, 60, 141

Gregory of Nyssa, 11 n23
Gregory Palamas, 10 n22, 18 n29, 92, 163

Hadot, Pierre, xi
Haldane, J. B. S., 167, 168 n7
Hawking, Stephen, 34–36, 171, 173 n21
Hebrew(s), x, 1–2, 7, 16, 18–19, 98, 182
Heinlein, Robert, 26
Heraclitus, 137
Hesiod, 12, 184
Hildegard of Bingen, 162
Hinduism, 138, 186
Hippolytus, 52 n19
Hoban, Russell, 176
Hobbes, Thomas, 144–45
Homer, 15, 55 n29, 57, 58 n35, 183
Hume, David, 21
Hunter, George William, 50 n17, 51, 94
Huxley, Julian, 127
Huxley, Thomas Henry, 80

Iamblichus, 67
Iblis, *see* Satan
Islam, 3 n9, 34, 138

James, William, 18 n28, 25 n10, 61 n41, 64
Jefferson, Thomas, 88
Jennings, H. S., 126, 150
Jesus, 3, 5, 9–10, 40, 60, 99, 113–14, 127, 164, 182 n41; *see also* Christ
John Chrysostom, 7
John of Salisbury, 154–55
John Paul II, 100–1, 111, 112 n49, 127
John Scotus Eriugena, 11 n23
Joseph Ashkenazi of Safed, 117, 125
Joyce, James, 172
Judaism, 109 n47, 138
Julian of Norwich, 180, 191
Jupiter, *see* Zeus
Justice, 8, 12, 44–45, 49, 59, 95, 102, 109, 144–46, 159, 181, 189 n49

Index of Names

Kabbalah, 6 n13
Kant, Immanuel, 70 n54, 110
Keith, Arthur, 94
Kipling, Rudyard, 177 n31
Kirby, William, 43
Kook, Avraham Yitshak, 188
Koran, 8, 152 n24, 156 n31, 194

Lanza, Robert, 173
Lash, Nicholas, 138 n50
Leibniz, Gottfried Wilhelm, 131
Leopold, Aldo, 107
Lewis, C. S., 22 n4, 49 n14, 65 n48, 66 n49
Li Gang, 155
Livy, 57
Lovecraft, H. P., 122–23, 124 n18
Lovejoy, Arthur O., 28
Lovell, Bernard, 119
Lovelock, James, 41 n1, 143
Lynch, Kenneth, 134 n39
Lyon, P., 150, 204

MacIntyre, Alasdair, 103, 104 n31
Macrobius, 129 n29, 161
Maimonides, Moses, 138 n50
Marcus Aurelius, 187
Marx, Karl, 60
McKibben, Bill, 44
Mendel, Gregor, 72
Meyendorff, John, 18 n29
Morris, Simon Conway, 82
Moses, 91–92, 181, 183 n42
Münsterberg, Hugo, 126

Neoplatonism, xii
Nilus the Scholastic, 158

Odysseus, 35, 67
Orwell, George, 61 n41, 157
Owen, Richard, 71, 79, 81, 119–20

Palamas, *see* Gregory Palamas
Panpsychists, 158
Pascal, Blaise, ix
Pausanias, 57 n32
Peirce, Charles Sanders, 171
Pheidias, 56–59, 61, 66
Phillimore, J. S., 9
Philo of Alexandria, 37 n34, 122 n13
Philokalia, 13 n25, 18 n30
Pindar, 185
Plantinga, Alvin, 22, 31, 32 n22, 181
Plato, 5, 14–15, 32, 56, 61, 67 n50, 69, 75, 77, 83, 125 n20, 136, 153–55, 159 n39, 170, 193
Platonism, Platonists, 1, 15, 19, 28, 33, 47, 60, 69–70, 77, 89, 107, 125, 163–64, 190
Plotinus, ix–xi, xiv, xvi, 15–19, 39, 55, 57, 66, 70, 71 n1, 98, 107, 132, 137 n48, 159, 161, 187, 192–93
Plutarch, 1, 35, 39, 42 n3, 57, 139 n52
Porphyry, xiv, 19 n31, 70, 107
Presocratics, 1 n3
Protagoras, 61
Pyrrho, 39
Pythagoras, Pythagoreans, 89, 109

Ratzinger, Joseph, *see* Benedict XVI
Ricoeur, Paul, 115–16
Roman(s), x, 1 n2, 13, 27, 57, 135
Rorty, Richard, 28, 61 n41
Russell, Bertrand, 53, 131, 132 n34

Sacks, Oliver, 142 n1
Satan, 8, 19, 127, 152
Schrödinger, Erwin, 171–72
Scopes Trial, 50
Sedgwick, Adam, 79 n8
Seidenberg, David, 6 n13, 6 n15, 45 n7, 109 n47, 117 n2, 118 n3, 125 n23, 133 n37, 189 n49
Shakespeare, 3, 188
Shestov, Lev, 39
Sidgwick, Henry, 146

Simulation, 29, 32, 147 n15
Slaves, slavery, 76, 88, 114, 132
Slime molds, 22, 148, 154
Smith, Logan Pearsall, 54
Social insects, 53, 56, 94, 143, 153; see also Eusocial
Sophists, 1 n3, 191
Spengler, Oswald, 109 n45
Spinoza, Baruch, 42
Sprat, Thomas, 62–63
Stapledon, Olaf, 69, 84, 122–23, 147, 155, 160–61, 167–70, 175
Stewart, Balfour, 30 n19
Stoicism, Stoics, xii, 6, 14, 51, 144

Tait, Peter Guthrie, 30 n19
Tegmark, Max, 28, 137 n48
Teilhard de Chardin, Pierre, 128, 165, 167, 169
Theophrastus, xiv
Thomas Aquinas, x, 3, 113
Torah, 44, 193–94
Torrance, T. E., 118–19
Traherne, Thomas, 4
Trees, 4 n11, 8, 17, 22, 78, 85, 102, 130, 149, 158, 159 n38, 160
Turkeys, 126–27, 148

Utilitarianism, 110

Vaughan, Henry, 187
Vilenkin, Alexander, 137 n48, 149 n20
Virgil, 13
von Uexküll, Jacob Johann, 121 n10

Wells, H. G., 47, 49, 93, 94 n13, 130, 152 n25
Whewell, William, 120, 129
Whitehead, Alfred North, xii
Wigner, Eugene P., 30, 171–72
Wilberforce, Samuel, 24
Wilmot, John, 37, 38 n35
Wilson, E. O., 48 n10, 145 n9, 188, 189 n49
Winchell, Alexander, 120, 121 n9, 122, 142
Wittgenstein, Ludwig von, 32 n23
Wohlleben, Peter, 159 n38
Woolley-Barker, Tamsin, 157 n36
Wren-Lewis, John, 127–28, 131, 132 n34, 182–83, 185, 186 n45, 187

Xenophanes, 1

Zeus, 12, 56–57, 61, 66, 164
Žižek, Slavoj, 115–16

ABOUT THE AUTHOR

STEPHEN R. L. CLARK is Emeritus Professor of Philosophy at the University of Liverpool, and an Honorary Research Fellow in the Department of Theology at the University of Bristol. His books include *The Mysteries of Religion* (1984), *God's World and the Great Awakening* (1991), *Biology and Christian Ethics* (2000), *Understanding Faith: Religious Belief and its Place in Society* (2009), *Ancient Mediterranean Philosophy* (2013), and *Plotinus: Myth, Metaphor and Philosophical Practice* (2016). His chief current interests are in the philosophy of Plotinus, the understanding and treatment of non-human animals, philosophy of religion, philosophy of psychiatry, and science fiction.

www.ingramcontent.com/pod-product-compliance
Lightning Source LLC
Chambersburg PA
CBHW030107170426
43198CB00009B/520